How Social Movements Can Save Democracy

How Social Movements Can Save Democracy

Democratic Innovations from Below

Donatella della Porta

polity

First published in 2020 by Polity Press

Polity Press
65 Bridge Street
Cambridge CB2 1UR, UK

Polity Press
101 Station Landing
Suite 300
Medford, MA 02155, USA

ISBN-13: 978-1-5095-4126-3
ISBN-13: 978-1-5095-4127-0(pb)

A catalogue record for this book is available from the British Library.

Library of Congress Cataloging-in-Publication Data

Names: Della Porta, Donatella, 1956- author.
Title: How social movements can save democracy : democratic innovations from below / Donatella della Porta.
Description: Cambridge, UK ; Medford, MA : Polity, 2020. | Includes bibliographical references and index. | Summary: "Leading political sociologist della Porta rehabilitates the role social movements have long played in fostering democracy. Bridging social movement studies and democratic theory, she investigates contemporary innovations of the progressive Left in times of crisis and reflects on the potential and limits of such alternative politics"-- Provided by publisher.
Identifiers: LCCN 2019029694 (print) | LCCN 2019029695 (ebook) | ISBN 9781509541263 (hardback) | ISBN 9781509541270 (paperback) | ISBN 9781509541287 (epub)
Subjects: LCSH: Social movements--Political aspects. | Direct democracy. | Right and left (Political science)
Classification: LCC HM881 .D46 2020 (print) | LCC HM881 (ebook) | DDC 303.48/4--dc23
LC record available at https://lccn.loc.gov/2019029694
LC ebook record available at https://lccn.loc.gov/2019029695

Typeset in 10 on 12 Sabon by
Servis Filmsetting Ltd, Stockport, Cheshire
Printed and bound in Great Britain by CPI Group (UK) Ltd, Croydon

For further information on Polity, visit our website: politybooks.com

To Alessandro Pizzorno, *amico e maestro*, in memoria

Contents

Acknowledgements

This volume is based on the assumption that democratic conceptions and practices need constant innovation. In a moment in which various crises converge in challenging existing institutions, it is all the more important to reflect on what can be done in order to save democracy. Progressive social movements have historically been carriers of democratic deepening, elaborating and prefiguring alternative visions that have often then been constitutionalized in democratic institutions. In a period in which attacks on democracy come from the populist Right, research on attempts to improve democratic institutions through increased participatory and deliberative qualities is most important.

Looking at some of these attempts, with a critical view aimed also at singling out existing limits and conditions for improvement, is my purpose. In this sense, this volume can be seen as building upon and developing some of my previous contributions on related issues: first and foremost in *Can Democracy Be Saved?* (Polity 2013) and *Social Movements in Times of Austerity: Bringing Capitalism Back into Protest Analysis* (Polity 2015), but also in *Movement Parties against Austerity* (Polity 2017), *Late Neoliberalism and its Discontents in the Economic Crisis: Comparing Social Movements in the European Periphery* (Palgrave Macmillan 2016) and *Social Movements and Referendums from Below: Direct Democracy in the Neoliberal Crisis* (Policy 2017).

In addressing this task, I rely on a long-lasting research programme on institutional involvement by progressive social movements, carried out at the Center on Social Movement Studies (Cosmos) that I direct at the Scuola Normale Superiore in Florence. In particular, on crowd-sourced constitutionalism, referendums from below and movement parties, I have collaborated especially with my colleagues at Cosmos Lorenzo Cini, Andrea Felicetti, Francis O'Connor, Martin Portos, Anna Subirats, Hara Kouki, Lorenzo Mosca, Joseba Fernandez, Daniela Chironi and Jonas Draege, as well as with Colin Crouch, Michael Keating, Ken Roberts and Sidney Tarrow, who have been our most welcome visitors. I am also grateful for the support I received from the Hertie School of Governance and for the conversations I had during some visits to Berlin with colleagues there, among them Helmut Anheier, Christian Joerges and Claus Offe. At Hertie, I also wish to thank Stefanie Jost, who helped me in developing the project for this book. Some important stimuli also came from presentation of parts of my work at seminars and conferences, in particular at the Stein Rokkan Lecture at the Joint Sessions of the European Consortium for Political Research in Mons in 2019. Herbert Reiter has helped me greatly, improving the text through his critical but constructive reading (as well as through his patience and support while I was writing this book).

1

Democratic Innovations and Social Movements

The Great Recession that hit the world in 2008 worked as a critical juncture, nurturing socioeconomic but also political transformations. Some of the political developments during the crisis have challenged civil, political and social rights, triggering a Great Regression (Geiselberger 2017). Increasing social inequalities have spiralled, with growing mistrust in established institutions fuelling a sense of insecurity and xenophobic reaction (Streeck 2017; Bauman 2017a). While scholars are debating how much inequality democracy can withstand without breaking down (della Porta, Keating et al. 2018), resistance to the backlash is also developing, with citizens mobilizing for social justice and 'real democracy' (Meyer and Tarrow 2018).

This volume will focus on some innovative proposals, emerging from progressive social movements, that aim at increasing participation and deliberation in order to save democracy. Exploiting windows of opportunity offered by institutions of direct democracy, social movements have promoted referendums or infiltrated 'from below' referendums promoted by other actors in a more top-down fashion (della Porta, O'Connor et al. 2017a). Party systems have been dramatically shaken, with the breakdown of mainstream parties and, in some cases, an unexpected rise of movement parties on the left (della Porta, Fernández et al. 2017a), as well as right-wing populist ones. Similarly unexpected success has come to candidates that appeal to social justice and citizens' participation within old-Left parties, among them Labour in the United Kingdom and the Democratic Party in the United States. In addressing these developments, I suggest that times of crisis are times of rapid change, presenting challenges to existing institutions but also, potentially, opening opportunities for a deepening of democracy.

This chapter will introduce the theoretical discussion on the potential innovative contributions by civic society that have indeed been addressed in democratic theory, as well as in various approaches within social movement studies. While movements have been studied mainly as contentious actors, fighting in the streets to resist or promote political change, social movement studies have also pointed at their capacity to nurture innovative ideas, as movements are constantly engaged in generating and spreading counter-expertise and new forms of knowledge. In doing so, social movements are endowed with specific ontological, epistemological and methodological preferences. This chapter therefore addresses the channels through which social movements' ideas enter institutions, singling out conditions that favour (or thwart) the development of innovative ideas and plural knowledge. It suggests that, by providing for alternative knowledge, progressive movements might contribute to the deepening of democracy through increasing the plurality of ideas.

Democratic challenges in the Great Recession

In the countries that have been most hit by the financial crisis, particularly in the European periphery, waves of protest have challenged the austerity policies adopted by national governments under heavy pressure from international institutions including the European Union (EU), the European Central Bank (ECB) and the International Monetary Fund (IMF). These protest waves – known as *Indignados* or Occupy movements – reflected but also strengthened a legitimacy crisis, caused by what protesters saw as a lack of concern by political institutions for the suffering of their citizens (della Porta 2015b). Protests took different forms in different countries, influenced by the different timing and characteristics of the financial crisis, as well as by the domestic opportunities and threats facing social movements (della Porta, Andretta et al. 2016).

The Great Recession had immediate and often dramatic political effects on what Robert Dahl (2000) dubbed 'really existing' democracies, especially on representative institutions. The crisis of institutional trust fuelled calls for constitutional reforms that could help refound the political community. Really existing democracies have certainly been under stress, but there is also potential for innovation. The multiple (financial, social, political) crises have in particular increased the tensions between those scholars and politicians who have considered citizens as too emotional and ignorant to make sensible choices, stressing the need for technical expertise, and those who have instead blamed an 'econocracy' that has taken over political decisions while pretending they are not political (Earle et al. 2017), as well as the idea of an 'epistocracy' in which only the most knowledgeable people can vote (Brennan 2016). Siding with a participatory and deliberative vision, I will suggest that what we need is more, rather than less, citizen participation in democracy, and look at some democratic innovations that could contribute to it.

The challenges to representative democracies during the Great Recession bring about a need to reflect on democratic qualities. Democracy has in fact a contested meaning, with different qualities stressed in different understandings of the concept of democracy itself and the evaluation of democratic practices. A concept with a long history, democracy 'has meant different things to different people at different times and places' (Dahl 2000, 3). In time, a minimalist definition of democracy as electoral accountability has emerged, and democracy has been identified with the current characteristics of Western polities (Held 2006, 166).

The widespread democratic malaise has, however, challenged the identification of the meaning of democracy with its minimalistic vision or currently existing institutions. While electoral accountability has been considered as the main democratic mechanism in the historical evolution of the discourse on really existing democracy, today's challenges to representative democracy focus attention on other democratic qualities (Rosanvallon 2006). The mainstream conceptions and practices of democracy are in particular contested in the name of other conceptions and practices, which political theorists have addressed under labels such as participatory democracy, strong democracy, discursive democracy, communicative democracy, welfare democracy or associative democracy (see della Porta 2013, ch. 1).

In particular, debates have emerged around two main characteristics often considered as at the basis of really existing democracies: delegation of power, and majoritarian decision-making (even if with different degrees of protection of minorities through constitutionalization of rights and institutional checks and balances). These two elements have in fact been in tension with other democratic qualities that constitute the building blocks of other conceptions of democracy.

First of all, participatory democratic theorists have long pointed towards the importance of creating multiple opportunities for participation by involving citizens beyond elections (Arnstein 1969; Pateman

1970; Barber 1984). While elections are seen as too rare, offer only limited choices, and can be manipulated in various ways, participation is praised as capable of constructing good citizens through empowering interactions. Participation in different forms and in different moments of the democratic process is considered as essential in socializing citizens to visions of the public good, also potentially increasing trust in and support for political institutions. Expanding the semantic meaning of politics, participatory approaches call for democracy not only within parliaments and governments, but also in societal institutions, from workplaces to neighbourhoods, from schools to hospitals, from the local to transnational institutions.

Majoritarian decision-making has also been criticized on several grounds. The power of the majority might jeopardize the rights of minorities, bringing about the need for the constitutionalization of some rights. In addition, there is no logical assumption that grants that the preferences that are more supported in terms of numbers are also the best for the collectivity. Considering these limits of majoritarian decision-making, deliberative normative theories have stressed the importance of creating high-quality discursive spaces, in which participants can exchange reasons and construct shared definitions of the public good (Cohen 1989; Habermas 1996; Elster 1998; Dryzek 2000). In this vision, the more the definition of interests and collective identities emerges, at least in part, through a high-quality discursive process, the more legitimate and efficient the outcome is expected to be. Legitimacy does not arise in fact from the number of pre-existing preferences, but rather from a decision-making process in which citizens can relate to each other, recognizing others and being recognized by them. Decisions are democratic not (so much) when they have the support of the majority, but rather when opinions are formed through a deliberative process in which reasons are freely exchanged. In high-quality discursive spaces, citizens, treated as equal, can understand the reasons of others, assessing them against emerging standards of fairness. In addition, public arenas with high discursive quality should help participants to find better solutions, not only by allowing for carriers of different knowledge and expertise (rather than just self-appointed 'experts') to interact, but also by changing the perception of one's own preferences, making participants less concerned with individual, material interests and more with collective goods. While the extent to which deliberation implies the actual building of consensus or the transformation of preferences is debated (Dryzek 2010), discursive quality requires a recognition of others as equal, with an open-minded assessment of their reasons.

Bridging participatory and deliberative conceptions of democracy, some scholars have pointed towards the importance of building enclaves free from institutional power (Mansbridge 1996) and developing 'processes of engaged and responsible democratic participation [which] include street demonstrations and sit-ins, musical works and cartoons, as much as parliamentary speeches and letters to the editor' (Young 2003, 119). In particular, subaltern counter-publics (including workers, women, ethnic minorities and so on) form parallel discursive arenas, where counter-discourses develop, allowing for the formation and redefinition of identities, interests and needs (Fraser 1990).

Participatory and deliberative conceptions of democracy challenge some of the main assumptions not only of really existing democracies, but also of technocratic alternatives to them. Supporters of what Colin Crouch (2003) has defined as the 'post-democratic' view the democratic malaise as related to too much participation. As neoliberal approaches stigmatize what they see as unreasonably high expectations about state responsibilities, in a rehearsal of the analysis already developed in the 1970s by the so-called trilateral report (Crozier et al. 1975), technocratic solutions are suggested to reduce the 'overload' of demands on the state. Building upon arguments that citizens are unable to understand political complexities and formulate sound opinions (e.g. Schumpeter 1943), the assumption is that electoral accountability puts elected representatives under the pressure of selfish individuals. The suggested solutions are therefore to reduce the competences of the state (freeing the market from state control), and to give power to electorally unaccountable institutions. Considering citizens as selfish, but also ignorant and therefore unable to pursue even their own private good, technocratic solutions are based on a fear of the brutal instincts of the masses. Lack of pressure from below is seen as favouring bipartisan agreements and reducing inequalities, movement pressures are considered as fuelling polarization and increasing inequalities (McAdam and Kloos 2016).

Contrasting the assumption that deciding on public issues is too complex a task to be left to the mass of citizens, participatory and deliberative conceptions on which the democratic innovations I am going to analyse are based trust citizens, their knowledge and their reasons. Public debates are considered as formative and, therefore, participation produces better citizens as 'people may become more competent and responsible if they are allowed to participate in public deliberation and actual decision-making' (Setälä 2009, 3). Direct forms of democracy might stimulate citizens by empowering them, increasing their sense of civic duty as well as their political efficacy (Smith and Tolbert 2004): they provide for 'education in democratic citizenship' (Dyck 2009, 540). While, in minimalist conceptions of democracy, ideas, interests, preferences and/or identities are assumed to develop outside of the democratic process, participatory and deliberative conceptions emphasize instead the capacity of democratic arenas to stimulate the development of inclusive collective identities. As the competence of experts is challenged by processes of politicization of science (della Porta, Keating et al. 2018), econocracy is not a solution to democratic stress; instead, it risks reducing not only the legitimacy of decision-makers but also the efficacy of their decisions. It does not help individuals to learn to be good citizens, but instead pushes them to the margins and makes them more responsive to populist leaders.

Even within really existing democracies, the suggestion that participation and deliberation must (at least) supplement representative and majoritarian institutions has been implemented through various democratic innovations (Barber 1984; Fishkin 1997). In their concrete evolution, existing democratic states and societies have mitigated the ideal-typical principles of representative democracy, mixing them with others that are linked to different conceptions of democracy (della Porta 2013). In implicit recognition of the limits of delegation and majoritarian decision-making, the really existing democracies have combined institutions privileging different democratic qualities. Participatory conceptions have penetrated the democratic state through reforms that have introduced channels of citizen participation in schools, in factories and in neighbourhoods, but also through the political recognition of movement organizations and of the 'right to dissent'. Referendums, once considered as a residual vestige of direct democratic procedures, are increasingly used, as are institutions in which the principle of delegation is limited, including in institutions based on representatives chosen by lot, as well as consensual decision-making. Democratic innovations – from participatory budgeting to deliberative mini-publics (Font et al. 2014) – have spread attempts to restore citizens' trust in democracy, as well as bringing in their expertise and knowledge.

As I have suggested elsewhere (della Porta 2013), the legitimation of really existing democracies required certain specific conditions that are less and less present nowadays. First of all, mass political parties allowed for linking delegation with some form of participation by citizens, contributing towards making representatives accountable in a long-term perspective (Pizzorno 1993). In addition, the majoritarian assumption needed a nation state, defining the border of the *demos* in whose name (and interest) decisions were made. Finally, even though representative democracy did not call for social equality, it still relied upon the assumption that political equality would reduce social inequality, which otherwise risks challenging the very principle of free access to political rights. The representative form of democracy developed, that is, in contexts characterized by party democracies, national sovereignty and well-established welfare states.

The weakening of political parties, nation states and welfare provisions has altered the functioning of representative democracies, but it may also have produced some opportunities for experimenting with other conceptions of democracies. In particular, it stresses the importance of involving citizens in the democratic process. As Pierre Rosanvallon (2006, 12–18) has suggested, in the evolution of democracy a circuit of oversight anchored outside of state institutions has developed, along with the institutions of electoral accountability. Growing societal powers of sanction and prevention have been reflected in an increasing organization of distrust.

In sum, the democratic innovations analysed here are justified by the belief that, in times of economic, social and political crises, more rather than less citizens' participation is needed. As a democratic malaise is fuelled by an increasingly elitist development within really existing democracies – particularly in their post-democratic version – what we need to restore democratic legitimacy and efficacy (on the input and the output side) is more involvement of citizens. Participation is not only essential to restoring trust in institutions, but is also a way to develop good citizenship. Crises require, and at the same time open opportunities for, change. Prefiguration of democratic participation is therefore even more important in and outside public institutions.

The backlash against democracy that is fuelled by right-wing populism cannot be addressed by declaring the people unfit for civic life and calling for technocratic solutions. Rather, an 'age of mistrust' requires an institutional adaptation that can transform challenges into resources. Social movements (along with judges and independent authorities), as instruments of external control and permanent contestation, act in what Pierre Rosanvallon (2006, 20) calls *counter-democracy* – that is, a set of formal and informal checks and balances, as well as counterpowers, that make sure that 'society has a voice, that collective sentiments can be articulated, that judgments of the government can be formulated, and that demands can be issued'.

Against this background, as I am going to argue in the next section of this introduction, progressive social movements are to be considered as promoters of democratic innovations that can improve participation and deliberative qualities. In this direction, the volume focuses on the involvement of progressive social movements in the ideation and implementation of innovations in institutional politics, addressing their potential but also the limitations on their capacity to improve democracy. As with political parties or interest groups, so too social movements may have different attitudes towards democracy, in some cases supporting and in others challenging democratic institutions. In a moment in which concerns are increasing regarding the potential disruption of a Great Regression led by xenophobic movements and parties, I address instead the potential for alternative politics and policy that progressive social movements might contribute in the direction of a deepening of democracy.

Bridging social movement studies and democratic theory, I analyse some democratic innovations promoted by progressive social movements, especially in the direction of participatory and deliberative practices. Focusing on recent cases, the analysis will thus highlight the role that progressive social movements can play in times that are characterized by crises, but also by transformation.

Progressive social movements as sites for innovation

While social movements have been studied especially as contentious actors, mainly taking to the streets to resist or promote political changes, some research has pointed towards their innovative capacity in terms of nurturing and spreading new ideas – about, among other things, demo-cratic institutions. Traditionally considered as actors 'at the gate' of the institutional system, social movements instead enter institutional arenas in various forms and through various channels.

Social movements have been considered as important actors in terms of their capacity to 'take the floor', building public spheres and participating in them. Clearly, not all social movements promoted democracy: some movements (particularly right-wing movements) have openly declared themselves anti-democratic; others (including left-wing movements) have produced authoritarian turns. There is, however, as Charles Tilly (2004, 125) has pointed out:

> a wide correspondence between democratisation and social movements. The roots of social movements are found in the partial democratisation that moved British subjects and the North-American colonies against those that governed them in the 18th century. Throughout the nine-teenth century, social movements generally blossomed and developed wherever further democratisation took place, decreasing when author-itarian regimes impeded democracy. This path continued during the twentieth and twenty-first centuries; the maps of the development of institutions and social movements widely overlap.

If democratization favoured social movements, the majority of these supported the democratic reforms that promoted their development.

In this volume, I am primarily concerned with what we might call progressive social movements. Even though progress is a contested term (Allen 2016), I would retain it to define actors that struggle for an inclusive vision of a just society and for deepening democracy. In doing so, I do consider that progress has a dialectical nature. It has been used to stress human emancipation as opposed to social domination, but also criticized as justifying domination by implying 'a universalist teleological form of thinking according to which some societies or groups have reached that telos earlier than others and thus have the authority, and maybe even the mission, to pull the less progressed people out of their "self-incurred immaturity" into the light of reason and freedom, possibly even overcoming their ignorant or indolent reluctance by force' (Forst 2019, 1).

While acknowledging the tension between a normative meaning and its historical use, I follow Forst's call for the development of a de-reified, non-teleological, non-dominating and emancipatory conception of progress. As he notes, differentiating between a technological vision of progress and moral–political progress:

> the decisive question raised by the concept of moral–political progress remains how the power to define such progress and the paths leading to it is structured. . . . Technological progress cannot count as social progress in life conditions without social evaluations of what it is good for, who benefits from it, and what costs it generates. Nor can true social progress as moral–political progress exist where the changes in question are enforced and experienced as colonization. Technological progress must be socially accepted, and socially accepted progress is progress which is determined and brought about by the members of the society in question. (Forst 2019, 1)[1]

In this direction, I define as progressive those social movements that share with the so-called left-libertarian movement family of the past a combined attention to social justice and positive freedom (della Porta and Rucht 1996). Progress is thus understood as:

> the liberation (or 'emancipation') of collectivities (for example: citizens, classes, nations, minorities, income categories, even mankind), be it the liberation from want, ignorance, exploitative relations, or the freedom of such collectives to govern themselves autonomously, that is, without being dependent upon or controlled by others. Furthermore, the freedom that results from liberation applies equally to all, with equality serving as a criterion to make sure that liberation does not in fact become a mere privilege of particular social categories. (Offe 2011, 79-80)

---

[1] As Forst noted (2019), 'If our critique of false notions of progress is *situated* and not merely abstract and empty, we also argue *for* progress, both in theory and in practice, because overcoming false progress is true progress. Being against progress, because one is motivated by an account of non-domination or emancipation, is also to be for it.'

In Forst's terms, I address 'empowerment initiatives', 'especially those where underprivileged groups . . . win participation rights through social struggles', thus aiming at expanding the scope of agency for individuals as well as collectives. Among them are movements that called for broader inclusion of citizens and reducing domination within and across national borders (Ypi 2012). While progressive movements are my main focus of analysis, I will argue that some of these actors' claims for broader participation and recognition in the public sphere can spread beyond the original promoter and be articulated by various actors with more ambiv-alent positions towards global justice. I will also discuss to what extent democratic innovations promoted by progressive social movements can be appropriated by regressive actors.

Studies of social movements have focused especially on their progres-sive variety, pointing at their emancipatory potential. At the onset of social movement studies, research on collective behaviour by scholars close to the so-called Chicago School stressed that collective phenomena do not simply reflect social crisis, but rather produce new solidarities and norms, which function as drivers of change, especially in the value system. Students of collective behaviour referred to these interpretations in looking at social movements in moments of intense social change (e.g. Blumer 1951; Gusfield 1963; Turner and Killian 1987). Rooted in symbolic interactionism, they gave particular relevance to the meaning attributed to social structures by actors, and focused on how social action based on new norms transformed institutional behaviour (della Porta and Diani 2006, 12–13).

Likewise in research within the new social movement perspective, which paid attention to macro-level social transformations, social movements have been considered as main actors of innovation. Opening the scientific debate on the emergence of new conflicts, Alain Touraine (1985) has considered social movements as constituting the opposition to dominant powers within different societies. In contemporary ones, social movements struggle for control of emerging *programmed* societies, in which knowledge is especially relevant. Within a resonant approach, Alberto Melucci (1982, 1989, 1996) has paid particular attention to movements as producers of norms in contemporary societies defined as highly differentiated and increasingly investing in the creation of indi-vidual autonomous centres of action, but also extending control over the motives for human action. In this perspective, rather than limiting themselves to seeking material gain, new social movements promote 'other codes' in order to resist the intrusion of the state and of the market into the everyday life of citizens. Conflicts have therefore been seen as oriented towards the control of meanings, the circulation of information, the production and the use of scientific knowledge, the creation of cultural models for individual and collective identities. Traditionally associated with disruptive forms of political participation, in the Habermasian account of social life movements assume a positive role in mobilizing to resist the invasion of the logics of the system (Habermas 1985).

More recent social science literature has considered social movements as 'learning sites' (Welton 1993), capable of building knowledge through discursive processes which consist of the 'talks and conversations – the speech acts – and written communications of movement members that occur in the context of, or in relation to, movement activities' (Benford and Snow 2000, 623). Addressing the importance of movements as producers of knowledge, Eyerman and Jamison (1991, 68–9) singled out three dimensions of their cognitive praxis: a cosmological dimension addressing the 'common worldview assumptions that give a social movement its utopian mission'; a technological dimension which addresses 'the specific technological issues that particular movements develop around'; an organizational dimension as 'a particular organizational paradigm, which means they have both ideals and modes of organizing the production and . . . dissemination of knowledge'.

Research on knowledge-practices within social movements singled out a broad range, moving:

> from things we are more classically trained to define as knowledge, such as practices that engage and run parallel to the knowledge of scientists or policy experts, to micro-political and cultural interventions that have more to do with 'know-how' or the 'cognitive praxis that informs all social activity' and which vie with the most basic social institutions that teach us how to be in the world. (Casas-Cortés et al. 2008, 21)

In fact, social movements are: '1) engaging in co-producing, challenging, and transforming expert scientific discourses; 2) creating critical subjects whose embodied discourse produces new notions of democracy; and 3) generating reflexive conjunctural theories and analyses that go against more dogmatic and orthodox approaches to social change, and as such contribute to ethical ways of knowing' (Casas-Cortés et al. 2008, 22). Practices of knowledge are both formal and informal, as the activist knowledge is formed through different types of knowledge-practices including concepts, theories and imaginaries as well as methodological devices and research tools. Moreover, they 'entail practices less obviously associated with knowledge, including the generation of subjectivities/ identities, discourses, common-sense, and projects of autonomy and livelihood' (Casas-Cortés et al. 2008, 28).

Social movements are first of all important actors in what Rosanvallon (2006) defined as counter-democracy, in that they criticize hegemonic thinking, especially its impact on subalterns. In fact, progressive social movements play a counter-hegemonic function (Freire 1996) as

> the character and relational mode of oppressed people tends to be marked by the identification with the oppressor and an often unintentional desire to emulate him/her in terms of identity, position in the social structure and ways of relating to the 'other'. If that often unconscious tendency is not identified and actively deconstructed, the odds are that the oppressive relationship will be reproduced, this time with new protagonists. (Motta and Esteves 2014, 2)

This critique of existing knowledge aims in particular at the unlearning of the dominant discourses, and the learning, instead, of oppositional and liberatory ones (Foley 1999, 4).

Learning is then oriented towards emancipation, going beyond the critique of hegemonic thinking and experimenting instead with alternatives. Being self-reflexive actors, progressive social movements acquire and produce knowledge in different stages of their activities. Learning is related to participation in the general activities of progressive movements, including meetings, protest, organizing, educational activities, as well as in self-reflection on their actions (Mayo and English 2012, 202–3).

Critical and creative approaches to knowledge aim at social transformation. Scholars have stressed the capacity of progressive social movements to offer alternative analysis and develop responses to situations of exploitation and exclusion starting from the direct experience of those situations. Thus, 'If scientific knowledge aspires to develop generalizable theoretical and methodological models (some of which is indeed often relied upon by movement actors), "peoples' knowledge" is based on grounded experience that can differently enhance particular processes of social emancipation' (Casas-Cortés et al. 2008, 48).

Social movement knowledge is in fact said to be situated rather than universal, committed rather than detached, focused on changes at the roots of the system rather than on the symptoms (Mayo 1999). It tries to provide useful skills; to develop a critical understanding of power and of agency (Foley 2004); and to connect the local and the global (Crowther et al. 2005). The knowledge produced is 'embedded in and embodied through lived, place-based experiences, [which] means that they offer *different* kinds of answers than more abstract knowledge: knowledges that are situated and embodied, rather than supposedly neutral and distanced (Casas-Cortés et al. 2008, 42–3). Movements generate knowledge which moves from practice to theory (Gordon 2007). Their knowledge is therefore considered as basically oriented to articulating theory and praxis, taking concrete realities as the point of departure: 'The goal is that of creating an appropriate and operative theoretical horizon, very close to the surface of the "lived", where the simplicity and concreteness of elements from which it has emerged achieve meaning and potential' (Malo de Molina 2004, 13).

The importance of social movement knowledge is also related to its emergence in action. In particular, movement theorizing is

> grounded in the process of producing 'social movements' *against* opposition. It is always to some extent knowledge-in-struggle, and its survival and development is always contested and in process of formation. Its frequently partial, unsystematic and provisional character does not make it any the less worth our attention, though it may go some way towards explaining why academic social movements theory is too often content with taking the 'cream off the top', and disregarding – or failing to notice – everything that has to happen before institutionalized social movement theorizing appears in forms that can be easily appropriated. (Barker and Cox 2002, 11)

Thus, theorization based on alternative knowledge and practices represents an aspect of citizens' engagement in creating collective institutions such as social movement organizations, which are expected to empower them in the pursuit of their aim of resistance and change (Barker and Cox 2002, 21).

In sum, progressive social movements have engaged and engage in democratic innovation. They experiment with new ideas in their internal life, prefiguring alternative forms of democratic politics, and they spread these ideas within institutions. They not only transform democratic states through struggles for policy change, but also express a fundamental critique of conventional politics, thus addressing meta-political issues and experimenting with participatory and deliberative ideas. Historically, progressive social movements have been the carriers of participatory and deliberative democratic qualities, calling for necessary adaptation through innovation in democratic institutions, playing a most relevant role in countering social injustice and struggling for democracy. In these struggles, they have produced innovative ideas and alternative knowledge. This has been, and is, all the more important in times of crisis, which old institutions appear unable to address. Rather than gradual change, these critical junctures require new ideas, even new paradigms, with which social movements may already have experimented. As mentioned, progressive social movements experiment with democratic innovations in their internal practices. In fact, their activities are oriented towards prefiguration of alternative forms of internal democracy. Self-reflexive actors, they experiment with new ideas of democracy, which are then the basis of proposed changes in democratic governance.

Triggered by dissatisfaction with centralized and bureaucratic representative democracy, since the 1970s so-called new social movements have pushed for various forms of participation in decision-making, spreading through a sort of 'contagion from below' (Rohrschneider 1993). Emerging trends within social movements that mobilized in the wave of protest against the financial crisis and for democratization illustrate this form of democratic innovation. Recently, the Global Justice Movement as well as anti-austerity protests have produced knowledge about direct democratic processes (Cox 2014, 965). In the beginning of the new millennium, with their reflexive practices inspired by Zapatistas and the building of deliberative spaces, the Global Justice Movement paid specific attention to knowledge production. More recently in the 2010s, those who protested in Tahrir, Porta del Sol, Syntagma Square or Zuccotti Park, and later in Gezi Park or Place de la République, have both criticized existing representative democracy as deeply corrupted and experimented with different models of democracy, stressing especially participatory and deliberative qualities. As a protest repertoire and organizational form, the *acampadas* – long-term camps in squatted public spaces – have been seen as the incarnation of a democratic experiment that has been adopted and adapted in different contexts. Aiming at participation and deliberation, the *acampadas* developed from previous practices of internal democracy, such as social forums, in the attempt to learn from their limits and try to address them (della Porta 2015b). In these activities, conceptions of participation from below, cherished by progressive social movements, have in fact been combined with a special attention to the creation of egalitarian and inclusive public spheres (della Porta 2013). With their emphasis on consensus, the *acampadas* privileged the participation of lay persons – the citizens, the members of the community – mobilized as individuals rather than members of associations of various types (Juris 2012), building on their personal experience and knowledge.

Contemporary progressive movements have considered transparency, equality and inclusivity as important democratic values. In particular, the setting up of camps in open-air space has aimed at enhancing the public and transparent nature of the process, expressing a reclaiming of public spaces by citizens. Choosing open spaces as the main site of protest, activists place a special emphasis on the inclusivity of the process, which involves the entire *agora*. The heterogeneity of participants is mentioned as a most positive aspect of the camps, in which people of different backgrounds, classes and ideology sit together and talk with each other (Gerbaudo 2012, 69). In this way, the *acampadas*, by occupying and subverting the use of prominent urban public spaces, aimed at reconstructing a public sphere in which problems and solutions could be discussed among equals (Halvorsen 2012, 431). Within the camps, the general assemblies aimed at mobilizing the common people – not activists but communities of citizens – through placards and individualized messages. Alternative practices were also developed in the everyday management of camp activities, including through free kitchens, medical tents, libraries, media centres and information centres for visitors and new participants (Graeber 2012, 240).

In all these activities, there were attempts at balancing the principle of direct democracy with a search for consensus. In the camps, consensual decision-making was built upon the practices devised by the horizontal wing in the Global Justice Movement (della Porta 2009), as collective thought was expected to emerge through inclusivity and respect for the opinions of all, even in large assemblies involving often hundreds of thousands of people. A consensual, horizontal decision-making process was based on the continuous formation of small groups, which then reconvened in the larger assemblies. Deliberation through consensus was in general seen as an instrument against bureaucratization, but also against the routinization of the assembly, and a way to construct a community (Graeber 2012, 23). So, the *acampadas* have been sites of contention, but also of exchange of information, reciprocal learning, individual socialization and knowledge building. Their ultimate goal was building a community through the personal knowledge of the participants and their direct experiences, including the expression of strong emotions. So, the occupied free spaces had to develop 'possible utopias', by attracting the attention of the media and inspiring participation, but also by 'providing a space for grassroots participatory democracy; ritual and community building, strategizing and action planning, public education and prefiguring alternative worlds that embody movement visions', as well as networking and coordinating (Juris 2012, 268). Camps were thus considered as places not only for talking and listening, but also for the building of collective identities, happening through the development of strong emotions and longer-lasting relations. Open public spaces were to create intense ties and sharing of a common belonging through encounters among diverse people. Camps therefore had to show opposition but also to prefigure new relations, experimenting with another form of democracy.

Some of the mentioned innovative ideas about democracy have been at the basis of institutional experiments that were indeed inspired by the same principles of participation and deliberation. Besides engaging in internal practices of democratic innovation, social movements are in fact also carriers of innovation in institutions, performing this role in a variety of ways and with different results. In short, social movements raise claims not only on specific policies, but more broadly on the way in which the political system as a whole functions: its institutional and formal procedures, elite recruitment and the informal configuration of power (Kitschelt 1986). Movements have often obtained decentralization of political power and channels of consultation with citizens on particular decisions; appeals procedures against decisions by the public administration; the possibility to be allowed to testify before representative institutions and the judiciary, to be listened to as counter-experts, to receive legal recognition and material incentives. Repertoires of collective action, which were once stigmatized and dealt with as public order problems, have slowly become legal and legitimate (della Porta and Reiter 1998), while direct democracy has been developed as a supplementary channel of access to those opened within representative democracy (della Porta, O'Connor et al. 2017a). Social movements also contribute to the creation of new arenas for the development of public policy, such as expert commissions or specific administrative and political branches, for example state ministries or local bureaus on women's and ecological issues in many countries. Within international organizations, such as the EU, movement activists have been co-opted by specific public bodies as members of their staff (Ruzza 2004) and opportunities for conflictual cooperation develop within regulatory agencies through consultation, to incorporation in committees, to delegation of power (Giugni and Passy 1998, 85). These institutions mediate social movement claims and even ally themselves with movement activists with whom they may have frequent contact.

In recent times, democratic innovations have included participatory arenas open to the participation of normal citizens in public debates on relevant (and often divisive) issues. Especially at the local level, there have been various attempts at increasing participation, through the creation of high-quality communicative arenas and the empowering of citizens. In fact, one can distinguish, with Graham Smith (2009), two main institutional formulas: assembleary, or oriented to the construction of a 'mini-public', usually selected by lot. The former in particular have seen the participation of social movement activists in neighbourhood assemblies or even thematic assemblies, neighbourhood councils, consultation committees, strategic participatory plans and the like. In particular, participatory budgets have spread from Porto Alegre, a Brazilian city of 1,360,000 inhabitants, to being recognized by the United Nations as one of the forty 'best practices' at global level (Allegretti 2003, 173). In order to achieve social equality and provide occasions for empowerment, citizens are invited to decide about the distribution of certain public funds through a structured process of involvement in assemblies and committees. The objectives of these institutions include effective problem-solving and equitable solutions, as well as broad, deep and sustained participation. The participatory budget has been credited with creating a positive context for association, fostering greater activism, networking associations, and working from a citywide orientation (Baiocchi 2002). Even though the intensity of participation, its duration and influence, vary greatly between the various participatory devices, they all point towards the limits of a merely representative conception of democracy. The aim of improving managerial capacities, through greater transparency and the circulation of information, is linked with the transformation of social relations, by reconstructing social ties, fostering solidarity and eventually 'democratising democracy' (Bacqué et al. 2005). Such instruments have been analysed as improving the capacity to address problems created by local opposition to the construction of big infrastructure (Bobbio and Zeppetella 1999). They are supposed to increase the legitimacy of public decisions as 'all potentially affected groups have equal opportunity to get involved in the process and equal right to propose topics, formulate solutions, or critically discuss taken-for-granted approaches, and because decision-making is by exchange of argument' (Baccaro and Papadakis 2008, 1).

Going beyond the discussion of democratic innovations within movements and existing research on participatory institutions and social movements (which I have addressed elsewhere, see della Porta 2013; 2015b), I want to analyse in this volume some institutional outcomes of contemporary progressive movements in terms of the spreading of their participatory and deliberative conceptions and practices in constitutional processes, direct democracy and party politics. In fact, as mentioned, a main assumption in this work is that, at a time in which tensions in democracies are increasing, progressive social movements might offer important resources for reinvigorating democratic participation and deliberation. Notwithstanding that institutional democratic innovations and social movements have been mostly considered in isolation from each other, the two often interact:

> Deliberative democracy and collective action have often been opposed as offering conflicting ways of constructing the common good, based on cooperative discussion on the one hand, and adversarial protest and negotiation on the other. Social movements have however shaped the inception and organization of democratic innovations to a large extent. Historically, the first wave of deliberative and participatory institutions appeared in the 1970s as a response to social movements' claims for a greater inclusiveness of the political process. Social movements also influence the way democratic innovations work, by participating in,

or on the contrary boycotting, new forms of democratic engagement. Finally, social movements' internal democratic practices and reflections about the limits of informal decision making have inspired the field of deliberative democracy, which has, in turn, influenced collective action research. (Talpin 2015, 781)

As I am going to argue in this volume, social movements can play a key role in introducing democratic innovations (which they experiment with in their internal practices) in public institutions, by using specific institutional mechanisms, such as constitution-building, direct democratic procedures and party politics.

In each of the following three chapters, I will therefore refer to the toolkit of social movement studies in order to account for some of the democratic innovations brought about by grassroots constitutional processes, referendums from below, as well as movement parties. Social movements need to challenge existing institutions, producing cracks (or at least turning points) in the system. Research in social movement studies has indeed focused on political opportunities, looking at both the contingent availability of potential allies (their dispositions and strength) and more stable channels of access to political institutions (mainly functional and territorial divisions of power) (see della Porta and Diani 2006, ch. 7, for a review). The main assumption has been that the opening of political opportunities influences collective mobilization and its forms, as rational activists tend to invest in collective action when their effort seems worthwhile. Broadly tested from cross-national (e.g. Kriesi et al. 1995; della Porta 1995) and cross-time (e.g. Tarrow 1989) perspectives, the political opportunity approach has suggested that protest is, by and large, more frequent and less radical when stable and/or contingent channels of access to institutions by outsiders are open. In fact, even in the face of economic crises and structural weakness of the lower classes, scholars have cited the opening up of political opportunities to explain the emergence of protest as well as its success (Tarrow 2011).

In their struggles, social movements mobilize material and symbolic resources. Social movement studies have thus looked at the capacity of horizontal networks to mobilize resources, as well as at the framing processes for mobilization, in particular at the bridging of specific issues to broader themes as well as the amplification of the importance of some topics for the everyday life of the people. Frames, defined as the dominant worldviews that guide the behaviour of social movement groups, are produced by the organizational leadership, which provides the necessary ideological background within which individual activists can locate their experiences. Frame analysis thus focuses on the process of the attribution of meaning, which lies behind any conflict. In particular, within progressive movements the quality of communication has been considered as of fundamental value not only for the development of informed opinions on a specific policy, but also for the quality of democracy in general (della Porta and Diani 2006, ch. 1).

More recently, within a more dynamic perspective, research on the political context for contentious activities has moved from a consideration of opportunities as structurally given into paying attention to the ways in which protest itself can create opportunities by challenging existing routines and destabilizing elite coalitions. The concept of repertoire of contention refers to what people know they can do when they want to oppose a public decision they consider unjust or threatening (Tilly 1986, 2). Initially focusing only on the more or less stable protest as a public display of disruptive action, Charles Tilly (2008) has addressed broader contentious performances, with some historical adaptations in the various forms of contentious politics. The characteristics of protest have often been connected with contextual opportunities and constraints, with the opening of opportunities favouring moderate forms of action. Beyond adapting to a changing opportunity structure, social movements can, however, also try to create their own opportunities through 'eventful protests', which constitute processes during which collective experiences develop through the interactions of the different individual and collective actors who, with different roles and aims, take part in it (della Porta 2008; 2017). Some protest events have a transformative effect, as 'events transform structures largely by constituting and empowering new groups of actors or by re-empowering existing groups in new ways' (Sewell 1996, 271). They put in motion social processes that 'are inherently contingent, discontinuous and open ended' (Sewell 1996, 272). Eventful protests have cognitive, affective and relational impacts on the very movements that carry them out as they affect structures by fuelling mechanisms of social change: organizational networks develop; frames are bridged; personal links foster reciprocal trust. Some forms of action or specific campaigns have a particularly high degree of eventfulness (della Porta 2008). During these intense times, signals about the possibility of collective action are sent (Morris 2000), feelings of solidarity created, and organizational networks consolidated. In fact, as Mark Beissinger (2002, 47) reminded us, 'not all historical eras are alike. There are times when change occurs so slowly that time seems almost frozen, though beneath the surface considerable turbulence and evolution may be silently at work. There are other times when change is so compressed, blaring, and fundamental that it is almost impossible to take its measure.' Eventful protests might therefore transform relations through causal mechanisms such as appropriation of opportunities, the activation of networks, and the increased resonance of some frames (McAdam et al. 2001; della Porta 2017a).

This volume

In sum, this introductory chapter has addressed the role of progressive movements as the most vocal actors in denouncing the democratic malaise in contemporary society. While various normative theories have pointed towards the importance of participation and deliberation for the legitimation of democracy, the historical role of social movements in deepening democracy is well documented in the empirical social science literature. Initially considered as a pathology of democracy (or, at least, a sign of dysfunction), social movements have increasingly been understood as a central component of democratic systems. In particular, movements are critical actors capable of promoting inclusion and fostering the epistemic qualities of social and political systems. Nonetheless, scholarship has given little attention to the specific contribution of social movements to democratic innovations, defined as new ways to address the malfunctioning of democratic institutions. To fill this gap, this volume builds upon social movement studies in order to address the potential of, but also limitations on, progressive movements' capability to innovate.

In each chapter, the theorization based on the bridging of social movement studies with studies of, respectively, constitutions, referendums and parties will be accompanied by the empirical analysis of a few specific cases. While focusing on the Great Recession, I have selected for each chapter what could be considered as 'most different' cases, in order to point especially at similarities in the mechanisms and dynamics of movement-based democratic innovations. Methodologically, I aim to go beyond most of the previously mentioned case studies and small-N comparisons of similar cases. A step I consider important at this stage in comparative research is to move beyond the analyses that trace dissimilarities between similar types, and look instead for similarities in the way in which different cases developed. Following McAdam, Tarrow and Tilly's *Dynamics of Contention* (2001), as well as della Porta and Keating's *Approaches and Methodologies in the Social Sciences* (2008), I will build my theorization in two steps, by first analysing a most paradigmatic case of the specific democratic innovation developed from within anti-austerity protests in Europe that I address in each chapter, and then assessing the robustness of the explanations in a few additional cases.

The empirical evidence comes in part from fieldwork conducted during comparative research projects carried out at the Center on Social Movement Studies (Cosmos) at the Scuola Normale Superiore in Florence, mainly using in-depth interviews and document analysis. Fieldwork has been carried out on the analysed cases in Iceland, Italy, Catalonia, Scotland and Spain (see della Porta, Andretta et al. 2016; della

Porta, Fernández et al. 2017; della Porta, O'Connor et al. 2017a, 2017b), while the Irish and the Bolivian cases are based on the analysis of existing literature. In all cases, I will rely on comparative historical analysis. As Daniel Ritter (2014, 107) has noted, most often:

> the objective is not to discover new facts, but to provide a new interpretation with the help of 'old' evidence. As a consequence, comparative historical researchers depend especially on the meticulous work done by historians and area specialists, but also on those produced by sociologists, political scientists, anthropologists, psychologists, diplomats, and journalists. As a rule of thumb, anything written from a social scientific or professional perspective could constitute evidence. The comparative historical scholar's task is in part to evaluate the credentials of other authors, and thus the credibility of the sources.

Indeed, following Ritter's lead, I used three categories of secondary sources: historical accounts of a country, texts focusing specifically on the research topic, and texts dealing more specifically with factors considered as causally relevant (Ritter 2014, 108).

The second chapter addresses forms of citizens' participation in constitution-making: what has been defined as *crowd-sourced constitutional processes*, focusing upon constitutional processes that explicitly aim at involving citizens in constitution-making. Constitutions are a fundamental element of the stable set of political opportunities that are often considered as particularly influential in defining the conditions for contentious politics, their characteristics and outcomes. In fact, in particular during transitions to democracy, participation by social movements promotes constitutions that not only are more open to claims from below, but also open up more channels of political participation. Besides in transitions to democracy, social movements contribute to creating constitutional moments, that in their forms and contents are resonant with their participatory and deliberative visions. If social movement studies have rarely addressed their constitutional effects, constitution-making has long moved out of the area of sociological inquiry altogether. As a time of 'constitutional acceleration' has been noted (and in part at least connected to the economic crisis), a recent wave of attention to constitutions has focused in particular on issues of legitimation through citizens' participation. Connecting this research to the study of contentious politics, the chapter addresses the constitutive powers of movements in terms of their impact upon the constitutional process by looking at cases of so-called crowd-sourced constitutional processes – especially the Icelandic one, but also the Irish.

The third chapter analyses the role of social movements as promoters of or main actors in direct democracy, with particular attention to *referendums from below*, defined as cases in which social movements have been promoters or main actors in the process. While there are very different types of referendums, some of which are used as an instrument of the elites rather than of challengers, there are several potential linkages between referendum politics and contentious politics. In recent times, several important referendums took place in Europe (and beyond) with broad participation of citizens not only in the electoral moment but also in the communication campaign that preceded it. In these cases, social movements affected the organizational forms, repertoire of action and framing of the issues at stake, opening up participatory and deliberative spaces. The chapter will combine insights from social movement studies and studies on direct democracy to investigate under which conditions social movements' mobilization in institutions of direct democracy can improve their inclusive and deliberative qualities. The cases chosen as illustrations are of highly participated referendums: against the privatization of water supply in Italy, on Scottish independence, and for Catalonian independence.

The fourth chapter looks at *movement parties*, defined by their tight connections with social movements, as potential innovators in party systems and electoral politics. Movement parties emerge as a sort of hybrid between movements and parties, participating in protest campaigns, but also acting in the electoral arena. As social movements are networks of organizations and individuals, movement parties can be considered as part of them, as testified by overlapping memberships as well as organizational and action links. Additionally, even if in different formats, they aim at integrating the movement constituencies within their organizations, representing movements' claims and appealing to movements' identities. Even if using (also) an electoral logic, they tend to be supportive of protest, participating in campaigns together with other movement organizations. Movement parties developing from within contemporary progressive social movements can therefore be expected not only to represent claims for social justice and 'real' democracy, but also to innovate their organizational models and action strategies in more participatory and deliberative democratic directions. While parties are important for movements and vice versa, the literature on relations between the two is at best sparse as research on parties moved away from concerns with the relations between parties and society, focusing on parties within institutions, and social movement studies mainly framed them as a social phenomenon, whose political aspects had to be located outside of political institutions. Referring to social movement studies but also party studies, the chapter develops some main expectations about the conditions for the rise and success of movement parties, with special attention to their potential for democratic innovation. In this endeavour, the Spanish Podemos is taken as a main case, with Bolivian MAS providing for a comparative perspective.

In the concluding chapter, I will summarize first the analysis of democratic innovations such as crowd-sourced constitutionalism, referendums from below and movement parties. Second, I will review some of the empirical evidence, research results and arguments presented in the three previous chapters in the light of their contributions to the main fields of knowledge in the social sciences: social movement studies (especially social movement outcomes) and empirical theories of democracy (especially democratic changes). Stressing the importance of concepts such as eventful protest and critical junctures, I will conclude with some reflections on moments of crisis as intense times, opening up challenges and opportunities.

2

Crowd-Sourced Constitutionalism: Social Movements in the Constitutional Process

Constitutions are a fundamental element of the stable set of political opportunities that are often considered as particularly influential in defining the conditions for contentious politics, its characteristics and its outcomes. During transitions to democracy, progressive social movements push for constitutions that not only are more open to claims from below, but also provide for more channels of political participation (della Porta 2017a). Besides in transitions to democracy, especially in times of perceived challenges or opening of political opportunities, social movements contribute to creating constitutional moments. Crowd-sourced constitutions are defined in this chapter as constitutional processes prompted by grassroots mobilizations and involving citizens in constitution-making.

In order to address the role that the participation of citizens in processes of constitution-building can have, we must begin with a definition of constitutions. In conceptions of democracy, constitutions set up the main rules about the relations between citizens and the state, as well as among various state institutions. In this sense, constitutions have the important function of protecting the fundamental rights of minorities – constitutionalizing those rights so that they cannot be easily withdrawn by a temporary majority. In a recent conceptualization, constitutions have been defined as:

> A legal order impacting on the exercise of political power that (a) contains an effectively established presumption of public rule in accordance with principles or conventions, expressed as law, that cannot easily (i.e. without societally unsettling controversy) be suspended; (b) is designed to constrain or restrict egregiously mandatory use of power in both public and private functions; (c) allocates powers within the state itself, and comprises some form of popular/political representation in respect of questions perceived as possessing importance for all politically relevant sectors of society; and (d) expresses a legal distinction between the form of the state and those persons assuming authority to borrow and enforce the power stored within the state. (Thornhill 2011, 10–11)

If social movement studies have rarely analysed their constitutional effects, constitution-making seems, for some time, to have moved out of the area of sociological inquiry altogether. As Thornhill (2011) noted, sociology itself promoted a critical view of power and order that went beyond its formal definition as deriving from constitutional law:

> If the political centre of the Enlightenment lay in the belief that political institutions obtain legitimacy if they enshrine constitutional laws translating abstract notions of justice and personal dignity into legal and normative constraints for the use of public and private power, sociology was first formed as a diffuse and politically pluralistic body of literature that opposed this belief. Sociology first evolved as a discipline that sought to promote reflection on the legitimacy of socio-political orders by elucidating the ways in which societies produce inner reserves of cohesion, obligation and legitimacy, without accepting the simplified view that these reserves were generated, and could be reliably authorized, by spontaneous external acts of reason. . . . At the centre of each of these theories was a negation of the principle that states acquire legitimacy from constitutional laws because these laws articulate simple promptings of universal reason to which states, in order to exercise their power in legitimate fashion, automatically owe compliance. (Thornhill 2011, 2)

When classical sociologists (such as Ferdinand Tönnies, Émile Durkheim and Max Weber) paid attention to constitutions, they located them within broader societal processes, within which they analysed the very origins of constitutions (Thornhill 2011).

While long forgotten in the social sciences, more recent sociological research has, however, addressed the evolution of constitutions and constitutionalism, with special attention to the challenges to processes of legitimation of political power. Indeed, a sociological approach has been promoted to analyse constitutions as developing through complex historical and functional processes, with constitutional moments presented as disjunctures (Thornhill 2011, 10).

In this sociological approach to constitutions, a Luhmanian interpretation has located constitutions within a process of functional differentiation that triggered the establishment of the political as a separate system. In particular, the historical evolution of constitutions is analysed as part of the formation of modern Western societies. In this vision, constitutions emerge and develop following intra-societal processes of functional articulation, with continuous differentiation in the functioning of societies and of political institutions. In these processes, constitutions regulate in particular the interactions and exchanges between different spheres of action, allowing the production and reproduction of power (Thornhill 2011, 372). At the onset, constitutions emerged as a legal set of norms that allowed states to acquire positive statutory functions by detaching their functions from the private sphere. In their evolution, modern constitutions granted states police power at the same time as constraining their range of intervention. In time, constitutions became guarantors of sovereignty and democratic procedure, constraining state power and separating it from external interference. In this process:

> the primary norms of constitutional rule, in consequence, can be seen as adaptive dimensions of political power itself. These are institutions generated within power as power became progressively sensitive to highly differentiated societal environments, and as society as a whole, shaped by its functional extension and differentiation, created and encountered a need for more inclusive and autonomous capacities for using power. (Thornhill 2011, 373–4)

Besides this reflection on long-term social transformations, a recent wave of attention to constitutions was triggered by the observation of an increase in constitutional activities. In fact, a time of *constitutional acceleration* has been highlighted, with a growing recourse to constitution-making, but also constitutional updating (Palermo 2007). This has been even more the case in Europe, not only because of the integration process in the EU as well as the transition to democracy in Eastern Europe, but also more broadly as a recourse to constitutional changes in order to address the political consequences of the financial crisis and of broader transformation in the role of constitutions themselves, even in already established democracies. More generally, research has analysed the judicialization of democratic politics and legislation, with a more and more prominent role for Constitutional Courts in contemporary societies, and the fading away of parliamentary sovereignty, sometimes explained as oriented towards protecting international economic elites (Hirschl 2004; Thornhill 2012).

The EU constitutional process has in particular been defined as a highly judicialized process, with EU courts intervening in interstate treaties. In this way, 'the courts, applying rights, act as primary bearers of constitution-making power. In consolidating interstate treaties as basic norms for legislation and defining jurisprudential norms to support the supremacy of European law, they routinely perform the acts of public-legal norm production that are imputed in classical constitutional polities to constitutional legislators authorised by an identifiable demos' (Thornhill 2012, 356). Responses to the financial and political crises, with the delegation of decisions to opaque institutions (such as the Eurogroup), have, however, challenged that constitutional balance, thus jeopardizing stability in the long term and, with it, the very legitimacy of the EU project (Dawson and de Witte 2013).

The aforementioned constitutional acceleration also triggered new visions of constitutions, which, first of all, moved beyond legalist constitutionalism, recognizing their political character. While legal constitutionalism had singled out some sort of essential conditions for democracy, *political constitutionalism* highlighted instead the contested nature of rights: 'Despite widespread support for both constitutional rights and rights-based judicial review, theorists, politicians, lawyers and ordinary citizens frequently disagree over which rights merit or require such entrenchment, the legal form they should take, the best way of implementing them, their relationship to each other, and the manner in which courts should understand and uphold them' (Bellamy 2007, 16). In fact, challenging the definition of basic norms, political constitutionalists see the main constitutional functions as lying in the provision of a shared framework in order to resolve disagreements about the right and the good. In this perspective, constitutions are to be dynamic since those shared frameworks need to be continuously revised and updated. The constitution is therefore conceived not as an 'entrenched set of fundamental principles, but rather as the framework for the articulation of and deliberation over conceptions of self-government and the common good' (Blokker 2017, 36). In this view, constitutions are not constraints imposed upon democracy, but rather limits that mature democracies have to place upon themselves (Bellamy 2007, 91). Given their political character, constitutions are in continual mutation, adapting to different contexts and cultures and, as such, they cannot be considered as an objective source of moral and political wisdom (Bellamy 2007, 166). Reflecting different norms and visions, they are open processes, with continuous reinterpretation prompted by societal and political changes (Hart 2003).

However, constitutions are not only political in the sense of being built upon political compromise from an instrumental perspective, they also have a symbolic value supporting collective identification in a political community. In this sense, a constitution is meant to represent the moral authority a political collectivity imposes upon individuals (Přibaň 2007), becoming a symbol of unity (Scholl 2006, 38). Thus, Paul Blokker (2010) distinguishes a dominant negative understanding of constitutionalism that points towards its instrumental, political function of limiting political power also by defining spheres of autonomy from it, and a conception that highlights instead a positive, cultural or symbolic dimension, as expressing core ethical values, oriented to promoting the identification and the participation of the citizen. It is especially this symbolic value of constitutions that is called into question in times of crisis as 'the symbolic dimension of constitutions invokes ultimate values, extra-societal markers such as natural rights, and societal traditions and identity which need to be protected and promoted by the constitution . . . The constitution articulates through its symbolic dimension a (constructed) collective unity and a form of collective self-understanding' (Blokker 2010, 75).

Constitutions are also seen as (more and more) in need of legitimation through popular participation, with the increasing involvement of social movements in constitutional processes seen as increasing citizens' participation in general (Blount 2011). This increasing role of popular participation in the production and transformation of the constitutional order has been noted in a growing number of cases. This is itself conceived as fundamental in order to address increasing political discontent, as well as its causes within broader challenges to democratic legitimacy. Constitutional revision is then implemented in a process which includes the voice of the people in order to respond to citizens' discontent and perceived institutional limits (Blokker 2017, 31). In Europe, such cases include constitutional processes in Iceland, Ireland and the Netherlands, as well as to a lesser extent in Romania, and with the Convention on the Future of Europe. Likewise, in the UK, proposals are currently being made to set up a Constitutional Convention including citizens. This recourse to the people is a countertendency to the previous move towards a so-called juristocracy within a 'new constitutionalism' that had grown since the end of World War II (Sweet 2008) but had also characterized the East European post-1989 constitutions, with a legalistic and rigid approach and limited attention to civic democratic engagement (Blokker 2013).

In a search for democratic innovation and legitimacy, a *popular constitutionalism* has supported extensive forms of popular engagement in constitutional politics (Blokker 2017). While, historically, some constitutional processes have also in fact been characterized by grassroots mobilization and politicization (such as, e.g., in the Italian constitutional process after World War II), this trend seems to have recently intensified. In particular, constitutional moments are in fact considered as particular times in which people more intensively and directly participate in the political process. In Bruce Ackerman's view, constitutional politics – in contrast to normal politics – develops out of exceptional circumstances in which some forms of grassroots engagement might take the forefront (Ackerman 1991, 171). In these creative moments, citizens' initiatives can became central drivers of constitutional change (Ackerman 1991), with high levels of civic mobilization. Interestingly, these moments are triggered by various crises as historic events (such as war, economic crisis or moral disruption) catalyse sudden and massive increases in political consciousness and appeal to broad commitment to public life (Ackerman 1995, 66).

Bruce Ackerman (2015, 705) singled out in particular three paths to constitutionalism in the modern world, each of them endowed with its own set of legitimation problems. In the first, followed in constitutional processes in countries such as India, South Africa, Italy and France, it is revolutionary outsiders that use the constitutional moment in order to channel into the new regime the claims that they had raised during their struggle. In the second path, as in Britain, insiders have used constitutions strategically in order to weaken revolutionary movements by making limited concessions. In a third path, as in Spain, Japan and Germany, it is political and social elites that form pacts around the constitutional process. Each path generates different problems as far as legitimation is concerned.

Particularly relevant for the debate on *grassroots constitutionalism* in moments of crisis is the first path, in which

> a movement of revolutionary outsiders mobilizes against the existing government at Time one. Many would-be revolutionaries are crushed at this point, but some have triumphed over the status quo. This sets the stage for the founding of the new regime at Time two. During the period of struggle against the old order, the insurgents issued public declarations justifying their sustained acts of resistance. Now that they have gained power, they translate these declarations into a constitution that commits the new regime to their revolutionary principles and organizes power to prevent a recurrence of past abuses. Since the revolutionaries challenge the status quo, they often gain ascendancy after a military struggle. (Ackerman 2015, 706)

The perception of a crisis can, however, also trigger insider constitutionalism when the insiders react to popular movements calling for change through strategic concessions. In the third path, social movements can be involved when insider elites need to build alliances with once-outsiders, in order to achieve compromises.

While the role of citizens is, in this theorization, the promotion of popularly elected conventions in which elites take the lead, in *democratic constitutionalism* instead a radical vision of democracy is put forward, developing from the idea that ordinary citizens should, as far as possible, be given a voice in proposing, discussing and deciding upon constitutional changes through the opening of various channels of participation (Colon-Rios 2011, 3). Against depoliticizing and juridifying trends, which are seen as contributing to generate problems of democratic legitimacy, there is a call for the creation of a multiplicity of sites in which citizens can participate in democratic practice (Tully 2008, 98). Constitutional law, then, should not be isolated from the passions of mass politics, but rather involve their constituent power (Colon-Rios 2013, 208–15), being able to 'propose, deliberate and decide upon important constitutional transformations through extraordinary mechanisms that work independently of a constitution's ordinary amendment procedure' (Colon-Rios 2013, 37).

Civic constitutionalism supports a democratic view of constitutional processes as requiring a more direct and substantive participation of citizens, especially highlighting the open-ended nature of the process, and the ultimately contested nature of rights. So, while modern constitutionalism considers constitutional processes as a 'social contract in which basic political definitions, principles, and processes are agreed upon', civic constitutionalism requires a conversation, which is carried out by all those who are concerned, and is open to new actors and issues (Blokker 2017, 41). From the normative point of view, civic constitutionalism struggles therefore for the 'extension of democratic process to include, free, open, and responsive discussion of the constitutional settlement' (Hart 2003, 5). Politics is here conceived of as the ruling of people, which extends to all matters, including the creation of fundamental laws (Colon-Rios 2009, 23).

It is exactly in this conception that the role of social movements as constitutive forces is more openly called for. As Bailey and Mattei observed, the 'constituent power' of social movements, as promoting and enforcing constitutional processes, has rarely been recognized. While formally assigning constituent power to the people, classical constitutional theorists have conceived popular sovereignty as legitimately exercised only through elected representatives. This raised the problem as to 'how can the state produce constitutional law when it is the constitution itself that produces the state? What segments of societal forms of political and civil organization are included in this category of the "people", and what is the "state" prior to the making of the social contract, which itself designates and constitutes their political status?' (Bailey and Mattei 2013, 969–70).

In this view, a constitution is an originary narrative, offering an account of the source of legal and political authority, and grounding it in the political will of a 'people' understood as capable of acting as a unified entity. In fact, the 'people' is itself defined by the constitution as a unified political entity which is constituted by the constitutional process, rather than having an a priori status (Buchanan 2006; Bailey and Mattei 2013, 970). So, 'The paradox of the constitutional narrative is that the origin has to "be" before and after the point of origination' (Bailey and Mattei 2013, 970). In this sense, the constitutional process allows for the shift from the multitude to the people, the former being defined as an unformed constituent power, capable of creating the very condition of possibility of the modern conception of popular sovereignty (Tully 2007; Bailey and Mattei 2013, 971).

In sum, recent research on constitutionalism points towards the relevance of crisis moments in constitutional change. In particular, crises require citizens' involvement in the redefinition of collective norms. As we are going to see in what follows, participatory values, spread during waves of protests, transferred (often through the work of translators within the political system) into complex dynamics in which movement and institutional actors interacted within newly created arenas. Given conducive institutional settings, mechanisms for constitution-making were activated that involved participatory and deliberative conceptions. In this process, political opportunities were appropriated in action, and resources mobilized within inclusive framing. Social movement involvement, in different forms and to different extents, had a procedural impact, with importance given to inclusivity as well as to the quality of the discourse that eventually facilitated the progressive contents in the end product of the constitutional processes. Even if the constitutional process is still ongoing and the results open-ended, these experiences seem to have had a long-lasting emancipatory effect, with a widespread sense of empowerment.

During the financial crisis in Europe, Iceland offers the best example of a constitutional process led by social movements in which 'citizens and social movements were not only the initiators of critique and change. Citizens played a constitutive part throughout the attempt at constitution-making that was set up in the wake of the protests' (Blokker 2017, 44). In what follows, I will reconstruct the conditions under which the Icelandic crowd-sourced constitutional process developed as a way to respond to a deep economic, but also social and political, crisis. In this disruptive moment, the massive mobilization of society took innovative forms within which the crowd-sourced constitutional experiment was conceived and carried out. In a similar way, in Ireland the financial and then political and social crisis brought about a participatory constitutional process, which was considered as a way to reconstitute a national community, its values and identity. In this sense, constitutionalism from below can be understood as a social movement outcome of a special type. For each of the two cases, I will look at the social and political context, characterized by a widespread conception of a crisis, as well as at the social movements that mobilized against the assumed causes of the crisis itself. Further, I will look at the constitutional processes, with particular attention to the activation of mechanisms of appropriation of opportunities, resource mobilization and collective framing. In this reconstruction, the participatory and deliberative qualities of the process will be stated, together with its empowering capacity.

Iceland in the crisis

In 2008 Iceland was the first European country to be heavily hit by the financial crash, after having experienced very high rates of economic growth between 2005 and 2007. It was in 2008 that the seeds of a grassroots constitutional process are to be found in the midst of massive protests and political turmoil. As a document of the Icelandic Citizens' Movement (2009) stressed:

> We must make radical democratic reform to ensure that the events of the last months will not repeat themselves. . . . We must build from the bottom up . . . initiate a discourse on what kind of society we want, what values we wish to uphold and how we want to distribute power to those that seek to represent us in government. Post collapse, the build up and investigation needs to be put on a certain path.

The crisis

With high private debt and the devaluation of the Icelandic currency, the crisis had indeed a severe impact on the everyday life of the people. By 2009 almost half of mortgages and bank loans, mostly taken out in a foreign currency, could not be repaid, and for this reason, between 2009 and 2013, about three families per day were being dispossessed of their houses because of debts (Hallgrímsdóttir and Brunet-Jailly 2015, 87). As a citizen explained: 'Because of the currency collapse, imports became too expensive. We have a small agriculture sector, a fishery sector, but we're not self-sufficient. So, a lot of consumer goods became inaccessible to the population. . . . We didn't have any imports coming into Iceland for two weeks. People started worrying, started panicking' (in della Porta, Andretta et al. 2016, 41).

The depth of the crisis was linked to the privatization of banking in the mid-2000s. Since then, Landsbanki, Kaupthing and Glitnir, the three main Icelandic commercial banks, had started to offer very high interest rates. In addition to this, Landsbanki established a subsidiary branch, Icesave, that collected deposits. Part of the banks' profits went to support the activities of centre-right political parties. The collapse of Lehman Brothers heavily affected the three banks, which were no longer in a position to repay their creditors. Their insolvency then brought about a collapse of the financial market, with ensuing depreciation by 50% of the Icelandic krona against the euro, a GDP breakdown, the sharp decline of the OMX15 Iceland stock index (by 90%), an increase in unemployment (from 1% to 9%), while over 65% of Icelandic companies became insolvent (Ostaszewski 2013, 61).

In this context, Icelandic citizens experienced a profound and broad disruption to their everyday life. In fact, the speed of the emergence of the economic crisis in 2008 was a highly important element in defining its dynamics, as the breakdown happened almost overnight. Within a few days,

> Iceland's three largest banks were placed into receivership and every day appeared to bring a new batch of bad news. Icelanders felt the consequences of the collapse of the banking system immediately. People who had invested in the banks' stocks saw their savings wiped out. While perhaps not significant in itself there was no way to get money in or out of the country for a few days, which bred feelings of isolation and helplessness among many. (Indridason 2014, 134)

Additionally, given very high domestic interest rates, many mortgages and other loans had been taken out in foreign currencies with lower interest rates. The significant devaluation of the Icelandic krona resulted in a substantial increase in the cost of these loans. As a result, 'the crisis did more than create widespread anticipation of personal economic loss. It produced a collectively experienced disruption in taken-for-granted reality; it disrupted taken-for-granted assumptions and ideas about Icelandic society, thus resulting in a shared experience of a problematic present' (Bernburg 2016, 41).

The financial breakdown reverberated across the political system, triggering a sudden drop in institutional trust (for example, trust in Parliament fell from 40% to 13%). The financial crisis, especially between early October and November 2008, affected institutional legitimacy as:

after liberating capital from state restraints and privatizing the banks, neither the present nor the previous government, nor the supervisory agencies (the Central Bank and the Financial Supervisory Authority) had sufficiently restrained the financial sector from outgrowing the Icelandic economy, threatening state insolvency and jeopardizing the country's welfare system. Ambitiously unleashing market forces, the authorities had seemingly done nothing to prevent the public from potential harm; they had stood by watching the banks accumulate risk at the expense of the public. (Bernburg 2016, 45)

The crisis also had political consequences, revealing a complex system of collusion between business and political parties, especially on the Right. It emerged that the conservative Independence Party (IP), when in power, had accepted controversial donations. A Special Investigation Committee, appointed by the Parliament, identified seven politicians and public officials who had neglected their duties as laid down by law – four of them from the IP, whose President, David Oddsson, was suspected of criminal negligence and then found guilty by the Court of Impeachment of violating the law on ministerial responsibility (Gylfason 2012). In addition, the former chief executive officer of the IP was sued by the Landsbanki (on whose board he was a member) for his responsibility in the bank's collapse (Gylfason 2012). The then prime minister was accused of lack of proper supervision of the banking sector.

In the midst of the economic crisis and related scandals, the party system was deeply shaken. At the local level, the newly founded Best Party performed unexpectedly well in the 2010 election in Reykjavik (Indridason 2014). At the national level, in 2009, the IP, which had led the government when the crisis had exploded, lost 13% of the vote while the Left parties increased their support, with 2% more for the Social Democratic Alliance (SDA), and an increase of over 7% each for the Left Green Movement (a left-wing party founded in 1999) and for the Citizens' Movement (which had been founded in 2009, asking for radical solutions to the crisis).

In 2009, a new government was formed by the SDA and the Left Green Movement that, initially within a minority coalition, eventually acquired a legislative majority (Indridason 2014). In reaction to the financial crisis, some steps were made in the direction of re-regulation, with increasing control over the banking sector and a new law separating investment activity from deposits, decreasing investment activities and shrinking bank assets almost to a fifth of their former levels. The decision to restructure the banks Kaupthing and Islandsbanki also signalled a clear turning point since, unlike in Greece or Ireland, 'the Icelandic government decided not to fund the bank deficit with taxpayers' money, which in the longer term seems to be a reasonable step in the Icelandic economic reality' (Ostaszewski 2013, 58). In addition, as mentioned, a parliamentary truth committee was constituted and ministers put on trial. Various interventions contributed to stabilizing the exchange rate, reigniting economic growth and decreasing unemployment.

What is more, the financial crisis of 2008 triggered a complex process of direct democracy in Iceland. The Icesave referendums in 2010 and 2011 were put in place by the president's decision to demand that the Icesave Bill, which essentially upheld collective national responsibility for private banking debts (mainly towards Dutch and British banks, which had invested in a local bank that had gone bankrupt in 2008), be submitted to a popular vote. Although passed by the Icelandic Parliament, the first Icesave Bill, which would have implied a repayment of approximately $17,000 for each Icelander (man, woman and child) in a country of only 320,000, was not signed by President Ólafur Grímsson. After invoking Article 26 of the Constitution on 5 January 2010, he put the resolution to a national referendum. It became clear that 'Icelandic voters believed, like Grímsson, that the taxpayers should not be forced to shoulder foreign debts incurred by the country's bankers' (Fillmore-Patrick 2013, 7). After the referendum resulted in an almost unanimous No vote on the repayments (of the 62.7% of registered voters who participated, 98.1% voted No), in 2011 a second referendum also rejected a reformed version of the Icesave Bill (with 75.3% of eligible voters participating, No received a lower but still resounding 59.8%) (Hallgrímsdóttir and Brunet-Jailly 2015). After British Prime Minister Gordon Brown announced that the UK government would take legal action using anti-terrorism legislation in order to freeze Iceland's properties abroad, in 2013 the European Free Trade Court ruled that Iceland was not responsible for repayment (Bergmann 2014).

Mobilizing for change

Among the conditions that allowed for addressing deep economic and political crises through political innovation was the development of an immediate and massive reaction by Icelandic citizens that started in 2008 and continued until 2012, creating not only disruption but also calls for a new identification. Organized horizontally, the protest activities empowered the Icelandic people, by producing innovative ideas. As Wade and Sigurgeirsdóttir (2011, 693) noted:

> From the normally placid and consumption-obsessed population an anxious, angry protest movement emerged. A handful of organizers, mainly people like singers, writers and theatre directors who had been

outside politics, called for rallies in the main square in front of the parliament building to demand a change of government. Thousands of people, all age groups and distinctly middle-class, assembled in shoulder-to-shoulder numbers never seen before in Iceland. . . . For all the fear and anger the protestors also felt a sense of elated solidarity.

In a country with very limited experience with contentious politics, the 'pots and pans revolution' – so called because of the use of kitchen utensils by the protesters – succeeded in mobilizing a large part of the population. The protests were innovative, from an organizational point of view to the forms of action and the collective framing.

The mobilizations, which started with a rock concert organized by a tiny and unpolitical group, spread quickly and massively. On 20 January 2009, thousands of people gathered in front of Parliament, in the central square of Reykjavík, remaining there for three days. Given the perceived lack of responsiveness by the political parties in power to the suffering of the citizens, disruptive protests multiplied, calling for the government to resign. Marches and meetings in downtown Reykjavík attracted growing numbers of individuals. Public spaces were created as

a platform for challenging the way in which the authorities framed the crisis as a global, as opposed to a local, problem. In the course of a few weeks, thousands of individuals began to attend the meetings, including nationally known intellectuals, critics, and activists, who argued that Iceland's political leadership had led the nation into crisis due to corruption and blind faith in market forces. Collective demands emerged: the ruling government was called on to resign, along with the Chairman of the Board of Governors of the Central Bank, and the Director of the Financial Supervisory Authority. (Bernburg 2016, 16)

Faced with the sudden crisis and a perceived lack of capacity of elected politicians to intervene, protests took massive and at times radical forms, in what came to be known as the 'pots and pans revolution': '[T]he protests went on for three successive days and created an atmosphere of civil unrest and disorder throughout the downtown area, and the noise could be heard kilometres away. In the evenings, bonfires were lit, and the demonstrations turned into riots; police used gas and batons to disperse the crowd' (Bernburg 2016, 7).

Confrontations were, however, rare. Rather, the innovation in forms of action included the use of pots and pans during demonstrations (following the Argentinian example), but also a bottom-up process of constitution-writing. In a virtuous circle, the massive involvement in the mobilization increased the sense of efficacy among protesters, fuelling further participation.

As for the framing, the activists developed a moral discourse that targeted the political corruption of an octopus-like elite, characterized by the collusion of businesspeople and politicians. Their greed was contrasted with a tradition of solidarity that was considered as deep-rooted in the country. Claiming back the state, with appeals to increasing regulation, the protesters, however, also developed a participatory conception of democracy, presenting themselves as a horizontal citizens' movement.

The protest was highly politicized, bridging moral opposition to injustice and claims for national sovereignty, but also for citizens' participation, as protesters complained about 'The moral injustice of it all!' (in Hallgrímsdóttir and Brunet-Jailly 2015, 84). In fact, 'while respondents often drew on sophisticated and technical arguments when discussing the Icesave debts, these arguments were generally presented within a highly normative framing of the issue that centered on moral reasoning, that is, questions of right and wrong. Key to this framing of Icesave was the idea that principles of natural justice were being violated through the Icesave repayment deals' (Hallgrímsdóttir and Brunet-Jailly 2015, 84–5).

National identification also strengthened, within a new vision of the nation. In a country that had fought hard for its independence, the perceived arrogance of foreign countries in their requests that the Icelandic people repay the debt of private banks reignited the anti-British sentiment that had been triggered in the past by the so-called Cod Wars. The debate on Icesave has been considered to be, in fact, 'an engagement with the larger global world where the "global" has become a part of most people's imagined world'. The 'social memory of past disputes was, thus, mobilised between the countries and the dispute contextualised by some Icelanders in light of Britain's imperial past' (Loftsdóttir 2016, 339). National sovereignty was often seen as being challenged by powerful countries – 'This is how they treat small nations' (cited in Loftsdóttir 2016, 352). In a David-against-Goliath narrative, protesters identified with the small Icelandic nation fighting against the global elites, particularly the banks, feeling under 'attack from the Dutch and Brits' (Loftsdóttir 2016). Identifying the struggle against the repayment as a 'struggle for independence', an activist noted: 'Our independence war was with Great Britain, the Cod Wars. . . . And the issue on Icesave was kind of a rerun of this thing where Great Britain was trying to take little Iceland by its fists and shake it around' (cited in Hallgrímsdóttir and Brunet-Jailly 2015, 85). The Icelanders were praised for 'standing up to the financial sector' and served as a 'role model in the battle that has now begun in Europe due to the debt crisis' (cited in Loftsdóttir 2016, 354). The refusal to use taxpayers' money to pay for the mistakes of private banks was defended through appeals to justice: 'We should never accept the state's obligation for the private debt of banks' (cited in Loftsdóttir 2016, 355).

In this context, citizens acquired constitutive power thanks also to institutional allies. Important (and unexpected) support for the protest came,
as mentioned, from the president of the Republic Ólaffur Grímmson,
who became a source of inspiration for the protest, having refused to
enact a law that had been passed by Parliament but which the majority
of the people found unjust (Ostaszewski 2013, 58). In particular, at
the onset of the crisis, he had responded to the activists' expectations,
expressed in a petition signed by more than 60,000 citizens (a quarter of
the electorate) (Curtis et al. 2014, 722). So:

> Backed by the President's decision, the society imposed a definite veto,
> which forced the Icelandic government to renegotiate the agreement, to
> hold a referendum twice and finally to be taken to court by the United
> Kingdom and the Netherlands. This phenomenon led to a process of
> developing direct democracy, which resulted not so much in changing
> the constitution top-down by a special constitutional committee as in
> appealing to the public, who decided about the shape of constitutional
> reforms in a referendum. (Ostaszewski 2013, 58)

After the national elections that followed the financial crash, the protesters also found some support in the new coalition government formed
by the Social Democrats and the Left Greens. It was also thanks to these
alliances that a grassroots constitutional process emerged.

The crowd-sourced constitutional process

What was later called a crowd-sourced constitutional process developed
from the combination of disruptive protests and institutional influence.
As mentioned above, the shock of the crash brought about a call for participation by citizens, so that the movement 'really opened up a space that
just simply wasn't there before the crash' (Hallgrímsdottir and Brunet-
Jailly 2015, 85–6). After a double defeat of the Icelandic goverment in
the two referendums on the Icesave law proposal, citizens' organizations
demanded a referendum on a new constitution to refound the nation,
reinstating core collective values that had been shaken by the financial
crash. This triggered a constitutional reform process that developed
through the National Assemblies of 2009 and 2010; the Constitutional
Assembly (which was later renamed the Constitutional Council) of 2011;
and a referendum in 2012 (della Porta, Andretta et al. 2016).

The referendums on Icesave were accompanied by a constitutional
process dubbed 'crowd-sourced', as citizens were invited to participate
in different forms. Aware of the need to re-constitute a social pact
that citizens considered as broken by the mainstream political parties,

before the 2009 election most parties promised to open a constitutional process 'outsourcing' some core and conflictual decisions to the people (Katrin Oddsdottir, in England 2015). The idea of writing a new constitution through a participatory process came from an MP for the Social Democratic party, Jóhanna Sigurdardóttir. Among the promoters of the process was the Association for Sustainability and Democracy (Alda), a civil society organization that aimed at democratic deepening through, for example, the introduction of institutionalized forms of public debate and participatory budgeting (Ársælsson 2012).

At the onset of the process, a network of liberal grassroots think tanks, the Anthill, held a National Assembly (*Thjodfundur*) on 14 November 2009 in Reykjavik. Stressing the importance of promoting participation, the Anthill declared that it would build upon the collective intelligence of citizens in order to redefine the core societal values and develop a new vision for the future. From the procedural point of view, 'the *Thjodfundur* process was meant to be an alternative national visioning process, providing an authentic space where citizens could participate in democracy' (Fillmore-Patrick 2013, 7). The National Assembly consisted of 1,500 people – 1,200 chosen at random from the national registry, and 300 chosen as representatives of companies, institutions and other groups – who met to discuss the core values on which Icelandic governance should proceed. In the following year, the Anthill then organized about 100 local *thjodfundurs* diffused across the territory, with a total participation of about 20,000 people. Randomly selected small groups and thematically specialized ones discussed constitutional issues with facilitators who were to guarantee participatory democracy as well as the quality of the debates (della Porta, O'Connor et al. 2017a, 177). The process was highly inclusive and plural in terms of the background of the participants.

Later, on 16 June 2010, Parliament passed a constitutional Act initiating the constitutional revision process, and on 6 November 2010, a Constitutional Committee of seven people, appointed by Parliament, organized a new National Assembly with the task of:

> identifying broadly what Icelanders wanted from a new constitution, identifying those values that should form the basis of the new constitution, and providing specific recommendations to the Constitutional Assembly. The Anthill and the polling company Gallup Iceland collaborated to select 1,000 citizens that represented Iceland in terms of gender, age, and geographic location . . . As with the 2009 National Assembly, professional facilitators moderated and enforced *thjodfundur* rules within the groups. Frequent votes and strict facilitation protected the essential participatory democracy of the *thjodfundur* process. (Dessi 2012)

The National Assembly decided that the new constitution had to include key provisions about electoral reform and the ownership of natural resources, which had been for some time the most contentious political issues in the country. As it stated, 'The image of Iceland shall be strengthened, multiculturalism encouraged as well as the separation between state and religion.'

Following the National Assembly's requests, the Constitutional Committee, including professionals such as lawyers, intellectuals and scientists, 'produced a 700-page report with detailed ideas concerning the composition of the new constitution, including suggestive examples of the text of individual articles as well as a thorough, clause-by-clause analysis of the constitution from 1944 and of specific issues, including the electoral system used in parliamentary elections and the management and ownership of natural resources' (Gylfason 2012, 13).

A special Act set up a Constitutional Assembly in charge of reviewing and rewriting the existing constitution, which dated from 1944, when it had been adopted as an adaptation of the Danish Constitution. The Assembly, formed by twenty-five delegates elected by direct personal election, had to convene by 15 February 2011, and to finish working no later than 15 April 2011. The revised Constitution was to be voted on by Parliament and then submitted to a referendum. The mandate was to examine the Constitution and, with the support of experts, to draft a legislative Bill for constitutional change to be submitted to Parliament. The debate had to include the following issues:

1. the foundations of the Icelandic Constitution and its fundamental concepts;
2. the organization of the legislative and executive branches and the limits of their powers;
3. the role and position of the president of the Republic;
4. the independence of the judiciary and their supervision of holders of governmental power;
5. provisions on elections and electoral districts;
6. public participation in the democratic process, including the timing and organization of a referendum, including a referendum on a legislative Bill for a constitutional Act;
7. transfer of sovereign powers to international organizations and the conduct of foreign affairs;
8. environmental matters, including the ownership and utilization of natural resources.

Membership of the Constitutional Assembly was open to ordinary citizens, with 522 of them running for election. On 27 November 2010, the 25 delegates were elected with the participation of about one-third of the electorate. Even if mainly from Reykjavik (only three delegates were not from the capital), overly educated, urban, wealthy, with over-representation of academics and underrepresentation of workers (only one farmer and one worker), the group included people with different experiences outside of institutional politics (Landomore 2017). Formed by ten women and fifteen men, the assembly included five university pro-fessors, three physicians, a lawyer and radio presenter, a mathematician, a farmer, a journalist, a manager, a pastor, the chairman of a publisher, a theatre director, a museum director, a trade unionist, a university student and a consumer spokesperson (Landomore 2017). It has been noted that 'the election campaign was exceptionally civilized, and quite different from parliamentary election campaigns' (Gylfason 2012, 12). That only 35.9 per cent of the eligible voters went to the polls has been explained by a complicated Single Transferable Vote system (voters were asked to list their candidates in order of preference), but also by the reduced trust in the approval of the Bill in the Parliament and by an abstention campaign by the IP (which, however, had the unexpected outcome of bringing about a very progressive Constitutional Assembly) (Gylfason 2012).

On 25 January 2011, the Supreme Court ruled the election to the Constitutional Assembly null and void because of procedural failures; however, Parliament decided nevertheless to appoint the candidates with most votes. The Constitutional Assembly then convened between April and July 2011. After having confirmed the need for a new Constitution, it split into three working groups in order to address the main issues, from the definition of basic values to the evaluation of the role of the president and ensuring democratic participation (della Porta, O'Connor et al. 2017a, 179).

Inspired by the anti-austerity protests, the constitutional process was characterized by the involvement of citizens in different times and var-ious forms in a bottom-up path. As a protagonist of the constitutional process stated:

> The street protests of 2008 and 2009 that followed the crash were mostly directed towards the government of the time and the demand for new elections. At the same time there was this very wide dialogue within the society of Iceland where people were trying to diagnose how they could make a better and fairer society. In the streets the loudest demand was not for a new constitution but for changes in the political landscape at the time. However, when those claims had been met, we still had to figure out how to change society to try and prevent the same thing from happening all over again. We were looking for big structural, big changes and then the constitution became part of the dialogue about

how we can fix this so we don't have the same disaster repeating itself after a few more years. (Katrin Oddsdottir, in England 2015)

In order to involve the population, various documents were published on the assembly's website with presentation of assessments of the 1944 constitution, the work of the assembly, the material it received, and the draft Constitution. Sessions of the assembly were broadcast and twelve drafts of the Constitution posted online. Crowd-sourcing was used, with input from outside called for by social media (YouTube, Twitter, Facebook and Flickr) or using regular email or mail, which brought about a broad response (as many as 3,000 suggestions were posted on the Council's Facebook page). The best proposals, shortlisted by the assembly, were presented for public debate on the website. Main issues addressed included the moral crisis of those in government, ways to improve political accountability, and the opening up of channels for democratic participation (Elkins et al. 2012; England 2015).

The broad participation of citizens in the drafting of the Constitution, through a massive use of new social media, was reflected in its definition as the world's first crowd-sourced Constitution (Elkins et al. 2012). As a key participant in the process stated, 'after participating in this experiment or project I became a huge believer in the wisdom of the crowds. You shouldn't be so afraid of allowing people to take their own decisions through whatever means are possible and that direct democracy – of course you cannot be voting on human rights and so on – but on certain things is the way to go forward because we need to be responsible for decisions we make as a group and that we can only do by making them as a group" (Katrin Oddsdottir in England 2015).

The Constitutional Assembly produced a constitutional Bill that incorporated the conclusions of the National Assembly, and was approved unanimously. According to the proposal, 10 per cent of the electorate can call for a national referendum to reject a law (Article 65) and propose a Bill to the Parliament (Article 66). Citizens are to be involved in the eventual removal of the president (Article 84) as well as in constitutional amendment (Article 113). There is also a very broad access to information (Article 15), a right to the internet (Article 14) and animal rights (Article 36). It is stated that natural resources belong to the people (Article 34), as well as nature having a right of its own (Article 33).

Eventually, a draft Constitution was approved unanimously and submitted to Parliament in July 2011. Its preamble, focusing on common fundamental values, reads as follows:

We, the people of Iceland, wish to create a just society with equal opportunities for everyone. Our different origins enrich the whole, and together we are responsible for the heritage of the generations, the land and history, nature, language and culture. Iceland is a free and sovereign state, resting on the cornerstones of freedom, equality, democracy and human rights. The government shall work for the welfare of the inhabitants of the country, strengthen their culture and respect the diversity of human life, the land and the biosphere. We wish to promote peace, security, well-being and happiness among ourselves and future generations. We resolve to work with other nations in the interests of peace and respect for the Earth and all Mankind. In this light we are adopting a new Constitution, the supreme law of the land, to be observed by all. (in Gylfason 2012, 18–19)

Parliament had then to approve the draft as a constitutional document, but postponed the decision (Landomore 2017). Only after more than a year had passed, on 20 October 2012, was a nonbinding national referendum on the constitutional proposal held, in which 49 per cent of the electorate participated, voting on six questions. The first question, on whether the draft Constitution should form the basis of a new Icelandic Constitution, was approved by 73 per cent of voters. The next five questions concerned references to the state church, change in the electoral system so to give equal weight to votes cast in all parts of the country, the public ownership of natural resources, the frequency of elections to the national Parliament, and citizens' referendum power (Elkins et al. 2012). With the exception of the question proposing the dis/establishment of the National Church of Iceland, all the other proposals were approved by large margins (80 per cent) (Ostaszewski 2013, 68). As has been noted, the referendum revealed that society was determined to change the system of democracy in favour of more direct democracy (Ostaszewski 2013).

The process of constitutional reform was interrupted in Parliament. After some changes to the formulation suggested by the Venice Commission of the Council of Europe, and statements by thirty-two out of sixty-three MPs in support of the Bill, the draft was supposed to be voted on by Parliament. However, in the days prior to the closing of Parliament for elections, the two conservative parties, IP and the Progress Party (PP), were able to stop the vote through filibustering.

After Parliament was dissolved on 27 March 2013, new elections brought the IP and the PP back to power, with the previous centre-left coalition losing support over, among other things, accession talks with the EU. On the other hand, the conservative parties' popularity was bolstered by opposition to the Icesave agreement. The European Free Trade Association (EFTA) decision in January 2013 to relieve Iceland of its Icesave obligations for good contributed to weakening the parties in government that had been seen as open to compromise on the debt repayment.

The 2009 election had produced the first overall majority for Iceland's two Left parties – the Social Democrats and the Left Greens – in history, with IP losing its dominant position for the first time. The 2013 elections, by contrast, returned Iceland to past equilibria (Indridason et al. 2016). With a record number of fifteen parties forwarding candidates, the combined vote share of the four established parties dropped from 90.6% in 2009 to 74.9% in 2013, with the Bright Future (BF, supported by many local Best Party activists) getting 8.2%, and the Pirate Party 5.1%, while the Greens lost half of their vote and the Social Democrats 16.9 percentage points. The centre-right IP and the PP won a slight majority (with 51% of the vote), thanks especially to an IP gain of 9.6 percentage points (Jonnson 2018).

The incumbent parties between 2009 and 2013 paid the price for their lack of capacity to propose an alternative politics. Notwithstanding some economic improvements, they were held responsible for austerity measures imposed by the national authorities (under pressure from the IMF), while only the PP (and, to a lesser extent, the IP) among the established parties had supported mortgage relief and opposed repaying the failed banks' debt (a position that found resonance in the decision of the EFTA Surveillance Authority in January 2013). After having opposed the turn towards neoliberalism, the Left Greens supported the IMF-sponsored austerity policies when in government. In effect:

> The Social Democratic Alliance joined the Left Greens in implementing the IMF's austerity policies, but at the same time fought fiercely for the cause of Iceland joining the EU and claimed that the Icelandic krona should be eradicated and the Euro should be introduced in its place in order to solve the problems of the financial system of Iceland for good. The Social Democratic Alliance still holds this policy despite the EU's chronic high levels of unemployment and the present Euro-crisis. (Jonnson 2018, 147)

Against this backdrop, the collective effervescence of the period of high mobilization tapered off to a huge extent, due to – among other things – activist fatigue, boredom, disillusionment, a decline in experienced grievances, or other motives, culminating in the return to power of the conservative actors who had caused the crisis to begin with. The failure to implement the popularly endorsed Constitution highlights the ambivalent relationship and power imbalances between direct and representative forms of institutional decision-making.

The constitutional process had been strongly opposed by part of the

Icelandic elite, expressed not only in the open criticism of the centre-right parties, but also by the lukewarm support offered by some in the centre-left parties. In particular, the statement about natural resources as the 'perpetual property of the nation' was fiercely attacked by the powerful fishing industry. The lack of involvement by political parties in the preparation of the text is also cited as a cause of discomfort (Thorarensen 2014). Criticism also emerged from experts, in particular lawyers, who stigmatized the proposed Bill on technical reasons. In addition, members of parliaments from outside of the capital opposed the reform of the electoral system (Gylfason 2013).

Nonetheless, even if objectives had not been achieved or implemented, the practices of collective mobilization and deliberation inherent in the campaigns resulted in greater transparency, and kept alive calls for reconstituting the people from below (della Porta 2015b). As a protagonist of the process stated, 'there will be a new parliament after this one. One day, most probably, the constitutional bill approved by the people of Iceland in the 2012 referendum or a similar one will become the law of the land. Stay tuned' (Gylfason 2013). While, in 2013, the centre-right parties in power had stopped the parliamentary vote on the new Constitution, after some stalemate, the pro-Constitution actors mobilized anew. Not only did the increasingly popular Pirate Party function as a sort of movement party, but so too did the pro-constitutional wing within the SDA. With 81 per cent of party members in favour of the new Constitution, and after heavy electoral defeat (from 30 per cent in 2009 to 6 per cent in 2016), the Social Democrats spoke up for its adoption. In parallel, especially since 2015, the Constitutional Society (a civil society organization) increased pressure on all political parties through targeted campaigns.

Opportunities seem indeed to have opened again with the new Parliament elected in 2017, after another financial–political scandal brought new elections. While expectations, fuelled by many opinion polls in the run-up to the election, of an increase in support for the alternative progressive parties were not fulfilled, and the Independence Party retained its position as the largest party in the Althing (national Parliament), nevertheless the Left Green Movement came second and the SDA doubled its vote share. As the conservative parties had lost their majority, a government was formed by a three-party coalition led by the Left Greens, including the Independence Party and Progressive Party. Left Green leader Katrín Jakobsdóttir was designated prime minister, and announced in January 2018 a new effort towards constitutional reform. In sum, while the approval of the crowd-sourced Constitution is still suspended, in a situation of deep and sudden crisis that dramatically affected the everyday life of Icelanders, massive protests were effective not only in opposing the public repayment of private banks' debt and imposing state intervention to alleviate the suffering of the population, but also in prompting a constituent process that represents a major experiment in popular Constitution-making.

Expanding the analysis: the Irish deliberative constitutional process

The Icelandic example is a main case of constitutional process driven from below, but it is not the only one. Some other examples of constitutional process with popular involvement also emerged in the midst of the financial crisis, following various expressions of massive political discontent (from street protests to electoral disruption). One of these is the Irish Constitutional Convention, held between December 2012 and February 2014, which was tasked with a partial revision of the Irish Constitution. As we will see, some conditions and mechanisms that influenced the Irish grassroots constitutional process were similar to the Icelandic case.

After a proposal by the parliamentary Joint Committee of the Constitution, a Citizens' Assembly was formed by sixty-six citizens, chosen by lot, plus thirty-three elected politicians, selected by political parties, with experts involved as mediators and advisors. Since January 2013, deliberative meetings were then called every month, lasting for a weekend, adopting thirty-eight recommendations of reform, including the introduction of citizens' initiatives (Suteu 2015, 267). While only consultative and top-down in its origins, the assembly has called for participation from citizens in the constitutional process, prompting a procedure that resulted in the promotion of four referendums in 2014, including the one that approved, with an unexpected 62%, same-sex marriage.

As with Iceland, Ireland too was hit hard by the crisis that here also was fuelled by a breakdown of the financial system. Differently than in Iceland, however, public debt drastically increased (from 40% of GDP at the beginning of the crisis in 2008 to about 120% in 2013) after the decision by the government to bail out the indebted banks (Hardiman and Regan 2013). Austerity policies followed, with dramatic cuts in public spending as well as a Great Recession, with an estimated total loss of as much as 20% of GDP between 2008 and 2015 (Hardiman and Regan 2013). At the same time, taxes were kept at a very low level (12.5% for corporate tax, with low social insurance contributions for employers) in order to continue to attract foreign capital. The low taxation rates contributed to a deficit of 7.3% of GDP in 2008, doubling to 14% in 2009, since foreign-based investors repatriated their profits rather than investing them in Ireland. In 2011, the coalition in government, comprising Fine Gael and the Labour Party, financed new tax breaks for the financial sector with pay cuts in the public sector (by about 15%) and in social welfare. While unemployment more than doubled (rising from 6.4% in 2008 to around 15% in 2012), early retirement was promoted, causing a drop in the number of employees in an (already small) public sector (Hardiman and Regan 2013). In particular, differently from Iceland, Ireland signed an agreement with the EC, IMF, and ECB for a loan programme in December 2010, which constrained domestic budgetary discretion, as 'all budget decisions must be cleared with the troika, fiscal performance is subject to quarterly reviews and troika personnel are embedded in the core government departments' (Hardiman and Regan 2013, 30).

Protest in defence of civil, political and social rights took initially more conventional forms, with strikes and mass demonstrations in 2008 and 2009, which, however, subsided when unions accepted austerity policies. With the Croke Park agreement, the trade unions, in exchange for a promise not to impose further pay cuts until 2014, granted 'industrial peace and productivity increases, reform of the bonus payment system, a recruitment embargo in the health and education sectors, and significantly reduced pay and conditions for new entrants to the public sector' (Hardiman and Regan 2013, 12). In March 2010, the Public Service Agreement 2010–2014 'copper-fastens previous unilateral pay reductions while containing a tentative commitment to avoid additional pay cutting measures, unless faced with a further economic crisis' (McDonough and Dundon 2010, 558). In 2011, some protest camps were organized following the example of Southern European citizens contesting similar austerity policies – in particular, in Spain and Greece. The most innovative forms of contentious politics developed, however, only after 2014, with the formation of social movement organizations such as Right2Water, which coordinated the opposition to privatizing the supply of water.

The most visible effect of the crisis was an electoral earthquake, as incumbent parties were heavily punished for what was seen as lack of capacity to prevent – or at least manage – the crisis. In particular, 2011 saw a most dramatic election with very high electoral volatility, shaking the traditional party system (Marsh and Mikhaylov 2012). While Fianna Fail fell from first to third position, Fine Gael became for the first time the first party in the country, forming a coalition government with the Labour Party, which had doubled its support, with the Left gaining a very high 31 per cent of the vote (Marsh and Mikhaylov 2012). It was noted, however, that electoral results represented 'a conservative revolution, one in which the main players remained the same, and the switch in the major government party was merely one where one centre-right party replaced another' (Marsh and Mikhaylov 2012, 161). The important role of personal ties in Irish politics, as well as a traditional localism-cum-clientelism, the weakness of the Left, and the feeble power of Parliament (Mair 2014) mitigated the intensity of the political changes, as did traditional ideological proximity among the main parties (Marsh and Mikhaylov 2012).

Following the crisis and the ensuing drop in institutional trust, all parties expressed a need to increase citizens' active engagement. In particular, there was a widespread perception that, faced with citizens' discontent, it was necessary to update the democratic model by increasing participation during periods between elections. In their campaigns for the 2011 election, all parties, in fact, mentioned proposals for citizen-oriented deliberative forums organized to discuss constitutional issues. Fine Gael especially developed a proposal for a British Columbia-style constitutional reform, putting forward the establishment of a constitutional convention in its Programme for Government (Farrell et al. 2013).

As in the Icelandic case, a non-governmental organization (NGO), We the Citizens, launched a deliberative polling exercise in order to debate core concerns of citizens on issues such as taxation and spending, educational reform and political change (referring to the role of MPs, freedom of information, party funding, and participation by women and young people). About 100 members were distributed between tables of 8 participants and joined by a facilitator. The experiment resulted not only in an increase in individuals' interest in politics and willingness to become more actively involved, but also in a growth of support for public spending, local services and property tax, and against the selling of state assets (Farrell et al. 2013).

In July 2012, the Houses of the Oireachtas (the Irish national Parliament) established a convention with the task of examining issues such as the reduction of the presidential term of office, the reduction of voting age, the review of the Dáil (the lower house of Parliament) electoral system, the right for Irish citizens overseas to vote in their embassies in presidential elections, the provisions for same-sex marriage, amendment to the existing clause in the Irish Constitution on the role of women in the home and encouraging greater participation of women in public life and politics, and the removal of the offence of blasphemy from the Constitution.

In December 2012, an Irish Constitutional Convention was put in place. Composed of 100 members (66 citizens, 33 representatives of the political parties, and a chair – a former NGO leader), the Convention met for its first session on 26–27 January 2013. Selected randomly and provided with travel and lodging expenses, the citizen-members had a plural composition in terms of gender, but also social background. Political parties were left free to decide how to choose their representatives, 29 of which had to be members of the Irish Parliament and 4 members of Northern Ireland parties (Fine Gael asked for volunteers and Labour held votes). The process explicitly aimed at favouring participation and deliberation.

Initial reactions were mixed. Critical voices addressed the topics, considered as too restrictive, as well as the process, given the participation of party delegates. As far as the topics to be addressed are concerned, it was noted, however, that 'the Convention proved quite inventive in stretching its remit beyond the narrow confines set by the government' (Suiter et al. 2016, 37). From the first meeting, the debate went beyond the initial definition – as observed, 'having read the briefing materials, heard from experts and advocacy groups and deliberated over the relevant arguments, the Convention members considered options that undoubtedly went beyond their brief. There was little dissent on this expansion of powers from the politician-members who belonged to the governing coalition that had initiated the Convention' (Suiter et al. 2016, 37).

Participation and deliberation were valued also beyond the specific groups of participants in the Convention. An Academic and Legal Support Group, including four political scientists and a legal scholar, suggested experts who could present different arguments on each issue, also helping in setting up the programme for each encounter. However, the Convention members retained control over the agenda through a steering committee made of politicians and citizens, which could recommend changes to the programme as well as speakers. The experts (policy-makers, academics, but also representatives of civil society organizations, etc.) had to make short presentations at the meetings, remaining available for plenary assemblies and small group discussions. Briefing documents, written by the experts, were distributed several days in advance of the meeting. In order to improve the information available to the participants, 'the experts were then asked to liaise with one another to draw up accessible "plain English" briefing documents on various aspects of each debate. These documents were emailed to all members in advance of the meeting, made available on the website and distributed in hard copy at the weekend meetings' (Suiter et al. 2016, 41).

The meetings of the Convention took place once a month, lasting all day Saturday, and Sunday mornings. Valuing deliberation as high-quality discussion, members were required to engage in respectful discussions, asking questions of each other and the experts, mentioning reasons for their preferences. In order to facilitate inclusive participation, the members sat in changing order at circular tables of about eight (with both politicians and citizens), with a note-taker and a trained facilitator who had to ensure all had an opportunity to speak, as well as reciprocal respect (Suiter et al. 2016, 42). The plenary debate was followed by small-group deliberation in non-public session. The participants then reconvened in plenary open session where the results of the small-group debates were reported. After further debate, recommendations were voted on by simple majority vote (Suiter et al. 2016, 45). Participants were then asked to assess the quality of deliberation.

Participation was expected also from citizens outside. Here, too, broadcasting, printed media and social media were used to inform and involve the public. Nine regional meetings were organized across the country in order to gather ideas on the issues to be discussed by the Convention, with the participation of about 1,000 people (Suiter et al. 2016, 37). In order to decide on which issues to discuss, the Convention encouraged suggestions, online and offline, from the general public, as well as from civil society organizations. Around 2,500 submissions were then grouped into topic areas, with short presentations on each prepared by the Academic and Legal Support Group of the Convention, with the task of ensuring full information for the participants. The discussion was followed by a vote by the Convention members. The plenary sessions, televised and live-streamed, were made available on the website (www. constitution.ie). The media were present at meetings, and civil society groups helped with publicizing the process (Suiter et al. 2016).

As for the format, according to some researchers, the inclusion of politicians in the Convention, initially criticized because of the risk they could dominate the discussions, had, instead, positive effects. Not only did politicians in fact try to avoid intervening too often, but their participation increased institutional trust and improved the public image of elected representatives (Suiter et al. 2016, 42). Thus, the process gained in throughput legitimacy – with increasing support from the media, which had been initially sceptical – but also output legitimacy, in terms of implementation of the decision. In fact, as the contents of each report came to be debated in Parliament, the presence of politicians within the Convention reduced the risk of a disconnection between the Convention and representative institutions (which had emerged, for example, in the case of Iceland) (Suiter et al. 2016, 46). On the contrary, politicians who were also members of the Convention supported its works and conclusions, referring to the Convention during parliamentary debates. So, for instance, a Sinn Féin politician, addressing the debate on same-sex marriage, stated: 'I congratulate the Constitutional Convention on its excellent work to date. I had some reservations initially but I am pleased to see the Constitutional Convention take on a life of its own and begin to undertake the task of making some much-needed changes to the Constitution . . . we are grateful to all members of the Convention who made this happen' (Suiter et al. 2016, 46–7). Some citizen-members, too, publicly expressed positive opinions on the work of the Convention, with one stressing that he would never have agreed to speak in front of such a large group if it had not been for his experience of doing so at the Convention' (Suiter et al. 2016, 47).

The work of the Convention resulted in forty recommendations for reform, eighteen of which seemed to require a referendum to be implemented (with a fixed Constitution, Ireland has had many referendums – thirty-nine since 1937 (Suiter et al. 2016)). After each meeting, a report was sent to Parliament for debate, and to the government for its consideration. The government had to respond through a formal ministerial statement to Parliament within four months, which it did (Suiter et al. 2016, 48). In fact, the government agreed to hold some referendums, among them the often-debated issue of same-sex marriage. Other recommendations were referred to appropriate parliamentary committees or government departmental taskforces. A second Citizens' Assembly was convened to discuss abortion laws in Ireland.

In sum, the work of the Convention has been considered as very positive, with both of the main opposition parties asking to continue the experience (Suiter et al. 2016, 48). In fact:

> Ironically, it is in two of the areas that were initially a target of strong criticism – its composition and remit – that the Convention has been truly innovative in ways that contributed to its input, throughput and output legitimacy. The inclusion of politicians not only ensured greater parliamentary buy-in for the process and its recommendations (output legitimacy) but politician-members were an important source of information on institutional/technical issues, as recognised by citizen-member feedback expressed in the Convention's final report (www.constitution. ie) (input/throughput legitimacy). The remit, although originally quite tightly prescribed, was stretched by the Convention from the first weekend – this, plus the fact that it could consider other amendments and its decision to recommend items for future consideration, meant it had strong agenda-setting powers (input legitimacy). Finally the inclusion of civil-society organizations in the weekend presentations and in the process of deciding the 'any other amendments' brought context and the lived experience to bear on the expert facts and analyses in ways that engaged Irish citizens nationally and internationally 'outside the room', 'throughput legitimacy'. They also, on occasion, were the means through which the interests of those who are traditionally marginalised from political processes were indirectly presented to the Convention (such as the views of homeless people during the discussion of economic, social and cultural rights) (input legitimacy). (Suiter et al. 2016, 50)

The constitutional process in Ireland, differently from the one in Iceland, already foresaw in the mandate of the Constitutional Convention a close dialogue between the Convention and the representative institutions, which helped in getting binding referendums successfully under way.

Concluding remarks

To sum up: while not always in the directions they would like to promote, social movements are relevant agents for constitutional innovation: they nurture new ideas and challenge old ones. In particular, they have an impact on legislation, addressing both specific policy areas and more general procedural issues, often pushing for more democracy (della Porta 2013). Especially in times of crisis, social movements can have increased capacity to exert constitutive powers. While legal studies and social movement studies have rarely interacted, the emerging field of the sociology of constitutions opens up space for an inter-disciplinary debate around not only the growing importance of constitutional processes, but also the conceptions of constitutions as political and contested. Moments of crisis pave the way for, and at the same time require, the involvement of citizens in the re-writing of constitutions, also as a way of restoring a collective identity based on shared values.

In sum, our cases confirmed the reflections in constitutional sociology on accelerated constitutionalism as prompted by crisis, and testified to attempts to bring the people back into the process, through the development of participatory and deliberative mechanisms. Important preconditions for the development of grassroots constitutional processes were widespread discontent, but also a willingness to resist collectively conditions which were considered as unjust. It is from citizens' movements that promoted horizontal involvement against social injustice that the crowd-sourced constitutional processes developed. The constitutional process acted then as a catalyser for change, allowing – given conducive institutional settings – for the building of broad alliances within the party system. The participatory and deliberative process facilitates a mobilization of organizational and symbolic resources, with long-lasting empowering effects. Procedural inclusiveness and high discursive quality tend to be reflected in progressive, emancipatory contents.

The crowd-sourced Constitution in Iceland is a major illustration of a process of transformation that was promoted from below in reaction to a deep social crisis, but also political and cultural crises. The Icelandic case shows, in particular, how critical junctures or moments of crisis can result in significant innovations in the tactical and strategic repertoire of movements, contributing to reconstitute the fundamental relation between society and the state. A precondition for citizens' movements to claim constituent power is the societal collective reaction to the financial breakdown. The opening up of political opportunities followed the electoral turmoil that the anti-austerity protests had contributed to intensifying. The claims for social justice, the rights of nature, citizens' participation, all emerged in the protests, and reverberated in the constitutional proposals. Crowd-sourcing also followed from the democratic conceptions and practices promoted during the 'pots and pans revolution'. The process was also facilitated by some specific characteristics of Iceland, such as its small, highly educated and spatially condensed population, as well as the inability or unwillingness of the security forces to repress protest elsewhere (della Porta, Andretta et al. 2016).

Some of the dynamics singled out in the Icelandic case I have also found in the Irish case, with a successful search for citizens' participation in constitutional processes as a way to address perceived crisis. Here, too, protests (even if in less dramatic forms than in Iceland) contributed to an attribution of the responsibility for the crisis to the political and economic elites, with ensuing electoral turmoil. A rewriting of the Constitution, sponsored by civil society organizations as well as political parties, emerged then as a way to re-gain political legitimacy, as well as reconstituting a social pact that was perceived as broken. If the crowd-sourced constitutional process emerged as more radical in Iceland, where established interests converged in halting its implementation, the Irish experiment was more effective, given also some adaptation in the format of the constitutional process, including the participation of MPs in the constitutional assembly.

Beyond the Icelandic and Irish cases, some further examples can be cited for the participation of social movement and civil society organizations in constitutional processes. While mainly top-down, the revision of the Romanian Constitution also included public debate, with the possibility to submit proposals for constitutional revision. The pro-democracy movement organization Asociaţia Pro Democraţia had started in 2007 to push for a grassroots constitutional process, aiming at increasing citizens' awareness of of constitutional reform, including provisions for referendum in case of amendment. The Convention on the Future of Europe, formed by representatives of the governments and parliaments from full member states and candidate states of the EU, which came together to draft a constitutional treaty (later to be rejected by referendums in France and the Netherlands), while steered top-down, also foresaw inputs from citizens, including those from the Convention's civil society forum (Oberhuber 2006).

Going beyond constitutions as understood literally, as Bailey and Mattei (2013) noted, social movements are acquiring constituent power as they defend constitutionally protected public interest against its increasing retrenchment, contesting the privatization trend dominant within the liberal constitutional order. In doing so, they develop alternative political channels for participation, reconstituting the public. In fact:

> Social movements have a long history of catalyzing change, not only by exerting pressure on politicians, but also on courts, resulting at times in major shifts in law . . . (1) they are liberating the concept of politics from the liberal constitutional form, which in turn is extending the concept of constituent power beyond representative politics; and (2) they are filling a crucial vacuum where representative politics have failed, offering alternative channels for political engagement. Social movements are expanding our understanding of politics as something more than a set of actions taken in formal political arenas. They are redefining 'what counts as political and who defines what is political', thereby reclaiming popular sovereignty. (Bailey and Mattei 2013, 275–7)

The reflection on social movements as constituent power can also contribute to the debate on the limits and evolution of institutionalized law and the importance of resistance and disobedience. Critical legal theorists have noted the subversive power of suppressed discourses (Teubner 1992), defined as hidden transcripts that challenge the dominant order (Scott 1985 and 1990). In a situation of alienation, resistance might take the form of open disobedience of the legal order (Thoreau 1948). The right to resistance has therefore been defended as the right to violate unjust current law, but also to contribute to strengthening law and rights in the long term (Douzinas 2014, 154). So, 'resistance is a peripheral externality of law, whilst simultaneously acting as the founding content and influence on the development of the state' (Finchett-Maddock 2016, 39).

A crisis can trigger resistance to the existing order, as well as a need for regeneration faced with collusion between private corporations and public powers that the crisis has made all the more visible (Bailey and Mattei 2013, 273–4). Citizens' participation is needed for a re-legitimation of the political order through a transformation in constitutional form and content. In this situation, social movement studies and constitutional studies could usefully interact in order to understand the ways in which the unrecognized people strive to exercise constituent powers, and how they sometimes succeed in exercising constitutional power. The reflections in legal theory on resistance to unjust laws, as well as on the need to develop new rights, such as the right to the commons, could inspire research in social movement studies on the conditions under which – as well as the forms through which – this happens.

The research also pointed, however, towards some constraining conditions, as well as limits in the crowd-sourced constitutional processes. First of all, deliberative qualities notwithstanding, some challenges became visible at times – as, for example in the Icelandic case, in the critique of an alleged low quality of the constitutional text or, in the Irish case, the limited remit of the issues that were left to citizens' deliberation. The main challenges, however, were political in nature. Given the difficulties in sustaining the processes through grassroots mobilization, political backlashes occurred, through the loss of party allies or the increasing power of parties who opposed the idea of a grassroots constitutionalism. Rather than a linear process of empowerment, we found a contested dynamic with stops and starts. Especially, the more radically emancipatory the content of the promoted Constitution, the more economic interests mobilized against it. Routinization of participatory procedures can also reduce their capacity for innovation. Even more deeply, the challenge is in ensuring that the appeal to the 'will of the people' is accompanied by a focus on emancipatory norms and values. As with other participatory processes, in order to strengthen equality rather than favour inequalities, participation needs to be inclusive. As the conception of the public good is contested – and a win-win solution is not always available – deliberation needs to be built upon public justification rather than populist rhetoric.

3

Referendums from Below: Direct Democracy and Social Movements

In recent times, several important referendums have taken place in Europe and beyond. In many cases, referendums were promoted by social movement organizations to oppose neoliberal policies. This was the case in a referendum against the privatization of the water supply in Italy, characterized by a grassroots campaign. In addition, nationalism became a focus of discussion with the referendums on Scottish independence, as well as the pseudo-referendum for Catalonian independence. In both cases, referendums that had been called by elites were appropriated by social movement organizations who exploited the campaigns in order to promote their ideas. In general, movements' participation also broadened the repertoires of action, as well as the number of organizations involved. Notwithstanding their different institutional settings, these referendums showed not only that late neoliberalism has challenged citizens' loyalty to their institutions, but also that dissatisfaction can bring about political activism, rather than apathy.

In this chapter, I will address *referendums from below* as a specific type of direct democracy, characterized by a substantial involvement of social movements and civil society organizations in referendum campaigns. In doing this, I aim at bridging social movement studies with studies of direct democracy. While there are many very different types of referendums, some of which are used as an instrument of elites rather than of challengers, there are in some cases several linkages between referendum politics and contentious politics, which have only rarely been addressed in the social science literature (della Porta, O'Connor et al. 2017a).

A very first observation, confirmed by much research on direct democracy, is that referendums, and especially those promoted by citizens, have increased in number. Not only have half of the 543 national referendums to take place in Switzerland between 1848 and 2006 happened since the 1970s (Kriesi and Bernhard 2014), but referendums are also being used more and more even beyond the traditional countries considered to be champions of direct democracy (de Vreese 2007; Qvortrup 2012). Additionally, the increase in the use of direct democracy is to a large degree *voter-driven*, as direct democratic procedures have often been initiated by demands from voters (Bjørklund 2009, 120).

The growing use of referendums has been explained by similar conditions to those observed as affecting social movement development. First of all, referendums are more frequent and increasing more in liberal democracies, with a clear statistical correlation with the quality of democracy (Altman 2011, 69–70). In recent decades, their importance has grown, however, exactly as a response to increasing political discontent. Given increasing dissatisfaction with the ways in which representative institutions work, referendums have been seen as a potential contribution to a reinvention of democratic government through more participation (Altman 2011). Together with referendums, various practices of direct democracy have developed to respond to the search for alternative or additional channels of legitimation of democratic institutions, faced with the insufficiency of electoral accountability (Bjørklund 2009, 133).

During economic, social and political crises that challenge in various ways other forms of institutional participation, referendums can be seen as an ever more needed channel to change politics and policies. In fact, a challenge to 'really existing democracies' comes from a combination of empowerment and disempowerment as citizens, during waves of protest, become at the same time more confident in their own capacity to affect politics from below and (much) less confident in the skills and motivations of professional politicians (Tierney 2012, 9). Faced with a drop in trust in the political system, referendums have been considered as capable of re-synchronizing political institutions with citizens (Altman 2011, 197), contributing to addressing the gap between increasing interest in politics and a decline in conventional forms and channels of participation (Tierney 2012, 302). Referendums work therefore as 'institutionalized, sporadic, safety valves of political pressure' (Altman 2011, 198). In the same way, various citizens' channels for direct participation can and do put pressure on decision-makers (Setälä and Schiller 2012; Fatke 2015).

Both resonant principles and the potential opening of opportunity have made referendum arenas interesting for social movements. From the normative point of view, referendums are main institutions of direct democracy, providing paths of access for social movements. In fact, referendums have been defined as 'a publicly recognized institution wherein citizens decide or emit their opinion on issues – other than through legislative and executive elections – directly at the ballot box through universal and secret suffrage' (Altman 2011, 7). Both popular initiatives, oriented to promoting new policies, and abrogative referendums provide citizens with some control capacity. They can contribute to making political processes transparent and deliberative, and governments accountable, as popular initiatives provide a surrogate for a lack of responsiveness by political elites, contributing to the articulation of new issues and proposing innovative policy options (Schiller 2009, 211).

Referendums, at times, give citizens the possibility to take part in various important decisions, between and beyond elections. This opening of channels of participation for citizens resonates with the conception of participatory democracy promoted by progressive social movements (della Porta 2013) as opposed to a delegation of power to a restricted political elite. Social movements have been said, in fact, to defend an ancient conception of democracy, at the core of which is the direct participation of citizens. In particular, with issues on which social movements have mobilized citizens beyond the indications of political parties, some referendums (such as the ones on divorce or abortion in Italy in the 1970s) have opened up space for the participatory and deliberative democratic conceptions cherished by progressive social movements.

At the strategic level, social movements can find additional opportunities in referendums, given that the public arenas that open up during referendum campaigns tend to be more open and dynamic than those which characterize normal electoral campaigns. As referendums focus attention on specific issues, they can help social movement organizations to promote new ideas and norms – as happened in the past on environmental problems or gender rights. The importance of participatory and deliberative campaigns has often been stressed. As the reception of arguments is influenced by the degree of awareness, and the acceptance of an argument is related to multiple and evolving predispositions (Zaller 1992; Alvarez and Brehm 2002), an intensification of political communication during electoral campaigns can make some issues more familiar and salient. While issue-specific awareness is certainly influenced by the mobilization of elites, there is also a potential for grassroots campaigns to focus attention on counter-arguments articulated by the opposing minority (Kriesi 2005, 177), which tend instead to be marginalized in the mainstream public sphere. The intensity of a campaign, together with the familiarity of an issue, increase, in fact, the general importance of plurality of arguments. Political elites, defined as all actors who contribute to public debate by speaking in the public sphere (Kriesi 2005), play a crucial role in campaigns but – especially if and when elites are divided – unpredictability increases. As Hanspeter Kriesi (2005, 239) noted, 'as long as the elite speak with many voices, as long as there is a conflict among the elite, as long as the elite form clearly structured coalitions and provide a diversity of arguments for the diverging points of view, the direct-democratic process does not risk falling into the populist trap'. As we are going to see, especially under some contextual conditions, progressive social movements can be successful in promoting referendums themselves or appropriating referendums which have been promoted by elites, introducing their specific strategies and framing into the public arena.

These potential and actual overlaps notwithstanding, the two fields of social movement studies and referendum studies have developed with almost no interaction with each other. While scholars of social movements have looked at political opportunities as an important determinant of protests, their forms and chances of success, they have, however, rarely considered referendums as channels of access to policy-making. Only occasionally have referendums been seen as a potential addition to repertoires of contention, and the presence of institutions of direct democracy seen as an indicator of open opportunities for challengers, with a moderating effect on the forms of contentious action. In particular, the presence of channels of direct democracy, together with a high degree of functional differentiation and territorial decentralization, have been defined as stable opportunities for challengers (Kriesi et al. 1995). Only recently has a systematic analysis started of the conditions under which referendums are called, or penetrated, from below (della Porta, O'Connor et al. 2017a).

For their part, studies on referendums have usually focused upon the elite (especially, party elites), the media and the public – the latter mainly considered as (more or less) passive recipients of top-down messages. In research on referendum campaigns, politicians, institutions and journalists have in fact been considered as producers of political communication targeting the public (Kriesi 2012a). Very rarely have studies addressed the contribution of citizens as producers of bottom-up communication messages. On the contrary, it is exactly the elitist character of referendum campaigns which is recalled in order to defend referendums from accusations of producing emotional and irrational results. As Hanspeter Kriesi (2007, 126) has observed, as an issue's salience is a strong predictor of participation, this tends to discourage those who are less committed, and strengthen instead the influence of political elites in the referendum campaign. It is this persisting role of elites that is referred to in order to placate the anxiety of those who are afraid that participation gives voice to the ignorant. Referring to sceptical observers, he notes in fact that they tend to underestimate the importance of elites. So, 'it is somewhat misplaced to deplore the lack of civism on the part of the citizens, if most of them do not participate in a vote. It is, as our results show, up to the elites to mobilize the citizens. If the elites do not mobilize, the citizens will not participate, because they lack awareness and motivation to do so' (Kriesi 2007, 137). Given that interest is the strongest predictor of participation at the individual level, and party attachment and institutional trust in government tend to increase participation in direct forms of democracy (Mottier 1993, 126; Sciarini et al. 2007), self-selection would therefore reduce the influence of those who are less competent and interested (usually, the least-educated).

While there is no denying that elites often control electoral campaigns (in referendums, as in other electoral processes), given the great variety of referendums – in terms of legal norms, but also contingent aspects – assessing the democratic quality of this specific institution is as difficult as it is for other electoral and non-electoral mechanisms of political participation. The purpose of this chapter is therefore not to discuss the pros and cons of the entire heterogeneous population of referendums, but rather to address the role that social movements (as missing players in research on referendum games) can have, and indeed have had, in some specific referendums, and the effects of their participation.

In doing so, cross-fertilization between referendum studies and social movement studies could be fruitful at both the theoretical and empirical levels. In particular, research on some specific referendums, which I call 'referendums from below', can be enriched by using the toolkit of social movement studies, with a focus on the role of specific repertoires of action, organizational forms and collective frames in the development of the referendum campaign. From research on referendums, social movement scholars interested in direct democracy can learn about the normative trade-off of direct democracy; the impact of different legal opportunities on referendum politics; the interplay of various players, including elites, in the referendum arena; as well as the motivations for participation at the individual level.

As I am going to argue in what follows, referendums from below were called for in moments of financial but also legitimacy crisis, involving social movements that had mobilized against austerity, calling for social justice and a deepening of democracy. Building upon a degree of institutional and political conduciveness, the referendums acted, then, as a catalyst for broader mobilization, as arenas for public debates were created through broad participation. Referendums triggered the appropriation of opportunities, as well as the mobilization of organizational networks and the development and spreading of resonant frames. The participation of social movements in the promotion of a referendum, in the electoral campaign, as well as in the aftermath of it, increased both the participatory and deliberative qualities of referendums. Even if not always bringing about the desired electoral result, referendums brought about long-term empowerment. Using concepts from social movement studies, I will reflect on the appropriation of opportunities, the mobilization of resources, as well as their collective framing, as important mechanisms in 'referendums from below' – that is, referendums that have been either initiated or highly participated in by social movements.

As illustrations, I will first analyse the referendum against the privatization of the water supply in Italy on 12–13 June 2011, mentioning then also the EU-wide popular initiative on the same issue. In the next section, I will address from a comparative perspective the referendum on Scottish independence on 18 September 2014 and the Catalan 'pseudo-referendums' on self-determination (in particular on 9 November 2014 and 1 October 2017). Importantly, all of these processes happened during the Great Recession and were influenced by late neoliberalism, becoming channels for expressing discontent (della Porta, Andretta et al. 2016). While the outcomes of the referendums differed (with an overwhelming success of the actors against water privatization in Italy, a narrow defeat of the independence option in Scotland, and a resounding but unrecognized victory for self-determination in Catalonia), all of these processes had empowering effects on the social movements that participated in them, as well as on the broader society.

'Water is not for sale': direct democracy against the privatization of water supply

With the *acampadas* ('protest camps') remaining marginal in Italy, the most important instances of anti-austerity protests mainly took the form of direct democracy. While the call for a referendum against the privatization of the water supply had developed within the European Social Forum at the beginning of the millennium, the referendum campaign on the issue grew in a moment characterized, also in Italy, by the financial crisis and the political turmoil linked to it. Held on 12 and 13 June 2011, the referendum resulted in an extraordinary success for the social movement organizations that had promoted it. Even if its results were hardly ever implemented, the referendum contributed to empowering the struggle for what were defined as 'the commons'. In what follows, I will analyse the ways in which activists created opportunities, the grassroots organizational model, the multiple repertoires of action used during the campaigns, as well as their innovative framing. I will conclude with some reflections on the campaign outcomes, at national and transnational level.

Appropriating opportunities through referendum

Social movement studies have given much attention to the appropriation of political opportunities as facilitating the emergence of contentious political actors, their development and eventual success. As previously mentioned (chapter 1), social movements can also prompt these opportunities through their actions. In this perspective, mechanisms of direct democracy have been considered as additional channels of access to institutions, which contribute to moderate contentious politics. Also as previously mentioned, however, research, mainly conducted in Switzerland or the United States, has questioned whether referendums increase the chances of success for movements, as campaigns appeared often to be dominated by the most resourceful actors, rather than involving the 'powerless' (Kriesi 2005). If the status quo is tendentially hostile to challengers, referendums break (or might break) with the routine, opening new discursive spaces with the potential to challenge power relations. While not suggesting that all referendum campaigns are open to the participation of social movements, I will investigate what happens when there is this irruption of the unexpected. Referendums, I argue, can create a positive momentum for the mobilization of citizens, which social movements aim to orient towards their aims. In this sense, also during referendum campaigns, social movement actors might appropriate opportunities that are created in action.

Research on referendums indicates that this type of election tends to be more open-ended than normal elections, as 'in a referendum, the campaign itself is frequently *more* important than in ordinary partisan or candidate elections. The dynamics of a referendum campaign can be harder to anticipate than those of an election, and the participation of the electorate varies more widely' (LeDuc 2007, 29). The institutional design influences the extent to which referendums give (real) power to the people (Altman 2011, 191). As the referendum campaign is an arena in which various players participate, social movements can promote referendum campaigns or appropriate them as an occasion to gain attention for their cause.

A first condition for the promotion of referendums from below is institutional conduciveness, as countries and other polities vary a great deal, not only in terms of allowing or not allowing referendums, but also regarding rules about how to call for a referendum, the potential content of the decision, and the validity of the decision. In particular, promoters of referendums might be citizens (usually through the collection of a certain number of signatures), political actors or institutions. The referendum can aim at maintaining the status quo or changing it, through propositive or abrogative questions. The effects can be binding (with often a threshold for participation) or not (in consultative procedures) (Altman 2011, 9). Different legal requirements for referendums tend to trigger different dynamics.

Besides institutional ones, contingent opportunities also have an important impact on referendum dynamics. In particular, issue complexity as well as issue familiarity, the strength of already-formed opinions, and the degree of party ownership of an issue all affect the campaign and its results (Kriesi 2012b). Opinions are more volatile on emerging issues on which there are usually weak(er) party cues (LeDuc 2007, 31), and party recommendations tend to be less important for those who already have information and/or opinions on a specific question (Font and Rodríguez 2009). In this sense, referendum campaigns vary in their capacity to interrupt routine politics depending on their issue content.

In addition, various players intervene in the referendum arena, using different strategies. Referendums initiated by governments can promote decisions by directly addressing citizens in order to circumvent parliamentary procedures and/or gain more legitimacy on topical choices. Citizen-initiated referendums, sometimes in the form of popular initiatives, may also aim at a decision on which parliaments and/or governments do not wish to take a position, in some cases because it cleaves parties internally (Sitter 2009). Actors can promote or engage in referendums with three potential goals:

> The first is *avoidance* of the need to make a decision in a certain framework. This may result from the fear that a decision might lead to a split within a unit whose cohesion the initiators and supporters of the referendum wish to sustain, be it a party, a coalition or party voters. The second is the *addition* of a decision-making forum to legitimize the decision and/or empower the initiator of the referendum. The third is a *contradiction*: blocking a majority decision or promoting a policy or reform that the majority in government and/or parliament rejects. (Rahat 2009, 99)

Focusing especially on the reasons for challengers to engage in a referendum campaign, Kriesi et al. (2007, 15–16) have observed the following:

> A challenger's *primary objective* may not necessarily be to win the vote in the subsequent referendum, i.e. to block the legislative proposal of the parliamentary majority with the help of the people. Alternative

objectives are possible. Thus, a challenger may anticipate a defeat and still decide to launch a campaign. He may expect to have an *indirect impact* on the issue-specific decision-making process: even if he fails to win a majority of the vote, he may still obtain the support of a sizeable minority of voters, signalling to the government that his position has widespread (although not majoritarian) support in the population. This may give him at least a *procedural* success (he may be coopted into the issue-specific political subsystem), or even a *partial substantive* success (he may obtain concessions in subsequent issue-specific reforms). A second alternative objective refers to the possibility that a challenger is not primarily concerned with the impact in the public at large, but with that in his own *constituency*. In this case, he intends to signal to his own constituency, and to potential allies, that he is defending their cause even if the chances of success are virtually inexistent. This objective takes a longer-term view and counts on *building up a reputation* for defending a given cause, which will pay off in the future (in the next elections, for example). Related to this second alternative objective, and difficult to distinguish from it in practice, is principled, value-oriented action, which does not calculate the costs and benefits of a campaign, but mobilizes independently of such considerations.

Social movement studies, in fact, suggest considering the impact of formal and informal political opportunities on contentious repertoires of actions, referendums being part of them. The formal institutional rules, but also the specific conjunctural political opportunities and constraints for actors from below, influence the propensity to use referendums for challenging the government and elites, as well as the forms and content of the campaign. Social movement studies have therefore pointed towards the relevance of political opportunities as facilitating elements of movement development, but also to the capacity of movements to appropriate, or create, opportunities.

The analysis of the referendum against the privatization of water in Italy shows mechanisms of appropriation of opportunities. The water campaign originated in a period of high mobilization around the Global Justice Movement in general, and the European Social Forum in particular, which had been able to produce openings at local and international levels. It was then around the call for the commons that various initiatives against the privatization of water supply developed, forging alliances with various relevant institutional actors at the municipality level, as well as promoting global campaigns which ended up with some important symbolic recognition (Fattori 2013; Mattei 2013; Bailey and Mattei 2013; Quarta and Ferrando 2015; della Porta, O'Connor et al. 2017a). Even when contingent national opportunities closed down, various forms of direct democracy included in the Constitution facilitated the maintenance of high levels of mobilization up to the victorious referendum campaign. While their ideas and strategies developed within a trial and testing of various ways to influence public decision-making, their courses of action were in turn shaped by conjunctural political dynamics that, together with the historical memory of referendums from below, played a crucial role for the Italian progressive movements, pushing towards the use of this specific form of contentious politics.

In Italy, as in Ireland or Spain, the crisis was driven more by low productivity than by public debt, as in the previous decade real GDP growth per capita had been among the weakest in the Organization for Economic Co-operation and Development (OECD) (Goretti and Landi 2013). The effects of very high public debt were buffered by high private savings, as net household wealth was €8.6 trillion in 2011, around 5.4 times GDP, and considerable primary budget surpluses had been run since 1991, with the sole exception of 2009 (Sacchi 2015). However, the fear of contagion increased given the presence of structural low growth already before the Great Recession (Sacchi 2015, 81). From April to July 2011, shortly after the European Council had endorsed a plan oriented to achieving a balanced budget in 2014, the price of Italian credit default swaps tripled (Sacchi 2015). Even if the country did not need to sign a Memorandum of Understanding with lending institutions in exchange for loans, it was still subject to heavy conditionalities, as 'while acting to ease the pressure on the Italian bonds by making purchases on the secondary market, the ECB imposed certain conditions that, despite not being formalized in MoUs, were nonetheless stringent and pervasive, as the ECB was setting the policy agenda, alternatives and instruments to be adopted in exchange for its support' (Sacchi 2015, 83).

At the political level, the Berlusconi government, given harsh internal conflicts, was unable to approve the austerity packages, as requested by the Council recommendation of 12 July 2011. Only after Berlusconi resigned did a government led by a so-called technocrat, Mario Monti, but supported by both main parties on the centre-right and centre-left, implement all the requests listed in a letter from the ECB to the Italian government, with particular emphasis on flexibilization of the labour market and the restructuring of the pension system. Demands by the ECB were in fact used strategically by Italian policy-makers to implement decisions that had previously been opposed by the trade unions.

The crisis implied a loss of domestic power and electoral accountability, given the supervisory role assumed by EU institutions. In particular, 'the labour market reform is monitored at every juncture, its contents thoroughly scrutinized, warnings are issued in a way that could easily make defenders of old-school democracy raise an eyebrow, and the parliamentary process is followed day by day' (Sacchi 2015, 89). After a year of government led by Mario Monti, the 2013 elections brought about a drastic loss for the main parties as, on the Right, the People of Freedom (PoF) reached only 21.3% (against 37.2% in 2008) and, on the Left, the Democratic Party (DP) achieved 25.5% (against 33.1% in 2008) – while the Five Star Movement (5SM), in its first experience with national elections, obtained 25.1% of the votes. Indeed, the electoral results were notable for the 'greatest vote-swing in the history of the Italian Republic, with an index of aggregate volatility of 39.1%' (Bellucci 2014, 244). A good percentage of the voters for the 5SM came in particular from former centre-left electors (Bordignon and Ceccarini 2013).

Protests then grew in defence of citizens' challenged rights, but overall in more reactive than proactive forms. In fact, the arena of anti-austerity protest was populated mainly by more traditional collective actors, remaining generally fragmented (della Porta and Reiter 2012; della Porta and Andretta 2013; della Porta et al. 2015). While labour conflict was sustained, it tended to remain isolated from the other types of mobilization that emerged over public education or the right to the city. Main unions called for strikes, but they were divided among themselves, as well as lacking connections to the social movement organizations that had emerged in the Global Justice Movement or in successive waves of protest. Innovative forms of protest, such as social strikes, were invented, but without any sustained empowering capacity. No strong social or political coalitions were formed to challenge neoliberal reforms. In a situation traditionally characterized by a large but not autonomous civil society, accustomed rather to searching for support in the centre-left parties and their collateral organizations, social movements had a weak capacity to mobilize against governments that were supported by the main centre-left party. This was reflected in the repertoire of protest, which remained in part anchored in the past tradition, with attempts to build camps in the city squares, after the Spanish examples, encountering very little success. The referendum in defence of water as a public good emerged here as a main result of those mobilizations, but also of a long-lasting process that had its roots in the European Social Forum.

On 12 and 13 June 2011, 27 million Italians (57% of the electorate) voted in a national abrogative referendum, thereby achieving the 50%+1 threshold required by Italian law. Two of the four questions submitted for the popular vote addressed the privatization of water – namely, the obligation of public authorities to select the providers of water services by way of bids open to public, private and mixed companies; and the inclusion in the water tariff of a quota (fixed by law at 7%) for the remuneration of the capital invested by the company managing the provision of water. The citizens who voted 'yes' (that is, for the abrogation of privatization of water supply, against the position of the government and

main parties) made up 95.4% on the question about the private management of water provision; and 95.8% were against the fixed remuneration
for private investors in water supply. This meant that as many as 25
million Italians voted against the government's position oriented towards
privatization (Chiaramonte and D'Alimonte 2012).

The abrogative referendum had been called by a coalition of social
movement organizations that had collected 1.4 million signatures, about
three times the number required by Italian law to initiate a citizen-induced
referendum. The collection of the signatures has been presented as 'an
incredible sign of vitality of the movement of the commons, which mobilized tens of thousands of volunteers, collecting nationwide signatures
in the most remote corners of the country. People usually sceptical of
political collections of signatures actually lined up, sometimes for hours,
to sign' (Bailey and Mattei 2013, 989). Started by the core organizations
of the Italian Forum of Water Movements, the campaign lasted eighteen
months, during which water rights were to become a core symbol only
not against privatization in general, but also for citizens' participation,
as synthesized in the slogan 'It is written water, it is read democracy'
(Fantini 2012, 16). In fact, far from being single-issue, the campaign
developed into a call for a definition of nature, culture, labour and
education as common goods (Bailey and Mattei 2013).

The referendum against the privatization of water developed from
pre-existing social movements as a way to appropriate opportunities
during a moment characterized by increasing austerity policies and
related retrenchment of citizenship rights, especially on issues of social
protection and public services, including energy, transport, health and
education. Between 1992 and 2000, Italy had in fact been the second
most active country in the world, after the United Kingdom, in the
privatization of public services (with a value of around €140 billion)
(Bailey and Mattei 2013). Since the mid-1990s, liberalization of water
management has transformed the formerly publicly owned municipal
corporations into a coexistence of different types of water suppliers and
an increasing presence of private companies, in the form of big corporations (Mazzoni and Cicognani 2013, 315).

Political opportunities for the water movement had seemed to open
up as, in 2007, a centre-left government had established a special commission in the Ministry of Justice with the task of proposing a reform
of the definition of public property in the Italian Civil Code (dating from
the fascist regime). Under the lead of Stefano Rodotà, former president of
the left-wing Partito Democratico della Sinistra (Democratic Party of the
Left, which then gave birth to the Democratic Party), the committee
singled out as in need of special protection what it defined as common
goods. Distinct from public goods and private goods, 'the commons' is

conceptualized as 'goods belonging to the natural and cultural patrimony of the country (such as rivers, streams, lakes, air, forests, flora, fauna) and goods of archaeological, cultural, and environmental relevance' (Quarta and Ferrando 2015, 269–70). After the abrupt fall of the centre-left government, and the entering into power of the centre-right coalition headed by Silvio Berlusconi in November 2009, the lower chamber passed a decree stating that, by 31 December 2011, local services under control of the public sector, including water supply, had to be placed on the market by public auction (Bailey and Mattei 2013). As political opportunities were closing down, a broad coalition of social movements and civil society organizations promoted a national referendum to repeal privatization, drafting the related questions and collecting the certified signatures to be delivered to the Constitutional Court for verification (Mattei 2013, 369). The coalition formed around a document posted on the web that called for a referendum procedure.

While building upon some alliances with the institutional Left, the water referendum also expressed the tensions with the centre-left parties that, in other historical moments, had channelled progressive social movements' demands into the system (della Porta 2013). As one of the campaign promoters stated:

> This movement born from the defence of the fundamental commons achieved a critical mass, both material and symbolic, which was able to sweep away that unique subculture of the Italian Right known as 'Berlusconismo', a mixture of ultramodern company culture and neo-feudal lordship-bondage relationships. The movement was also able to dismantle the part of the reformist Left that had fallen in love with 'privatism' and was no longer able to distinguish between the area of profits for the few and that of the rights of everyone, between the market sphere and the life sphere, between commodities and commons. (Fattori 2013, 381)

Confronted therefore with the closure of institutional opportunities, with a centre-right government in power, and international (especially ECB) pressures for austerity policies, the social movement opposing the privatization of water management created its own opportunities through the promotion of an abrogative referendum.

Referendums within contentious campaigns

Some referendum campaigns can change the perception of time, triggering a sense of urgency. Referendum campaigns can be considered as eventful, as they trigger an intensification of attention around some issues, creating specific public spaces in which relations between collective and individual actors develop. Research on direct democracy has also pointed towards the influence of contingent events with a strong impact on public opinion. While often presented as second-order elections (Franklin 2002, 756), signalling attitudes more towards the government than towards the specific issue at stake, referendums on salient topics might help in focusing attention, encouraging issue voting. Turnout in referendums is in general influenced by demographic variables (such as education, income, age, length of residence in a community, ethnicity) and attitudinal ones (such as political interest, knowledge and competence) (Neijens et al. 2007), but contingent events can work as catalysts. Sympathies for political parties have at times been important predictors for the direction of the vote, when parties give indications; nevertheless, referendum campaigns are in general more open arenas for opinion formation than those for political elections (LeDuc 2002), with therefore more space for agency. Strategic choices for campaigning address, then, the building of coalitions with collective actors, as well as the population to be targeted, with the option of either focusing on pre-existing constituencies or trying to mobilize those who are undecided (Kriesi 2012a). More than normal electoral campaigns, referendum campaigns might in fact affect the final choice, as predispositions might be changed by arguments, especially when the sources of those arguments are considered as credible and succeed in bridging the specific topics with core cultural themes (Kriesi 2012a).

Social movements can, therefore, play a significant role in referendum campaigns by focusing attention, through disruptive action, on the questions about which the referendum is called. They can do this, especially, by using their skills in moving beyond conventional repertoires of action. Massive mobilization in protest actions, as well as the multiplication of smaller events, can draw the attention of public opinion to the preferred choice. Social movement organizations may therefore create turning points in conventional politics by the use of unconventional means.

Social movement studies have often stressed the importance of existing resources for collective mobilization. The involvement in campaigns of movement organizations with more or less formal structures tends to increase the attention given to an issue through processes of block recruitment, as each works as a multiplier mobilizing its own constituency into various types of protest campaigns. Referendums, as tools of direct democracy, are part of movements' repertoires, resonating with their aspirations for the direct participation of citizens. In recent times, research on protest campaigns has distinguished between more formal processes of networking, often involving existing associations, and aggregative forms, connecting individuals, often through social media.

The campaign against the privatization of water supply combined both strategies, with the aims not only of mobilizing in large numbers, but also of advancing prefigurative forms of democracy. They succeeded so well in creating multiple forums of high discursive quality that they empowered their participants well beyond the end of the referendum campaign.

In the Italian water referendum, the promoters adopted from the very beginning a horizontal logic, pushed by both instrumental and normative concerns (Fantini 2012; Carrozza and Fantini 2013; Cernison 2014; Bieler 2015). The organizational structure of the campaign mixed various organizational forms promoting high levels of participation, through a very horizontal network of various groupings that had mobilized under the banner 'Water is not for sale', opposing the conception of water as a 'service with economic value'. As a leading activist in the campaign, Tommaso Fattori (2013, 378) summarized:

> it was not a completely sudden awakening: behind the victory in the referenda was a long molecular process and the steady construction of the largest social coalition ever seen in the country, which brought together thousands of local networks and national organizations, united by a pact to defend water, which became the symbol of the commons. The referendum was just the final stage along a road walked for more than a decade, born at the dawn of the new century, from a double need that arose in the social movements: the specific defence of the commons of water from looming privatization policies and also the need to find a weak link in the material and symbolic construction of privatistic globalization.

At the start of the protest against water privatization was, in 2000, the foundation of the Italian Committee for the World Water Contract (Comitato italiano per un Contratto mondiale sull'acqua – CICMA), following a Water Manifesto that had been published in 1998. The Committee initially involved some development NGOs, the cultural association Punto Rosso ('Red Point'), an Environmental Forum, and some members of the Partito della Rifondazione Comunista ('Communist Refoundation Party'). Later on, they were joined by organizations for 'another globalization', such as ATTAC and Rete Lilliput, as the water issue had acquired symbolic value at the first World Social Forum in 2000 – with frequent references to the 'water war' in Bolivian Cochabamba – and in the first European Social Forum held in Florence in 2002. Groups linked to the Social Forums then networked with several local committees against the privatization of the water supply, contesting increases in price and decreases in quality. Several Catholic groups participated in the campaign in what has been defined as part of a Catholic awakening and renewed activism in public affairs, with the frame of 'water as human right and commons' considered as particularly resonant with the Catholic Social Doctrine (Fantini 2014).

The logic of building a broad and horizontal network followed that experimented with during the Social Forums at various levels (Fattori 2013, 379–80). As Matteo Cernison (2014, 65) summarized, the 2011 referendum 'was part of a broader, long-lasting process, which pitted two distinct and conflicting paradigms against each other: a market-oriented, neoliberal view on resources and services, and an anti-neoliberal view, which considers water as a public resource and a human right'. After the experience of the Tuscan Water Forum, in 2006 a national Forum was created which included: social movement organizations; trade unions (old and new); Catholic, environmental, critical consumers' and pacifist groups; as well as the recently founded Five Star Movement (later to become a political party) (Bieler 2015). Workers in the water provision sector were also active participants, together with water consumers and some municipalities. Several networks converged in the struggle, but were also formed during its development. In 2008, an alliance including local administrators launched the campaign 'Salva l'acqua' ('Save the Water') and a Coordinamento degli enti locali per l'acqua pubblica ('Network of Local Municipalities for Public Water'), with the aim of modifying the municipal statutes of cities and provinces by introducing a reference to water as a human right and a common good – with some successes in this direction in the Region of Valle d'Aosta, the Autonomous Province of Trento, and the towns of Venice, Cuneo and Ancona.

What is more, the campaign involved various very informal groupings of activists. Sport associations, parishes, scout groups, student organizations and artists all mobilized in a creative form, together with left-wing squatted social centres (Fantini 2012, 18), as did small ad hoc groups. In fact, 16 per cent of voters in the referendum declared that they had actively participated in the campaign, which had represented for 60 per cent of them their first experience of political activism (Fantini 2013). Even if the Democratic Party (Partito Democratico – PD) had initially refused to support the campaign, hopes were raised after the positive electoral result for the centre-left in the Spring 2011 administrative elections, particularly for some of the referendum's supporters. Several local administrators and the youth organization Young Democrats (Giovani Democratici – GD) opposed water privatization, while other leaders of the party promoted a counter-campaign for privatization.

With a flexible structure, the Forum italiano dei movimenti per l'acqua (FIMA, 'Italian Forum of Water Movements') developed to coordinate many actors, differing in size, action-scale, previous political experience and specific goals (Cernison 2016). In fact, the normative conception of the commons was reflected in an inclusive organizational structure characterized by 'a decentralised and non-professional structure, based on local committees of volunteers and activists; horizontality and equality among all participants, translated in the practice of decisions taken by consensus and in the refusal of charismatic leadership; transparency of the procedures, exemplified for instance by the decision of repaying back the public electoral reimbursement to the private citizens that financially supported the referenda campaign' (Fantini 2012, 37). Run through a national assembly, the assembly of the Italian Forum of Water Movements was open to all activists, and met about once a year to define the general political line. A small national coordinating group, with members from regional committees and national associations continuously active on the water issue, met about once a month in order to implement the political decisions of the assembly, while an 'operative office' in Rome, with no decisional power, had the task of coordinating the various activities. Thematic working groups and local bodies also spread (Fantini 2013), with a FIMA mailing list functioning as a space for debate for activists that continued after the referendum.

The conception of democracy within the movement resonated with the ideas developed not only from the Global Justice Movement, but also from anti-austerity protests in Southern European countries, with an emphasis on transparency and horizontality, opposition to financial capitalism, and an emerging focus on elites and the people (Fantini 2013). In order to address internal tensions, the FIMA

> adopted the consensus decision-making rule in its local and national meetings. Furthermore, when a vote was nonetheless required, the voice of large organizations – such as the national trade unions – counted [the same] as the voice of smaller associations and committees. Second, the assembly assigned the central office of the Forum only operative tasks, and the local committees constantly monitored its dimension, its internal composition, its relationship with other organizations. . . . Third, the FIMA explicitly created separated spaces of participation for some powerful and resourceful actors, giving life to the committees of support for local authorities and, in particular, political parties. Fourth, but probably most important, the FIMA granted a particular centrality to the local committees, and to the territorial struggles that they represent. (Cernison 2016)

The activists stressed, in fact, the presence of 'sovereign local committees, but of course with a political commitment to unity' (in Cernison 2016), comparing the local committees to the roots of a tree. National action was deeply rooted at the local level, as the Forum is characterized by the manner in which policy and initiatives emerge as the local nodes share their experiences and proposals. . . . Indeed, the key strengths of the movement are its deep roots and diffusion in the territories; its ability to aggregate different experiences and cultures and to connect the local struggles with the national dimension of the mobilization; the dialogue, openness and collaboration with the institutions. (Ciervo 2009, 159–60)

A very horizontal and decentralized action strategy followed, as communication resources (fliers, web elements, posters) and symbols promoted by the national coordination were sometimes disregarded by the activists, who developed their own symbols and forms of communication (Cernison 2016). Adapting to this trend, the central office of the FIMA gave up on attempts to homogenize the campaign messages, focusing instead on 'the creation of actions, messages and symbols that the activists could easily readapt and personalize, and in gathering and sharing on the web or at the national level contents independently produced by the local committees' (Cernison 2016). It is exactly this lack of strong coordination of the contentious campaign that activists considered to be key to the success of the movement, which praised a 'creative chaos':

a total mess, which essentially was the richness of the movement, in the sense that we were able to structure and propose to the territory some things, and to construct tools such as the posters or, let's say, the web banner. Yet, then, some of these things were taken, readapted and transformed, we received suggestions from the territories, the territories themselves produced things. . . . So, I mean, it was a sort of a creative chaos from this point of view. It's not by chance that a massive use of the social networks [emerged], probably for the first time in Italy they had the capacity to promote a message in such a viral way. (in Cernison 2016)

The campaign on the water referendum in Italy included various forms of action, from more conventional participation to disruptive protests. At the outset, the movement launched grassroots information and educational activities for the promotion of an alternative water culture, raising awareness about the effects of the lack of access to clean water and of the privatization of water provision around the world, and involving schools and parishes, with frequent collaboration with local authorities and various associations. In fact, 'these initiatives were built on expertise and practices of development NGOs on education for "global citizenship", with water issues analysed within the broader analytical notion of sustainable development and the normative framework of international solidarity' (Fantini 2012, 19).

International events, such as the Peoples' World Water Forum (whose first two meetings were held in Florence in 2003), worked as counter-summits to the World Water Forum, an event on water usage which opponents claimed was controlled by business. Specific actions were also undertaken inside the companies in charge of water provision, including the creation of workers' committees, which collaborated with user organizations. In this, an alternative model of democratic management, based on demands for participation by workers and consumers in the running of water companies, was developed.

The Forum experimented also with various channels of direct democracy, including a popular-initiative law proposing public management for water services in Tuscany; a referendum to repeal the regional water law, proposed by activists and local governments in Lombardy; and a Citizens' Initiative Bill for a Water Reform statute, which in 2009 collected more than 400,000 signatures, eight times the required 50,000. Beyond the mobilization involved in the massive collection of signatures, writing of proposed bills through bottom-up participation also took place, as social movements and citizens became legislators themselves, writing their own laws directly. In doing so, they implemented a participatory model of democracy for the management of the water supply, which was considered to be resonant with its nature as a common, thereby transforming the 'consumer-users' not only into citizens, but – especially – into *commoners* (Carsetti 2014).

Street politics was also important. National protest marches were organized in Rome in 2010 and 2011, while local committees promoted the H2Ora, with public initiatives taking place at the same hour across the country (Cernison 2014, 92). In December 2010, twenty coordinated demonstrations, decentralized to the regional level, took place. Within a process of adaptation to the different needs of the various phases of the campaign, large marches were combined with educational work.

Especially innovative was the movement's use of its own communication channels. Websites allowed for the development of a dense network of organizations in which a 'low level of centralization testifies to a relatively levelled knowledge of the network' (Cernison 2014, 18). Also at the local level, websites allowed for high levels of participation (including an online poll to choose the campaign logo) and self-financing (Cernison 2014, 93–4). Informal groupings of activists (often younger ones) created blogs and Facebook pages, using the web not only for the top-down distribution of information, but also as a space for interaction, connecting online and offline communication. During the last months of the campaign, appeals to vote were spread through pictures and videos (Cernison 2014, 150).

The perception and conception of online technology developed over time, from a mainly instrumental view as a cheap tool to coordinate a broad community of activists through the sharing of information and advertising material, to the appreciation of its deliberative potential. Thus:

> together with this generalized tendency of conceiving of the 'digital' as an environment, the idea of a sympathetic and alternative online space opposed to the traditional and closed mainstream media emerged. Therefore, militants adopted the web, Facebook and email chains as platforms for alternative communications efforts, to oppose the silence of Italian television and of the main national and local newspapers. In other words, activists perceived digital technologies as 'their own' environments of action, a place where their opponents were less prepared to communicate. (Cernison 2014, 152–3)

Especially in the last days of the campaign, Facebook pages such as 'Acqua Pubblica' ('Public Water') were used to contact potential voters and mobilize them, as images and symbols were included as banners on personal Facebook accounts, while the 'Vendesi Mamma' ('Mum for Sale') campaign developed on YouTube, ironically spreading the message that 'privatizing water is like selling one's mother'. Facebook's event tool was used to invite citizens to turn out to vote, to organize free transport services for going to vote, and also to organize bicycle rides at the local level (Cernison 2014, 209–10). The new social media acquired a special function at the peak of the campaign, allowing for a massive and decentralized mobilization that contributed to the results of achieving the quorum and winning the referendum with the support of more than 95 per cent of the voters.

In sum, the need for coordinating a large network of very diverse organizations and individuals pushed towards a loose network, with significant autonomy at the periphery. The experience of the social forum interacted with that of the anti-austerity protests in the normative stress on broad participation, managed through consensual methods. The tensions between national and local groups, with their own organizational peculiarities, were addressed through a complex mix of aggregative and networking instruments. The broad network included, indeed, very different organizational forms: from unions to squatted centres, from formal associations to citizens' committees, from movement organizations to institutions. The movement's experiences with forms of direct democracy (including petitions, as well as laws promoted from below) favoured the choice of the referendum as a way to react to the formal closing of opportunities in representative institutions at national level.

Framing the right to water

Framing strategies have been addressed in both referendum studies and social movement studies. Research on referendums has stressed the importance of the ways in which an issue is presented. Especially when the issue is complex, citizens do rely on arguments (Kriesi 2012c), as well as on emotions (Wirth, Schemer et al. 2012). Ostensibly single-issue, in reality referendum questions are often multifaceted, so that the definition of what is at stake can be very relevant to the result. Issue ownership (e.g. by political parties) is also challenged in referendum campaigns – at least, more so than in normal elections. While, in ideologically polarized referendums on highly salient and well-known issues, voting behaviour is expected to be more likely structured by factors such as party identification and ideological beliefs, opinion formation is more open on other topics (LeDuc 2002). Referendum campaigns are particularly important in informing citizens as well as in motivating them to invest energy in the campaign, as more information increases the salience of an issue, and hence exposure and related participation (Binzer Hobolt 2007; Marsh 2007). The arguments articulated around the referendum's question are particularly important, as positions on an issue also explain the level of turnout (de Vreese and Boomgaarden 2007, 197–8).

In parallel with the attention in referendum studies to issues at stake in terms of their degree of resonance, technicality, party ownership, and of the presentation of the issue during the campaign, social movement studies point to the importance of framing. Referendum campaigns organized from below are therefore occasions for social movement organizations not only to bridge a specific referendum question with broader issues of justice, but also to articulate a different vision of politics based on participation and debate within democratic public spheres (della Porta 2013). Social movements, especially those with more explicitly inclusive positions, might contribute to introducing new (and often broader) arguments, linking specific issues to broader ideals of social justice and democracy. In doing so, they might also politicize and even polarize the debate, creating new public spaces. In particular, my research shows the importance of frame bridging between the issue at stake in the referendums and broader topics. Frame bridging takes place in fact between the referendum issue and the values and claims traditionally addressed by the progressive social movements, not only at the substantive level (such as dignity and equality), but also at a procedural one (such as participatory and deliberative democracy). Moreover, when called in relation to typical social movement claims, referendums can have the effect of frame intensification, identifying broad norms with non-negotiable aims.

Framing and frame bridging were extremely important in the Italian campaign on the water referendum, through which activists were able to convince electors well beyond left-leaning ones.

During the campaign, a growth in universality of the frames, as well as the bridging of different issues, fuelled organizational networking around the defence of human rights and the creation of the commons. In fact, 'many activists had entered the movement on the basis of their particular organizational background, but as a result of the struggle they started to broaden their approach and were transformed into water activists, leading to a more homogeneous organization' (Bieler 2015). Participation in various transnational campaigns fuelled the development of a discourse around the universal rights of citizens (Petrella 2001; Mazzoni and Cicognani 2013; Mazzoni et al. 2015). The commons was then an important concept elaborated within the movement itself.

In the movement discourse, the right to water was considered as part of citizenship rights, and the social costs of privatization were denounced, as 'the theme of water also included symbolic power, as water is understood as a fundamental source of life, a human right, and part of the commons' (Bieler 2015). Access to water was framed neither as an economic good, nor only as a response to a human need, but rather as part of the human right to life (Petrella 2001). Water was presented as a symbol of life ('we are water') as opposed to the culture of death of neoliberalism (Muehlebach 2018). So,

> the movement gave voice to widespread popular moral perceptions, putting forward at the same time political claims with legal implications. . . . Support for the identification of water as a natural human right, inherent to human nature and dignity, stems from widespread moral perceptions and common sense recognising water as an essential element for life, recalling that the human body is made of water for more than 70%, and acknowledging the central role played by water in the broader material-symbolic domain shaping culture and societies throughout places and times. (Fantini 2012, 24–5)

Following pressure from the movement, in 2010 the UN General Assembly and UN Human Rights Council approved two resolutions that acknowledged the human right to water and sanitation (Fantini 2012, 27–8).

The definition of the commons was a building block in the campaign. According to the Rodotà Commission, the commons are resources that require special legal protection, which should be stronger than that already provided for public goods (Quarta and Ferrando 2015, 270). Water was thus framed as a common good, locating it beyond the individualistic conception of human rights. The commission proposed a management of natural resources characterized by 'i) the active and direct involvement of local population through decentralized and participatory management, ii) the exploitation of traditional knowledge and customary practices, iii) the emphasis on the cultural dimensions of the management schemes promoting social accountability and harmonious relation with the whole ecosystem' (Fantini 2012, 31–2).

Given the non-competing and non-exclusive nature of resources such as water that are necessary for the fulfilment of fundamental human rights, special legal protection was needed in order to guarantee their sustainable and intergenerational preservation in order to avoid over-exploitation and exhaustion. The conceptualization of the commons enabled the overcoming of a dualism between the private and the public, by stressing the rights of a community to have access to and benefit from them. The commons must therefore be kept *extra commercium* and be put under diffused ownership and widespread responsibility to protect them, as 'any individual, for the sole fact of having an interest in or a contact with the resource, becomes responsible for the way in which it is managed, and holder of a right of action against any form of *mala gestio*, independently from the fact that the good is under public or private management' (Quarta and Ferrando 2015, 271). The commons is so defined as 'those goods – natural resources like water, air, parks, basic social services . . . – that are functional to the promotion of fundamental human rights and the free development of peoples. . . . The law should therefore guarantee direct, collective and universal enjoyment of these goods, taking into account also future generations' needs' (Fantini 2012, 35). Redolent of the UNESCO concept of a 'world common heritage', the reference to water as a 'common good (or shared resource) of human-kind' resonated with a cosmopolitan vision of a community. It inspired the movement's self-representation, fostering the sense of belonging among the participants (Fantini 2012, 32).

The management and delivery of such goods must include local communities and cooperatives of water users, as well as customary governance, as 'in the discourse and practices of the Italian water movement, both references to human rights and the commons uphold the claim for an assumption of responsibility by public authorities, against their perceived withdrawal in front of economic interests and market logics. Moreover, activists demand the renewal of public institutions towards a more participatory and effective democracy' (Fantini 2012, 39).

Water became, then, a symbol for the commons of humanity, peace, international cooperation and solidarity (Carrozza and Fantini 2013). Not by chance, a sense of community, as well as outrage over violated rights, were important motivations for activists (Mazzoni and Cicognani 2013). The framing of rights also had high mobilizing potential, pointing towards 'the importance of the perceived violation of a principle (i.e., the right to water) as a specific psychological process underlying activists' moral motivation to identify with the Water Movement and act on its behalf' (Mazzoni et al. 2015, 324). The right to water acquired a 'sacred value', being 'seen as absolute, non-negotiable, and inviolable, thus leading individuals to respond strongly to any violation of it (Mazzoni et al. 2015, 324). In the words of an activist, 'water is a fundamental human right. Indeed, it means life. In this sense, like other human rights, it cannot be violated' (cited in Mazzoni and Cicognani 2013, 320).

Another important motivation against water privatization was the preservation of community ties, regaining a 'sense of community' – as an activist put it, 'this is actually the reason, sense of community, and the fact of being able to handle things in common and dealing with them together' (Mazzoni and Cicognani 2013, 321). The issue of water acquired in fact an aggregating power, allowing for going beyond 'the fences of political affiliation, party, association and movement, and we just give birth to an initiative where everyone can bring his/her content' (Mazzoni and Cicognani 2013, 321). The struggle itself allowed for the creation of a community by increasing friendly relationships. As activists stated, 'being in the street among the people . . . allowed everybody (even the elders) to forget their loneliness and stand up for their common rights' (Mazzoni and Cicognani 2013, 321), as 'the sense of a community spirit and the involvement in the committee's initiatives produce a nice feeling, such as "just staying with other people"' (Mazzoni and Cicognani 2013, 322). In the words of one activist, 'one motive more, which is tightly linked to this particular campaign, is not just to try to get back the civic sense but also to join a sense of collectivity, which sometimes may also mean you have some laughs!' (Mazzoni and Cicognani 2013, 322).

An additional frame revolved around the claim for a participatory and deliberative conception of democracy (Petrella 2001). Not only did re-municipalization re-empower local government, but publicly managed water was considered a sign of democracy, while privatized water was seen as a sign of dictatorship (and illegality) (Muehlebach 2018). Against those who stole sovereignty from the people, 'the referendum, a fundamental tool of democracy, was hence the final stage of a process that started focused on the subject of water but more generally is trying to recover pieces of a sovereignty that formally belongs to the people but in substance has been hijacked by oligarchies' (Fattori 2013, 381). Because 'the private management also hinders the ability of citizens to make their voices heard' (Mazzoni and Cicognani 2013, 320), activists realized that 'through water, they could present to the rest of the society the ideas of participatory democracy, the common good, alternatives to privatization and, in general, a new social paradigm opposed to the dominant neoliberal one' (Cernison 2014, 83).

The proposal to increase the direct participation of citizens developed not only against privatization, but also against the previous, overly centralized and top-down experiences of public management. As one activist put it:

> commons is everything we share, gifts of nature and creations of society that belong to all of us equally, and should be maintained for future generations. These are goods that escape the idea of exclusive use and build social bonds. These goods must not allow discrimination in access to them according to individual wealth, but reintroduce the element of equality, as well as a relationship of care – rather than one of domination or subjection – between humanity and the rest of nature of which it is a part. (Fattori 2013, 384–5)

In this vision, the commoners 'are all the members of a community or loosely connected group of people who steward and care for the shared goods, adopting a form of self-government based on their capability to give themselves rules (and incentives and sanctions to make them be respected) called commoning' (Fattori 2013, 385). *Commoning* is thus presented as 'an open, participatory, and inclusive form of decision making that produces and reproduces commons in the interest of present and future generations and in the interest of the ecosystem itself, where natural commons are concerned' (Fattori 2013, 385). *Commonification* refers then to the self-government of the good by the citizens within public management bodies, with the aim of granting universal access to the good and protection of the resource.

The adversary is, in contrast, framed as a cohesive economic and political elite. In its struggle, 'the movement opposed speculators, entrepreneurs, investors and shareholders of corporations, that is those who exploit their power to make profits by selling water', as well as the politicians who are colluding with those interests (in Mazzoni and Cicognani 2013, 323). In the words of an activist, 'what I really hate is the idea of somebody getting richer with water. Personally, thinking that somebody else takes advantages from this situation makes me really angry' (in Mazzoni and Cicognani 2013, 323). Privatization is therefore immoral, as it implies 'profiting from the sale of an article that should be shared by everyone' (Mazzoni and Cicognani 2013, 321).

Beyond the referendum: long-term empowerment

The referendum results did not end the water struggle in Italy, as its outcomes have not been fully implemented. In the midst of the financial crisis, as the European Central Bank demanded that the Italian government adopt austerity measures, a few weeks after the referendum

Parliament approved a law called 'Dispositions to adjust the law to the referendum results and to European law', which reintroduced provisions for privatization of public services abolished by the referendum, except in regard to water (Mattei 2013). After the referendum, Acea SpA, a partially privately owned water corporation in Rome, stated that no legal obligation followed from the referendum. Through various treaties and memorandums, the EU continued to push for privatization. In 2017, a new law from the Democratic Party, the so-called Madia Law, reintroduced the principle that an adequate remuneration for invested capital had to be granted to private investors, while the collectively written Citizens' Bill in favour of water supply has never been discussed in the Chamber of Deputies.

This resistance to implementing its results notwithstanding, the referendum did have significant consequences. First of all, there was an important constitutional victory as, in July 2012, the Italian Constitutional Court declared 'for the first time in Italian history, that the will of the people expressed in the form of direct democracy by the referendum could not be overturned by means of representative democracy (that is, by the Parliament) at least for a reasonable period of time' (Mattei 2013, 372).

The memory of those participatory processes, assembleary and based on consensus as the main decision-making method, also remains imprinted as an empowering legacy. The struggle for the implementation of the referendum results then continued, as the organizational networks formed during the campaigns remained active online and offline. Since the autumn of 2011, a campaign of civil disobedience invited consumers not to pay part of the water fees (Carsetti 2014). Even after the referendum, activists continued to meet in various squatted spaces to discuss how these could be transformed into commons through 'moments where people attempted to make democracy a lived experience', and 'a kind of "slow democracy" was performatively enacted and lived' (Muehlebach 2018, 352). The activists stated that the political and legal universe had been transformed forever: 'While the concept of *bene comune* never became law and never passed as a reform of the civil code as had been intended by the Rodotà Commission, it has nevertheless become a concept that continues to be deployed in courts of law, including the Italian Supreme Court. It thus continues its life within Italian legal culture and has been inscribed in many municipal and regional statutes' (Muehlebach 2018, 355).

Certainly, the resounding success of the water referendum was 'a blow to the neoliberal establishment' (Mattei 2013, 371) as water as a commons became a metaphor for democracy (Carrozza 2013), expressing the will of citizens to participate in decision-making (Fantini 2013). As one of the promoters of the water referendum recalls (Fattori 2013, 378–9),

'the vote was symptomatic of a strong desire for connections and participation, beneath the ashes of social atomization: the attempted absorption
of the commons realm into the processes of capitalistic valorisation will
find ever larger obstacles and social conflicts mounted before it by the
efforts of the commons movement'. The referendum also affected party
politics as, in the words of an ATTAC activist, 'the result of the referendum accelerates the crisis of the parties, introducing through its
social practices the need to overcome representative democracy, towards
substantial democracy based on social activism and direct participation'
(cited in Fantini 2012, 36). Thus, the referendum became, in the activists'
memory:

> a new starting point from which to construct a counter-hegemony and
> place a spoke in the wheels of the mechanisms for the decommodi-
> fication of the commons realm. . . . The risk of the commodification
> of water – universally seen as the symbol of life and what we all have
> in common – in effect worked as the trigger for a broader process of
> rediscovery and defence of the commons, which is still in full swing
> today. . . . Thanks to the powerful symbolism of water, today in Italy
> a new and wide-ranging debate has developed on the new enclosures
> of the commons, from culture and knowledge to energy. It is necessary
> to rediscover and refer to the symbolic dimension, to provide new
> narratives of the world, moving well beyond the dry notions used in
> technocratic parlance. (Fattori 2013, 378–9)

The concept of the commons continues, in fact, to be a central reference
for the movements that followed, inspiring other progressive campaigns.
The idea of a participatory form of democracy in the running of water
services certainly challenges 'the capitalist focus on commodifying ever
more areas and submitting them to the profit logic of the market, implying a move towards a new economic model' (Bieler 2015). Indeed, 'the
legal and political actions of the *beni comuni* movement reinvigorated
the constitutional debate . . . reopening the debate about what ought to
be the space for the "public" and the constituent role of the people in the
constitution' (Bailey and Mattei 2013, 980).

Water remained a politically highly contentious symbol for direct
democracy outside of Italy as well. Launched in 2009 by the European
Public Services Union (EPSU), the Right2Water European Citizens'
Initiative (ECI; 'Water and sanitation are a human right! Water is a
public good, not a commodity!') collected enough signatures in enough
member states to force the EU institutions to react, bringing water access
onto the agenda. Announced at the Marseille official and alternative
world water forums in March 2012, registered with the Commission
on 1 April and confirmed on 10 May 2012, the campaign spread in the

autumn of the same year through various movement events, as well as within local struggles against privatization. The number of signatures greatly exceeded the required 1 million, and reached the quotas in thirteen countries (1,236,455 in Germany), beyond the required minimum of seven EU member states. In September 2013, around 1.9 million signatures were submitted for approval to member-state governments; and on 20 December, the petition was presented to the Commission. In June 2013, citing the ECI, the Commission excluded water from the Concessions Directive, maintaining, however, the possibility of reviewing the exclusion three years after implementation of the Directive.

The organizational structure remained networked. A major role in the mobilization was played by the European trade union EPSU, which had been involved in protests against water privatization in Central and Eastern Europe in the 1990s, forming the Reclaiming Public Water Network, and had mobilized successfully against the privatization of water as part of the EU Services Directive in 2002 and the Public Procurement Directives in 2003/4. For the purpose of the campaign, EPSU built an alliance at the European level with the European Environmental Bureau (EEB), the European Anti-Poverty Network (EAPN) and the Social Platform. Most important was the support of a broad alliance of trade unions, social movements and NGOs across the whole 'social factory' (Bieler 2017, 309).

Influenced by the Italian experience, the campaign was framed in terms of commons, democracy and rights. The petition aimed in fact at securing recognition of water as a human right in the EU, and stimulating related legislation to protect water as a public good not to be privatized. Referring to the Right2Water European Citizens' Initiative, Louisa Parks (2014) noted that 'with a strong presence, expertise and resources in Brussels, this umbrella organisation could also rely on developed networks of national and local members for the collection of signatures'. Three key objectives were stated at the launch of the ECI in May 2012: '(1) The EU institutions and Member States be obliged to ensure that all inhabitants enjoy the right to water and sanitation; (2) water supply and management of water resources not be subject to "internal market rules" and that water services are excluded from liberalisation; and (3) the EU increases its efforts to achieve universal access to water and sanitation' (Bieler 2017, 315).

Following a public hearing held on 17 February 2014 in the European Parliament (EP), on 19 March 2014 the Commission released its Communication on the ECI, promising to strengthen existing instruments and to launch an EU-wide public (non-binding) consultation on the Drinking Water Directive. It refused, however, to introduce water as a human right into EU legislation, claiming that the Commission was not responsible for the issue, which remained in the competence of the member states (something, activists noted, the EC had not respected when pushing for further liberalization and privatization in Greece, Portugal and Italy). While stating that it would not further pursue the liberalization of water, no EU legislation backed that statement (Bieler 2017). As the private water corporations complained about the exclusion of water from the Concession Directive, some successes were noted for the ECI. In particular, in late 2014, the European Economic and Social Committee (EcoSoc) asked the EC to implement the ECI's demand through legislation establishing access to water and sanitation as human rights, excluding them permanently from the commercial rules of the internal market. Towards the end of 2015, the EP passed a resolution criticizing the EC for having disregarded the ECI's demands, and asking that water not be part of any future Concessions Directive, nor of trade deals negotiated by the EU.

In sum:

> The ECI, based on a broad alliance of trade unions, social movements and NGOs, was successful at a time when austerity policies were enforced across the EU member states, including pressures towards further privatization especially on the countries in the EU's periphery such as Greece and Portugal. It, therefore, went completely against the trend and in opposition to dominant forces pushing for further neo-liberal restructuring. (Bieler 2017, 318)

The aim is now to extend similar protection to other public services such as health, education, energy and transport.

Expanding the analysis from a comparative perspective: referendums in Scotland and Catalonia

Some of the dynamics singled out in the Italian case also emerged in two other recent cases of referendums on independence: an official referendum held in Scotland in 2014, and two unofficial ones held in Catalonia. As for the former, in November 2013, following an agreement between the Scottish government and the government of the United Kingdom, the Scottish Parliament approved the Scottish Independence Referendum Act 2013. On 18 September 2014, a very high 84.6% of the Scottish population participated in a vote on the question 'Should Scotland be an independent country? with 55.3% answering No. In the latter, on 9 November 2014, after more than 500 municipal-level non-binding consultations on independence held from 2009 to 2011, about 2.3 million people cast their votes in a symbolic, non-binding referendum supported by the Generalitat (della Porta, O'Connor et al. 2017a). Following up on this experience, challenging a decision of the Constitutional Court, on 1 October 2017 the regional government of Catalonia held a referendum on independence, whose result they considered to be mandatory. As many as 2,266,498 citizens voted, 92% of them supporting independence.

The importance of movements' appropriation of opportunities emerged clearly also in these two cases. As for Scotland, at the national level the Labour Party had been more open to devolution than the Liberal Democrat–Conservative coalition that was in government at the time of the referendum campaign. After the coalition government, headed by David Cameron, had rejected an enhanced devolution option (so-called Devo-Max), the closing down of political opportunities pushed Scottish nationalists towards a mass mobilization, combining claims for independence with issues of social justice. The hard-line reaction of the UK government, with some support from within Labour, and the ensuing media campaigns against the Yes vote, polarized the public. Electoral propaganda for the No vote was dominated by attempts at spreading fear, with economic disaster threatened in case of a victory for independence. When coupled with the ongoing financial crisis, this contributed to increased support for the No vote, but also outraged many Scots, who felt expropriated of their sovereignty.

In fact, the shift from calls for devolution to calls for independence radicalized positions also within the Scottish Nationalist Party (SNP), which had initially favoured a compromise on devolution, with the continued acceptance of the monarchy, NATO membership and the pound as currency. While closing down at the national level, opportunities for change opened up at the local level instead. The election of an SNP government in Scotland gave democratic legitimacy to the call for a referendum. The Conservative Party in government at the national level, and its closure to claims for devolution, boosted support for the pro-independence parties and movements. The effect was a polarization between the right-wing Westminster government and the (assumedly progressive) Scottish population.

In the Catalan case, the pseudo-referendum campaign was also triggered by a closing down of opportunities after an initial opening. Since 2003–4, the centre-left governments at both regional and national levels had been sympathetic towards demands for devolution, opening up a process of constitutional change in the Statute of Autonomy. In particular, opportunities opened up as the presence of the Partit dels Socialistes de Catalunya (PSC) in the Catalan governments between 2003 and 2010, and of the Partido Socialista Obrero Español (PSOE) in government in Madrid between 2004 and 2011, made possible a re-negotiation of Catalonia's institutional relationship with the central Spanish government. A massive mobilization was fuelled by the closing down of opportunities in 2010 and 2011, as the conservative government that took office in Spain opposed the reform project. While closing down at the national level, opportunities remained open, however, in Catalonia, with a process of polarization similar to the one observed in the Scottish case. The moderate Catalan nationalist forces repositioned themselves as, in particular, not only Convergencia i Union (CiU), but also the centre-left Esquerra Republicana de Catalunia (ERC), openly embraced pro-independence stances and promised, once in government, to hold a referendum on independence (Rico and Liñeira 2014). In January 2013, the Catalan Generalitat adopted the Declaration of Sovereignty (later declared unconstitutional), which defined Catalonia as a sovereign political subject (Orriols and Rodón 2015). In 2015, the main pro-independence civil society organizations and parties (ERC and CiU) ran in the Catalan election on a joint electoral platform, *Junts pel Si* – 'Together for the Yes', committing to hold a referendum, with an ensuing unilateral declaration of independence provided it obtain the support of more than 50 per cent of the votes (della Porta, O'Connor et al. 2017a).

A massive protest campaign spread within this complex mix of multilevel political opportunities. As – given the strong opposition of the Partido Popular and a long-awaited decision by the Constitutional Court – a negotiated solution started to be seen as unrealistic, a contentious campaign for independence grew after, in June 2010, the Constitutional Court nullified provisions regarding Catalan status and language, as well as a range of economic and political competencies (Basta 2017). Support for an independent Catalan state, increasing at first slowly, from 13.6 per cent in June 2005 to 19.4 per cent in February 2010, skyrocketed to 48.5 per cent by November 2013.

Also here, the call for a referendum became a way for Catalan independentists to create their own opportunities by fuelling a polarization with Madrid and ensuing radicalization of the traditionally moderate positions of the Catalan nationalists, with claims moving from autonomy to independence. The campaign evolved together with a long and intense wave of protests against austerity policies, adopted by Spanish governments under international pressure. Notwithstanding the high rate of economic development in Catalonia, the financial crisis in fact hit hard, with a rise in unemployment from 6.5 per cent to 25 per cent between 2007 and 2014. As the financial crisis triggered political and social crises, Catalanism succeeded in moving beyond its historical rootedness in the middle classes and rural areas, as well as among Catalan-speaking workers, expanding its urban and working-class constituencies (della Porta and Portos forthcoming).

In sum, a crisis of political legitimacy underpinned the mobilization campaigns in both Scotland and Catalonia, as the closing down of political opportunities interacted with socioeconomic difficulties. The traditional tensions between centre and periphery, with frequent calls for more autonomy, interacted with discontent with the financial crisis and the ensuing recession. In a remobilization of multiple cleavages, centre–periphery conflicts were intertwined with socioeconomic ones, as more just policies were promised in the new polities. Electoral de-alignment (especially on the left wing of the ideological spectrum) and the availability of allies (especially at the regional level) transformed latent potential into action. The referendums around independence acted then as critical junctures, which the nationalist movements exploited in order to focus attention on their claims.

As in the Italian water referendum, in both mobilization campaigns for independence a complex organizational repertoire developed, including conventional and unconventional forms. In Scotland, a conventional organizational structure characterized the Yes campaign led by the SNP, using traditional forms of electoral propaganda and canvassing. Innovative, participatory and unconventional forms of contention were adopted instead by a grassroots component of the pro-independence campaign. An influential role in promoting participation and open debate was, in fact, played at the local level by networks of social movement organizations active in different arenas on environmental issues, women's rights, immigrant rights, neighbourhood collectives, students, artists and intellectuals (Black and Marsden 2016; Dalle Mulle 2016). Within the grassroots and multi-layered mobilization developed by local community groups, forums for open information and debate were set up, promoting political education and socialization. The campaign became highly participatory and the quality of the deliberation increased, with the provision of information and public arenas for the exchange of arguments. Especially in the most deprived neighbourhoods, mobilization for the referendum campaign contributed to empowering social groups that had long remained at the margins. The action repertoire also included mass protests and direct action that mobilized for the Yes campaign, especially among the young (who voted 62.5 per cent in favour of Yes) and also the lower class (the Yes vote being particularly high in those areas with the highest levels of unemployment) (Curtice 2014). In this way, the referendum functioned as a transformative mechanism for Scottish civil society.

The Catalan case also shows a gradual organization of discontent from below. Existing resources, in terms of the presence of a rich civil society tradition, also played an important role here, allowing for widespread participation in several local non-binding consultations on independence. The campaign, however, also produced its own resources, with new grassroots groupings and coordination committees (Muñoz and Guinjoan 2013; Crameri 2015). Already since 2006, the Plataforma pel Dret de Decidir ('Platform for the Right to Decide') had been created to coordinate dozens of associations, municipalities and individual protest activities, while a large demonstration took place in July 2010, after the Constitutional Court rejected some parts of the Statute of Autonomy. It was during these actions that the movement succeeded in pushing more traditional organizations, such as Òmnium Cultural and various professional and recreational associations, to participate in the mobilization, with a sort of organizational appropriation of existing associations. During the campaign, a move towards an unconventional repertoire accompanied the growth of pro-independence positions. The civil society organization Assemblea Nacional Catalana (ANC, 'National Catalan Assembly') then took the lead in coordinating mobilization efforts.

The campaign for independence also largely relied upon a contentious repertoire based on a logic of numbers, with massive marches of hundreds of thousands of participants characterized by a high deployment of nationalist symbols, used as a way to show force. Especially, from 2012 to 2015, *diadas* (National Days of Catalonia) were launched by civil society organizations such as Òmnium Cultural and Assemblea Nacional Catalana. In September 2013, following the example of the Baltic movement for independence, a human chain of 1.6 million people – many wearing T-shirts with the slogan 'My place in history. The Catalan path towards Independence' – covered the entire 400-kilometre Catalan coastline in what was reputed to be the largest human chain ever. The following year, about 2 million protesters filled the streets of Barcelona, marching in alternate colourful rows that reproduced the Catalan flag *Senyera*. Semi-conventional forms of action (such as petitions) were broadly used, but so too was civil disobedience, notably in the performing in 2014 and 2017 of non-binding consultations on independence, which the Constitutional Court had declared illegal.

Unlike in Italy or Scotland, repression fuelled escalation. Although Spanish authorities had by and large tolerated the non-binding voting performance that took place in 2014, the organizers of the 2017 referendum were hit by the harsh policing of the various protest events. According to della Porta, O'Connor et al. (2017b):

> Events in the weeks preceding the referendum, however, triggered renewed grassroots mobilisation. On September 20th, Spanish *Guardia Civil* officers raided several offices of the Catalan regional government, arrested 14 senior officials, and confiscated 9.6 million referendum ballot papers as part of an operation to prevent the referendum from taking place. Spanish authorities also threatened judicial measures

against the organisers of the referendum, blocked websites, froze regional financial assets, limited credit and imposed central supervision over payments for non-essential services by the Generalitat and other public institutions ... thousands flocked onto the streets of Barcelona blocking major roads in the city chanting the slogans '*no tinc por*' (I am not afraid) and '*fora les forces de la ocupació*' (occupation forces out). In the wake of the hard-line actions taken by the Spanish authorities which prevented the Catalan government from logistically preparing for the vote, the organisational burden was taken up by ordinary citizens. People were organised through local '*Comitès de Defensa del Referendum*' (Referendum Defence Committees) that coordinated through Twitter, WhatsApp and Telegram.

In addition, juridical action led to the arrest of various Catalan pro-independence politicians, high-ranking officials and prominent figures. The determination by the Spanish government not to allow the referendum called by the Catalan government to happen was expressed as well in the searching of newspaper offices, printing offices and mail services in order to seize material that was to be used for the referendum, as well as closing websites and assumption of controls on finance and control of police operations (Cetrà et al. 2018, 128, 133).

On 1 October 2017, 2.2 million Catalans turned out to vote in the referendum, notwithstanding harsh repression, including the use of batons and rubber bullets with police interventions that shut down about 400 out of a total of 2,315 polling stations, which were all defended by citizens, including through the building of human shields (della Porta, O'Connor et al. 2017b). The Observatory of the Penal System and Human Rights registered a total of 844 citizens who required medical assistance as a consequence of the intervention of the 9,000 Spanish police officers, in what Human Rights Watch dubbed an excessive use of force. Concerns were also expressed regarding violation of freedom of expression, assembly, association and due process. Activists and independentist party leaders, moreover, increasingly became the target of state repression, which included arrests on charges of sedition of the main leaders of pro-independence civil society organizations, as well as elected representatives (Cetrà et al. 2018, 135). Not only was repression not effective in discouraging separatist sentiments (Barceló 2018), but direct or indirect experiences of victimization during police and judiciary repression even increased support for independence, in particular among the young and the better educated, while also increasing dissatisfaction regarding the actors (among them the Spanish police and the monarchy) who were seen as representative of the Spanish state, or – such as the EU – who refused to condemn the crackdown on the independentists (Balcells et al. 2018).

On 10 October, the President of the Catalan government, Carles Puigdemont, signed a declaration of independence (initially postponing its coming into force in order to develop a negotiated path), followed on 27 October by the Catalan Parliament declaring independence. The Spanish state then suspended Catalonia's political autonomy, imposed direct rule, and disbanded the Catalan government and Parliament. New elections, however, returned an independentist majority. The main Catalan nationalist parties formed a new Catalan government, while at the national level a successful vote of no confidence paved the way to a minority government of the PSOE, with external support from independentist and left-wing parties. Given the ambiguity of the Spanish Constitution, which grants the right to autonomy to 'nationalities', the legitimacy of a referendum on independence remains contested (Cetrà et al. 2018, 128).

From the organizational point of view, a horizontal and loosely structured model spread in the pro-independence movement, with the ANC as a platform made up of more than 500 territorial assemblies, 50 thematic assemblies, and 50,000 members. With the support of institutional and semi-institutional actors (e.g. Association of Municipalities for Independence, pro-independence parties, unions, etc.), two major social movement organizations, Assemblea Nacional Catalana and Òmnium Cultural, were central to all secessionist mobilizations in Catalonia until the summer of 2017. As the cycle of contention developed, there was a downward scale-shift, and the organization of dissent decentralized beyond these major organizations. New actors then emerged to coordinate the mobilization, among them the Comitès de Defensa de la República (CDRs) or the umbrella organization Universitats per la República. Moreover, neighbourhood committees mushroomed, together with collectives of parents, who occupied the schools where the elections were to take place. As repression increased:

> there was a need to build broad coalitions and engage in grassroots work in order to keep the intensity of mobilization high. In part due to the preceding cycle of mobilization and prior instances of collaboration, such as the *diadas*, the CDRs became spaces for cross-cutting mobilization and brought different generations and milieus together in local spaces . . . By embracing more disruptive tactics, CDRs aimed to halt the circulation of traffic, block access to cities, motorways and to the French border. The CDRs were also key actors involved in the general strike in Catalonia on 8th November 2017 against the implementation of article 155 of the Constitution, which led to the suspension of Catalan autonomous powers. Blockades, occupations, occasional clashes with the police happened that day and recurred during the

subsequent weeks as reactions to the arrests and imprisonment of some members of President Puigdemont's government and the leaders of civil society organizations. (della Porta et al. forthcoming)

In sum, the analysed referendum campaigns had eventful effects, with small and large protest events accompanying more conventional forms of canvassing. In Scotland, even if the No vote eventually won, the referendum campaign had a transformative power, spreading a taste for politics all over the region. Participation in the campaigns brought about self-education in political skills, stimulating political learning. Even if it failed to obtain independence, the Yes campaign succeeded in awakening Scottish civil society, with long-lasting effects on citizens' political imagination. Also in Catalonia, the use of social movement strategies was pivotal in increasing attention for the pro-self-determination and pro-independence actors, with polarization and politicization fuelling a broad and loose network of traditional and new groupings that served to extend the mobilization to the entire territory and all social groups.

Innovative framing allowed for the spreading, but also the transformation, of the nationalist discourse, as the referendum campaigns worked as discursive critical junctures in both Scotland and Catalonia. In the former, the pro-Yes forces have been successful in changing Scottish political debate, stigmatizing austerity and neoliberalism as English values which remain foreign to the social values of the Scots. The definition of Scottish identity was re-vitalized thanks to the bridging of nationalist discourse with appeals to social justice. Together with the rejection of austerity policies, there was the promise of enhanced democracy in an independent Scotland. In a traditionally quite inclusive nationalist discourse, in the midst of the crisis, frames of social justice and participatory democracy converged in the vision of another Scotland. In fact, the definition of social justice went well beyond the traditional social-democratic view of the SNP, as historical memories of Scotland as the birthplace of the labour movement were revived during the campaign. The slogan of the Radical Independence Campaign, 'Britain is for the rich, Scotland can be ours', contributed to bridging a re-configured class discourse with some more traditional nationalist arguments.

In Catalonia, too, the referendum campaign enriched the traditional discourse of Catalanism with a growing emphasis on a continuum from self-determination up to independence. During the campaign, with the radicalization of the conflict with Madrid, independence became more and more legitimated, not only within traditional Catalan nationalism but also on the Left, which had historically been sceptical about self-determination and independence. During and after the campaign, there was, therefore, an innovative bridging of issues of independence and social justice, while the position of self-determination became dominant on the Left, even among those who did not support independence. In fact, terms such as 'progress', 'social state' and 'redistribution' spread within the campaign, linking left-wing frames with nationalist ones up to the point that ideological self-positioning on the Left came to be a strong predictor of support for independence in general, and the unofficial consultation in particular (Palà and Picazo 2014). In the revisitation of the history of the Catalan struggle for independence, an innovative framing connected sovereignty and social justice, the bridging of nationalist and social claims allowing for a growth of mobilization that went well beyond the traditional Catalan cultural networks.

Addressing the conception of democracy, the framing of the campaign also had a strong motivational capacity – as testified, among others, by the slogan 'Together we make history', and the call for a second democratic transition. The hope for deep changes is reflected in slogans such as 'Now is the time' ('Ara es l'hora'), 'Will–Voting–Victory' ('Voluntat–Votar–Victòria') and 'We shall vote and win' ('Votarem i guanyarem'). The framing of the objectives of the struggle was radicalized given further repression and spiralling processes of solidarization with its victims (the injured and the imprisoned activists). The repression also impacted upon the framing of the struggle – as the ERC's spokesman in the national lower chamber declared: 'If we are imprisoned, we will be released by the Catalan people' (in Barrio et al. 2018). More generally, *el proces* for Catalan independence has been accorded a constituent character: the subject mobilized for independence 'was produced by its own agency and wants to decide on its own future ... What is at play is not (just) a cultural or identitarian logic but the will of a broad sector of the Catalan population to form a new political structure, a new state' (Letamendia 2017, 23).

Concluding remarks

To summarize, in a context of deep socioeconomic and political crisis, the referendums from below I have discussed in this chapter have mobilized social movements through calls for social justice and self-government – either in the version of the commons, against their enclosure, or in the independentism version. Relying on some institutional conduciveness in the form of either historical experiences with referendums, or a strong claim for the 'right to decide', the calls for referendums acted, however, as catalysts for the appropriation of opportunities as well as the mobilization of material and symbolic resources. In comparison with 'normal' referendums, in referendums from below grassroots involvement helped spread participatory and deliberative values, also allowing for long-term empowerment.

Social science literature on referendums and other mechanisms of direct democracy has pointed towards their increasing use, especially as a result of a malfunctioning – on the input side – of the institutional system and the de-alignment of the party system (Qvortrup 2014a; 2014b). Referendums proliferate especially where parties are becoming weaker and weaker but, increasingly, they are also supported by the forces of the Left (parties and social movements) as an opportunity to promote citizens' political engagement and participation. Referendums have been praised for their capacity to extend constitutional safeguards against the excessive power of politicians (Qvortrup 2014c), and as the most direct expressions of people's will (Marxer and Pállinger 2007). Referendums from below have in fact developed in moments of crisis in the attempt to promote change.

The choice of engaging in referendums reflected some general norma-tive predispositions within those progressive social movements towards participatory and deliberative democratic qualities. Direct democracy, as put forward in referendums, resonates with some aspects of democratic norms as promoted by progressive social movements. Normative theories of democracy have emphasized the importance of equality in the capacity to influence decision-makers, and of autonomy in opinion formation. Some degree of equality is considered as an important precondition for the participation of the *demos*. As carriers of a participatory conception of democracy, progressive movements criticize the monopoly of media-tion through mass parties and a strong structuration of interests, aiming to shift policy-making towards more visible and controllable places. To this, they oppose democracy as participation and self-management, which has been much discussed among social movements in various historical periods. As instruments of participation and, potentially, of deliberation, referendums could be considered as resonant with progres-sive social movements' search for alternative conceptions and practices (della Porta 2013).

Through their involvement, social movements increased the participa-tory and deliberative quality of the referendum campaigns, by making them more inclusive in terms of number of citizens involved and also of arguments addressed. Defining direct democracy as 'an umbrella term for a variety of decision processes by which ordinary citizens vote directly on policy matters', Hobolt (2009, 5) noted that, while 'proponents of direct democracy celebrate citizen engagement and the responsiveness of the political system to citizens' wishes', 'many scholars of voting behaviour have pointed out that voters lack the interest, sophistication, and infor-mation required to make reasoned decisions in elections' (Hobolt 2009,

5–6). A main argument against citizens' participation in complex decisions, recently emerging in arguments against electoral accountability and for technocracy instead, is that, usually, citizens are poorly informed and lack the necessary competence and qualifications. Additionally, those who fear the 'tyranny of the majority' (Setälä 2009) also suggest that citizens might have little reason to incur the cost of informing themselves, and polarization might ensue from heated campaigns. Debate on Brexit has pointed towards the impact of fake news and emotional polarization on a volatile public. A populist paradox has been mentioned, with referendum results influenced especially by the powerful and the rich, as not only do they more frequently take part as electors in referendums, but also they are more likely to fund campaigns, speak up in public arenas and generally influence the referendums' results.

While admitting some weaknesses, research on referendums has singled out a more varied scenario. There is, first of all, the observation that direct forms of democracy can by themselves stimulate participation (Smith and Tolbert 2004, 33), educating to democratic citizenship by socializing to the public good (Dyck 2009, 540). First and foremost, some research on referendums has challenged the argument – famously put forward by Schumpeter (1943) – that citizens are unable to understand political complexities and formulate sound opinions, building instead on the idea that participation and deliberation have to be (at least) added to representative and majoritarian institutions (Barber 1984; Fishkin 1997). Much research has also noted that electors tend to be able to make well-informed, or at least reasonable, choices at referendums (Hobolt 2009). Voters tend to choose following their ideological beliefs and are also capable of distinguishing between propaganda and information (Mendelsohn and Cutler 2000; Bernhard 2012).

What is more, research stressed the legitimizing capacity and integrative functions of referendums (Caciagli and Uleri 1994; Ranney 1994; Uleri 1994; Papadopoulos 2001). Several studies noted that citizens are interested in and capable of casting a sound vote, especially as being exposed to public debate increases not only the understanding of complex issues but also empathy with others, so improving public deliberation. Contrasting visions of referendums being hijacked by the most powerful, research has indicated that voters are more competent than usually expected and direct democracy potentially enhances political interest and competence. Referendums can also work as a school of democracy (Fatke 2015).

Referendum campaigns have also been said to improve, under some conditions, the quality of decisions. In particular, research indicated beneficial consequences for the many, as well as better macro-economic performance, better public services, and lower public debt in contexts in which referendums were frequently used. There is, in fact, some empirical evidence that direct democratic procedures increase responsiveness to voters' preferences (Sager and Bühlmann 2009; Maduz 2010). Participation through referendums has been praised as a way to increase accountability, especially faced with the weakening of other channels of institutional access (Setälä 2009).

The qualities of each referendum certainly vary with institutional design, and also the political and social dynamics in which it is embedded (Qvortrup 2014a). Direct democracy, in general, has been linked to values such as political and social equality, as well as assumptions about citizens' capacity to learn within deliberative arenas – even though problems related with the size of these arenas have been highlighted when combining deliberative and direct democracy conceptions (Schiller 2007). Empirical research has disclaimed the three main arguments by opponents of referendums – namely, that citizens are unable to make considered judgements, that parliaments defend minorities better, and that referendums delegitimize representative institutions (Caciagli and Uleri 1994). However, a striking variation in referendum practices has been noted, which shapes their effects on citizens and institutions.

In all our cases, referendums emerged within a process of closing and opening of windows of opportunities for the causes promoted by movements. Allies were present at different levels of institutional politics, sometimes even as main promoters of the referendum, which then became a turning point for consolidating broad coalitions. Referendums from below – that is, those which involve a larger degree of extra-institutional mobilization, either through citizen-initiated referendums or by the wide-scale appropriation of state-endorsed ones – provide particularly conducive opportunities to broaden participation and enhance political engagement and understanding amongst the electorate. Importantly, they also bear a number of normative commitments, including encouraging mass participation, and an emphasis on configurative practices and deliberation. Referendums do offer social movements the chance to make a decisive contribution to issues of substantial political importance. By looking at these movements' resource mobilization, appropriation and forging of opportunities, and capacity to develop resonant frames, I have highlighted how movements have successfully changed political debates and, in the Italian case, have triggered constitutional processes.

The research has, however, also pointed towards constraints and challenges for the development of referendums from below. As already noted, when talking about grassroots constitutionalism, the mobilization of civil society, which is so important for improving the participatory and deliberative qualities of direct democracy, goes in waves, with ups and downs. As referendums are quite long-lasting processes, the mobilization from below during campaigning, as well as after it, could be difficult to sustain. A drop in mobilization then puts at risk the delicate equilibrium of participation and deliberation that has emerged as very important for high-quality direct democracy. Also, as for grass-roots constitutionalism, the more challenging the potential results are for the establishment, the more counter-mobilization can be expected, with forms varying from restriction of communicative channels (as in Italy), to counter-campaigning based on mobilization of negative emotions (as in the Scottish case) or plain repression (as in Catalonia). Also, as the Italian case shows, even resounding victory does not lead to automatic implementation of the referendum's results. Rather, the economic and political actors that oppose those results can rally to block the implementation process, especially if the movements are not able to keep up the mobilization, and if their opponents instead increase their political power.

4

Movement Parties in the Great Recession

While parties are important for movements and vice versa, the two fields of study have been characterized by a reciprocal indifference, which was as research on parties moved away from concerns with the relations between parties and society, focusing instead on elections and party activities within institutions, and social movement studies mainly located them outside electoral institutions. This notwithstanding, institutional politics is permeated by social movements as a most important actor in the normal functioning of a political system: 'parties and movements have become overlapping, mutually dependent actors in shaping politics to the point that long-established political parties welcome social movement support and often rely specifically on their association to win elections' (Goldstone 2003, 4). Relations between the parties and movements are frequent as 'movements compete with parties. Movements infiltrate parties. . . . Movements become parties' (Garner and Zald 1985, 137). Social movements have, in fact, pushed for party changes through programmatic challenges, by proposing new issues; through organizational challenges, by promoting a participatory model; and through electoral challenges, by raising support for some emerging topic in public opinion (Rohrschneider 1993). Movements introduce new forms of collective action that influence election campaigns, join electoral coalitions, engage in (proactive or reactive) electoral mobilization, polarize political parties internally or even turn into parties (McAdam and Tarrow 2010).

Party studies have addressed relations between parties and interest groups (including movements) within reflections on organizational linkages. In general, interactions with external actors are important, as parties are not in complete control of the political agenda. Organizational linkages between elite action and citizens' preferences in fact connect the rulers with the ruled (Lawson 1980, 3). Of particular importance, linkages with interest groups make it possible that 'a considerable part of interest selection and aggregation is achieved without the involvement of party elites. Appropriate organizational environments like, for example, trade unions, religious organizations or a party's own youth organization, select and aggregate relevant grievances into reasonably coherent packages of political demands which then become the object of negotiation between organizational and party elites' (Poguntke 2002, 45). Through their linkages with societal organizations, party elites become informed about relevant claims: 'as long as organizational integration is high, organization members may cast their vote according to their leaders' recommendation even if they disagree with individual elements of the deal, because their prime loyalty is to the organization' (Poguntke 2002, 46). So, political parties aim to draw the support of a majority of voters, and interest groups pressure the government to enact policies that advance the substantive agendas or ideological perspectives of their constituencies. Both actors might value reciprocal influence through overlapping leadership or other forms of exchanges, while also providing brokerage for reaching beyond their own networks (Heaney 2010). The sharing of that control with other organizations is not a problem as long as parties have systematic linkages with them. However, 'a weakening of these links . . . and/or the emergence of new, non-party associated organizations, and/or a weakening of the agenda-setting role of those associated non-electoral organizations that do exist, could imply a challenge to the hold of party systems on the mass public' (Mair 1983, 420). New parties might therefore emerge to represent unrepresented claims.

Building upon the two streams of literature, we can define *movement parties* as characterized by particularly intense relations with social movements. In a broadly accepted definition, social movements are conceptualized as networks of groups and individuals, endowed with some collective identification, that pursue goals of social transformation, mainly through unconventional forms of participation (della Porta and Diani 2006). Political parties are free associations built with the aim of achieving institutional power (Weber 1922), mainly through participation in elections (Sartori 1976, 64). Movement parties emerge as a sort of hybrid between the two. As organizations, they participate in protest campaigns, but also act in electoral arenas. In Kitschelt's (2006, 280) definition, 'movement parties are coalitions of political activists who emanate from social movements and try to apply the organization and strategic practice of social movements in the arena of party competition'. Even if using (also) an electoral logic, they tend to be supportive of protest, participating in campaigns together with other movement organizations, combining their activities within the electoral arena with extra-institutional mobilization (Kitschelt 2006, 281). As social movements are networks of organizations and individuals, movement parties can be part of them, as testified by overlapping memberships as well as organizational and action links. Movement parties also aim at integrating the movement constituencies within their organizations, by representing movements' claims. In their framing, movement parties have been said to be driven more by ideological militancy than by pragmatic considerations (Tarrow 2015, 95).

Social science research indicates that the emergence of movement parties is facilitated by certain conditions. First of all, there is a *transformation in the cleavage structures*. Research has underlined the role of emerging cleavages, as new parties tend to appear when there are neglected issues, especially in moments in which problems become more visible and politicized (Kitschelt 1988). As neoliberal globalization has eroded protected property rights and increased cultural diversity, a cleavage between winners and losers has been identified as triggering the development of populist right-wing parties (Kriesi et al. 2008; 2012), but also of counter-movements towards social protection (van Cott 2005; Yashar 2005; Silva 2009; Roberts 2015a). Also, in Europe, neoliberalism has transformed the cleavage structure that was at the basis of domestic party systems by a precarization of labour, as well as a proletarianization of the middle classes (della Porta 2015b). Movement parties have emerged where the dynamics of the crisis have been faster and where they have more radically challenged everyday life (della Porta, Andretta et al. 2016).

Second, *conducive conditions in the electoral field* act as facilitators. Party studies have linked institutional conduciveness to the formation of new parties with electoral rules referring to degree of decentralization, proportionality, reserved seats for minorities, low barriers for registering parties and low thresholds for earning seats (van Cott 2005). Vice versa, majority electoral systems with single-member districts discourage the emergence of new parties (Harmel and Robertson 1985). Contingently, electoral volatility increases chances of new parties being born. As Kitschelt noted, movement parties tend to appear when: '(1) collective interests are intensely held by a large constituency, willing to articulate their demand through disruptive, extra-institutional activities, (2) established parties make no effort to embrace such interests for fear of dividing their own electoral constituency and (3) the formal and informal thresholds of political representation are low' (Kitschelt 2006, 282). New parties emerge especially when, given low barriers to entry, movement entrepreneurs realize a need for deep reforms and assume there is a constituency. They are then successful when interests or opinions, which are salient and widespread, are not channelled within the established party system, as existing parties are unwilling to address claims that they think will soon fade – thus, the action of mainstream parties affects the electoral fortunes of emerging ones (Meguid 2005, 347).

A third facilitator is *the delegitimation of political parties*, especially of the party family to which social movements traditionally referred. As for progressive movements, in Latin America new parties emerge on the Left in those countries in which centre-left parties had been leading forces in the implementation of neoliberal reforms (Roberts 2015a). Movement parties rose as established parties were most dramatically losing citizens' trust. The relations of cooperation between centre-left parties and social movements had in fact been challenged as left-wing parties increasingly moved towards the centre, while movements more and more frequently addressed social issues. In the case of parties of indigenous people, the relevant characteristics of party systems include de-alignment, frag-mentation and, especially, the decline of once strong left-wing parties (van Cott 2005). Similarly to the Latin American cases, in Southern Europe, too, movement parties emerged and succeeded when centre-left parties were perceived as compromising with austerity policies. During the economic crisis, the Panhellenic Socialist Movement (PASOK) in Greece, the Democratic Party in Italy and the PSOE in Spain all turned towards neoliberal policies based on structural reforms and privatization programmes, which translated into cutting social spending, increasing the retirement age, reforming the labour market, and reducing the public sector, etc. Syriza, the Five Star Movement and Podemos emerged and grew from the dissatisfaction with mainstream parties, in particular (but not only) of the centre-left (della Porta, Fernández et al. 2017).

Fourth, *increasing exogenous constraints*, such as responsibility towards international and market-related conditionalities, fuel a general loss of representative capacity in mainstream parties, reducing their elec-toral support (Mair 2009; Streeck 2014). In Europe, the mobilization on the right of the losers in globalization seemed a major phenomenon at the electoral level, but since the 2000s the critique of globalization (especially in its neoliberal form) has developed on the Left as well – in this case, more within contentious politics.

Finally, movement parties tend to develop during *massive movement mobilizations.* Their emergence and, especially, their success are influenced by the characteristics of the social movements they are connected to. In recent times, the legitimacy crisis of late neoliberalism has fuelled anti-austerity protests, which have pointed towards the corruption of an entire political class as the mechanism through which the profits of the few prevailed over the needs – the very human rights – of the many. In opposition to the corrupt elites, the protesters defined themselves as part of the large majority of those suffering from social and political inequalities. Social movements became, in fact, more and more critical of representative democracy. While these attitudes reflected a drop in trust in existing parties, which was widespread in the electorate, social movement activists remained, however, convinced of the need for political intervention to control the market, campaigning for a return of the public (della Porta 2015b). This brought about the – almost paradoxical – choice to create new movement parties, whose electoral affirmation was then favoured by the widespread mistrust of the existing political parties.

Movement parties can be located within a broad trend of organizational party transformations, characterized by continuous approaching of the parties to state institutions and growing detachment from society. In nineteenth-century Europe, after *parties of the notables* had represented elite constituencies in pre-democratic societies, the *ideological mass parties* emerged, endowed with a stable bureaucracy (Weber 1922) in order to represent the collective interests of those who had hitherto been excluded. Various concepts were then proposed to describe the autonomization of parties from their linkages with a specific social base (*catch-all parties*), a focus on getting votes (*electoral parties*) or an interpenetration of party and state based on inter-party collusion (*cartel party*) (della Porta 2015a). In particular, the cartel party literature singles out a trend for parties to collude with each other in order to get more and more state support – thus, however, losing more and more the relationship with their members (Katz and Mair 1995). These tendencies seem to peak in what I have named *neoliberal populist parties* – organizationally light, heavily personalized, split into non-ideological factions, characterized by heavily manipulative use of mass media but also by a power rooted in the occupation of institutional positions, often used for clientelistic or corrupt exchanges (della Porta, Fernández et al. 2017). As relations between parties and civil society organizations are further weakened (Allern and Bale 2012), party activists are substituted as channels of communication to potential voters by the mass media, while membership tends to decline (van Biezen et al. 2012). At the same time, the party discourse changes, becoming less and less ideological, with an 'anti-political' language. In a vicious circle, the decrease in trust and identification in parties further pushes for personalization as a strategy to win back consent (Diamanti

2007). In sum, the current mainstream model of party organization is shallow, weak and opportunistic; ideological appeals are (at best) vague, with an overwhelmingly electoral orientation: *personalistic* parties are once again formed to offer leaders with an instrument to win elections and exercise power (Gunther and Diamond 2003, 187).

While party studies focused on dominant party models, one could parallel these by looking at movement-sponsored, party-challenging models. Looking at the Latin American case, Roberts (2015a, 39) has distinguished the following models of party/movement relations: (a) a vanguard model – with party control of social movements; (b) an electoral model – with relations only mobilized at elections; (c) an organic model – with a deliberately blurred distinction between party and movement. Paralleling the evolution into mainstream party types, I have suggested singling out specific movement parties in different historical periods that at the same time opposed and adapted to dominant party types (della Porta, Fernández et al. 2017). First of all, the party of the notables can be contrasted by parties of (left-wing) cadres that, in conditions of limited representation, tended to defend the interests of the excluded, within a conception of the party as a vanguard of the proletariat. This type of party emerged and survived where institutional opportunities for the expression of left-wing positions were more closed. As labour organized, class-based, mass, ideological parties emerged, characterized by a hierarchical relationship with the labour movement within an integrated interaction of parties and unions, with leadership and membership overlap and interchange (Allern 2010, 37). Born in Europe in the nineteenth century from within the labour movement, these parties raised claims for political and social rights, contributing to the development of the very conception of democracy (della Porta 2013, ch. 2). Mainly originating outside of Parliament, with the aim of bringing in the claims of the workers, class-mass parties (particularly social democratic ones) have been characterized by collateral, ancillary organizations, strongly linked to their party by overlapping memberships and mutual co-determination rights (Poguntke 2002, 49) and capable of attracting sympathizers. The developments of the then-movement parties were influenced by reactions by elites. In the Scandinavian countries and the United Kingdom, open elites refrained from repressing the workers, facilitating the growth of large and moderate labour parties. Deeper cleavages in some historical periods in Germany, Austria, France, Italy and Spain, with related repression of the emerging workers' movements, pushed towards the creation of *soziale Ghettopartei*, with radical ideology and a consolidated but also isolated membership (Rokkan 1970). In general, the higher the obstacles to entry into representative institutions, the less appealing was a strategy of gradual reform (Bartolini 2000, 565–6) and the more divided the Left

(Marks 1989). Especially since the 1950s, with a clear acceleration since the early 1980s, class-mass parties have, however, dramatically transformed themselves, due in particular to a decline in party linkages with workers' organizations: 'parties everywhere began to withdraw from old programmatic priorities, yet the pace, extent, and direction of that strategic transformation have varied across countries ... New priorities have begun to complement, if not eclipse, conventional social democratic concerns with social security and income equality' (Kitschelt 1994, 3).

It was from the critique of the bureaucratization of the ideological class party that a new form of movement party emerged with the development of new social movements: the left-libertarian party family, often identified with the Greens (Müller Rommel 1993). As new social movements called for a more horizontal relationship, left-libertarian parties have reflected this mood, with attempts at developing more participatory conceptions of politics (Kitschelt 1989, 3). Their stress on internal democracy can be read within a dialectic process, in which 'each new party type generates a reaction that stimulates further development, thus leading to yet another party type, and to another set of reactions, and so on' (Katz and Mair 1995, 6). Left-libertarian movement parties were in fact characterized by open membership, loose networks of grassroots support, heterogeneous clientele (Gunther and Diamond 2003, 188–9), a call for social solidarity relations, and participatory structures (Kitschelt 1989, 64; also Frankland et al. 2008). At their origins, these parties adopted a non-conventional repertoire of action, including forms of protest (Poguntke 1993, 81; also O'Neill 1997, 43). Green parties were more likely to form within strong environmental movements, from problem push (Rüdig 1990) but also opportunity pull, being, however, perceived as just one node in a (usually) horizontal network (Rootes 1995). Linkages between Green parties and new social movements are mostly informal, unstable and influenced by cycles of protest (Poguntke 2002, 22). A tendency towards institutionalization has also been noted in the Green parties, being 'drawn into the normal party political game of negotiation and compromise' (Poguntke 2006, 402). Moving in the direction of a professional-electoral party, Green parties have even looser ties to movements.

As we are going to see in this chapter, contemporary movement parties on the Left reflect an evolution in the organizational structures, identity frames and repertoires of action of progressive social movements. However, this adaptation is not without its tensions, as movement parties have to balance the different logics and pressures present within party systems and social movement networks as main fields of intervention. As van Cott (2005) noted with reference to indigenous parties, among the positive effects for the social movements that support them is their promotion of a non-exclusive, healthy society based upon values of recognition and respect for diversity, more transparency in politics, internal democracy and increased participation. Potential negative outcomes are, however, present as well, as participation in party politics increases division in social movements – since factionalism tends to be widespread in parties with grassroots participation (Kitschelt 1989). As well as producing risks of contamination of indigenous culture by Western models of parties and the destabilization of collective identities, 'successful new parties may reduce the effectiveness of indigenous social movements by distracting them from past priorities, such as the defence of territorial autonomy and the construction of new political institutions rooted in indigenous values and modes of self-government and participation' (van Cott 2005, 234).

In sum, when the economic and political crises produced grievances that did not find channels of representation in the existing party systems, and powerful mass mobilization put forward claims for social justice and democracy, new movement parties emerged on the Left. Reflecting the movements' values, these parties appropriated opportunities and mobilized material and symbolic resources, experimenting with new participatory organizational structures, repertoires of action and collective frames. In what follows, I will develop these points, looking at, first, Podemos as a main illustration of movement parties in Europe, then expanding the analysis to Latin America, mobilizing the main toolkit of social movement studies to look at exogenous opportunities and endogenous resources.

* * *

Podemos as a movement party

On the European continent, the Great Regression has accelerated a long-term and multidimensional crisis of political parties, which has especially challenged their capacity to mediate between political institutions and citizens (della Porta 2015a). For several decades, research has in fact pointed towards the rapid decline in attachment of citizens to parties (Diamond and Gunther 2001, ix), in party membership and in electoral participation, as well as in the trust of electors in the competences and abilities of their own parties (Dalton 2004, 28 and 149). Neoliberal globalization and then the financial crisis catalysed discontent, as unregulated free markets and international conditionalities constrained parties' action, and the representation of the citizen entered into tension with the responsibility towards external actors, from corporations to international organizations (Mair 2009). As the financial crises exploded, the promises that economic growth would follow from the privileging of responsibility towards external actors over responsibility towards the citizens failed, resulting in increasing mistrust of parties, as well as of parliaments and governments at different territorial levels. Distrust, indeed, doubled in countries such as Greece, Italy and Spain, with distrust of parties rising in 2013 to 94 per cent in Spain, 95 per cent in Greece, and 87 per cent in Italy (della Porta, Fernández et al. 2017). During the most critical period, the distance from the European average reached almost 10 percentage points in Italy and 15 in the other two countries.

In the 2010s, distrust of existing electoral institutions was expressed in a global wave of protest. Protests followed the geography of the emergence of the economic crisis, developing into a crisis of political legitimacy, which hit the different European countries with different strengths and at different times. While the aforementioned mistrust of institutional politics initially discouraged an engagement in elections, the opening of spaces within the party system stimulated the foundation and strengthening of parties that voiced the claims emerging in those movements, used forms of direct action, and also innovated in terms of organizational models.

The main example of this type of party in Europe is Podemos in Spain. As Fernández and Portos (2015, 1) noted, the rise of Podemos can be linked to three processes: first, institutional closure, which led to the exhaustion of activists and protest activities; second, the opening of windows of political opportunity, given the inability of the mainstream parties to channel citizens' claims and the neoliberal turn of the PSOE; and third, the availability of organizational resources, including the symbolic capital gained by some activists during the mobilization.

The many crises: challenges and opportunities

In Spain, the crisis hit fast and deep, dramatically affecting the everyday life of citizens. While initially limited, public debt increased dramatically after the collapse of the housing market and the related fall in revenue. After the first year of the recession, Spain had the highest level of unemployment and one of the highest public deficits in the entire Eurozone (Conde-Ruiz and Marín 2013). Public accounts shifted from a 2% surplus in 2007 to a deficit of 11% in 2009; public debt jumped from 36% of GDP in 2007 to 54% in 2009 (Conde-Ruiz and Marín 2013). Reductions in public investment (dropping by 60% since 2009) and in public employees' wages, along with increases in VAT and in personal and corporate income taxes (Conde-Ruiz and Marín 2013), were accompanied by a further deregulation of an already deregulated labour market (Picot and Tassinari 2014) and the stripping of workers' rights in the once protected main labour market. Bank customers who could not repay their mortgages were evicted from their homes at a rate of two per day (Romanos 2014). After EU institutions increased pressure for austerity policies and the flexibilization of the labour market, the new regulations facilitated dismissals, reducing compensation in cases of unjust dismissal. Agreements with social partners were sought only occasionally, and disposed of in case of disagreements, with a decline in union rights and the decentralization of collective bargaining.

The dramatic socioeconomic conditions triggered a crisis of political legitimacy. In an institutional system based upon a powerful executive, balanced by territorial decentralization and alternation between the two main parties, who controlled a very high percentage of the electorate, the economic recession and austerity policies brought about the decline of those parties (Torcal 2014). Already shaken by a series of scandals related to political corruption, institutional trust dropped, with very high levels of electoral volatility. During democratic consolidation, political parties had acquired a central role as state institutions, given that the 1978 Spanish Constitution promotes parties within a tendentially two-party system, favouring strong and stable governments and political turnover (Gunther et al. 1988; Gunther et al. 2004). The party system had in fact remained quite stable, with a bipolar structure of competition characterized by low levels of party fragmentation and inter-bloc volatility (Linz and Montero 1999; 2001; Gunther 2005), though both party identification and membership remained low (Mair and van Biezen 2001; Torcal 2006). The crisis further weakened party loyalties, with a growing critique of what was perceived to be a corrupted and unreliable political class (Feenstra and Keane 2014). As in other countries, the party in government in the first stages of the crisis, the centre-left PSOE, which, after some initial resistance, had supported austerity measures, was particularly punished in electoral terms (Bartels 2014). With very high electoral volatility (Rashkova and van Biezen 2014), support for the PSOE dropped from 43.8 per cent to 22 per cent between 2008 and 2015. The breach of trust with its own electorate was said to be twofold: 'first, at the level of the "ideological contract" and, on the other hand, related to the confidence in their effectiveness in overcoming the crisis' (Lobera 2015, 101). As the leader of Podemos, Pablo Iglesias, was to state, the 'political space of social-democracy was empty and we have occupied it' (Iglesias 2015a).

Against this backdrop, on 15 May 2011 the occupation of Puerta del Sol in Madrid started a long and massive wave of contention that came to be known as the 15M movement (the movement of 15 May). Although including some more traditional forms (among them, prominently, strikes and marches), the protest repertoire was largely transformed by the emergence of new forms, such as the *acampadas*, but also the re-emergence of old tactics, similar to *charivari*, which singled out alleged perpetrators for public shaming rituals. Discontent further increased as the traditional closure towards social movements, reflected in high levels of repression of the peaceful protests, back-fired, fuelling collective action (Fishman 2011). At the organizational level, there was a strengthening of a horizontal, inclusive, assembly-based model that had already spread during the Global Justice Movement (della Porta 2007), with, however, further innovations promoted in particular by young activists, who played a most important role in the mobilizations. The collective framing included a defence of citizenship rights, but also proactive visions of progressive transformations of the welfare system towards conceptions and practices of the commons. Strongly oriented to denouncing the immorality of the corrupt institutional system, protesters also imagined ways to overcome existing state and market institutions. The movement's ideas and practices, nurtured within local assemblies and self-managed collectives, also influenced labour conflicts in the public sector through the so-called waves (*mareas*) that followed the decline of the camps. Values of equality, inclusiveness and dialogue were practised within deliberative and participatory conceptions of democracy. Experimenting with different strategies and playing within different arenas, the Spanish cycle of anti-austerity protests politicized and empowered citizens, who participated en masse, also having transformative effects on the party system (della Porta, Andretta et al. 2016).

While the positions of the two major parties had approached each other on many economic issues (Fernández-Albertos and Manzano 2012; López 2012; Sampedro and Lobera 2014), the massive wave of protests broke that consensus. In particular, 'Podemos aimed at reorganizing the political map around this new axis and promoting a new double and mixed cleavage: "the caste" against "the people", and "the old" against "the new" politics' (della Porta, Fernández et al. 2017, 50). While the electoral laws had discouraged the emergence of new parties, 'the success of Podemos (and Ciudadanos on the centre-right) results, however, from the perceived crisis of the mainstream parties, which spread the belief that successful participation in the electoral arena was possible, especially in the European elections' (della Porta, Fernández et al 2017, 50). As the European elections, with proportional representation, allowed for a first success, the visibility thereby acquired facilitated a positive outcome in national elections as well. Twitter and Facebook were also used to mobilize a large number of citizens (Toret 2015), resulting in May 2014 in an unexpected 8 per cent of votes and five representatives in the European Parliament (EP), while PSOE and PP lost 2.5 million votes each in comparison with the previous EP elections. The EP elections were therefore considered 'a sign of a very possible electoral and party-system de-alignment in forthcoming elections' (Cordero and Montero 2015, 358). In May 2015, Podemos and allied lists were very successful in the local elections, gaining several highly important cities, among them Barcelona and Madrid. In the December 2015 general elections, Podemos came third, with 20.7 per cent of the vote (Podemos lists won forty-two seats and the allied Confluencias, twenty-seven). In the new national elections in June 2016, in coalition with Izquierda Unida (IU, United Left) (Schavelzon and Webber 2018), Podemos and allies confirmed their third place, with a similar percentage of support to that of Podemos alone in the previous elections (21.3 per cent). The coalition Unidos Podemos obtained seventy-one seats, against eighty-five for the PSOE, with, however, very high levels of support among the under-35s (twice as high as PSOE's) as well as among the unemployed and students (Gillespie 2017).

Mobilizing resources

The 15M movement contributed to preparing the terrain for Podemos through a critique of the parties and the party system that were identified with the Spanish democratic transition (Sampedro and Lobera 2014). As one of the leaders of Podemos, Íñigo Errejón, noted, the party 'constituted a new political identity by articulating heterogeneous and dispersed demands in a basic narrative frame, which is massive in the extent that it is transversal and with extremely porous ideological borders' (Errejón 2015, 128). As institutions remained closed and mobilization in the streets declined, a 'destituent' process, based on protest, mutated into a constituent process, based on the 'assault on institutions', also through participation in the electoral process (Subirats 2015a, 164), at both the national and local levels (Arribas Lozano 2015). Podemos was born in a deliberate choice by movement actors to create an electoral tool that could eventually exploit the new energies which emerged during the peak of the protest cycle, channelling them into institutional politics (della Porta, Fernández et al. 2017, 49). Referring to a transnational mobilization, Podemos was bolstered by the victory of Syriza in Greece that, conquering the national government, focused attention on the potential for European progressive governments or parties. As Pablo Iglesias stated during a speech at a Syriza rally: 'The wind of change is blowing in Europe. In Greece it is called Syriza; in Spain, it is called Podemos.' The same message emerged from the *Marcha por el Cambio* ('Rally for Change'), held at the Puerta del Sol in Madrid, in which about 100,000 sympathizers took part to express the 'joy of being together'. Pablo Iglesias stressed in particular the possibility of political change: 'It is necessary to dream. But we dream, taking our dream very seriously' (in Agustín and Briziarelli 2018, 5).

Organizational resources were mobilized from within progressive social movements. At the birth of Podemos, a group of activist-scholars with previous experience in the alter-globalist and anti-austerity protests joined forces with the small leftist Izquierda Anticapitalista ('Anticapitalist Left', now Anticapitalistas – 'Anti-capitalists'). On 17 January 2014, some Podemos founders promoted the collection of signatures in support of the manifesto *Mover ficha: convertir la indignación en cambio político* ('Making a Move: Turning Indignation into Political Change'). Launched by twenty-eight social movement activists, the manifesto collected 50,000 signatures on a leftist programme, an alternative to what was dubbed the 'two-party regime of the PSOE and PP'. Aiming at achieving broad electoral success, Podemos defined itself as a 'tool for "popular and civic unity" understood as the articulation of floating discontent and for popular activation oriented to recovering sovereignty and democracy, kidnapped by the oligarchical "caste"' (Errejón 2014, online). Podemos succeeded, then, in rooting itself at the local level, with as many as 400 circles (both territorial ones and sectorial assemblies) already in place before the European elections. Open to participation and horizontal, they succeeded in involving thousands of citizens in the electoral campaign, in what an activist described as 'a kind of 15M of politics' (in della Porta, Fernández et al. 2017, 51).

The visibility Podemos achieved in the European elections largely increased popular support, with a significant growth in the number of participants in the activities of the circles, as well as of followers in social media (from 200,000 to 610,000 on Facebook, and from 60,000 to 200,000 Twitter followers in just one week). With strong media visibility, Podemos then organized its Constituent Assembly. As della Porta, Fernández et al. (2017, 51–2) summarized, in the constituent phase, between October and November 2015, '107,488 people elected the members of the various organizational bodies. Ethical, political, and organizational documents were also voted by 112,070 people between 20 and 26 October 2014. . . . During this constituent process, different ideas and visions emerged, especially about the organizational model of Podemos.'

The organizational choices and evolution in the party testify to the influence of the 15M, but also of some tensions between party and movements. First and foremost, two different organizational models competed from the beginning: a more traditional one and a more innovative one. The first model (supported by Pablo Iglesias and approved with a resounding majority of 84 per cent in the online ballot) was more conventional, foreseeing a general secretary, and a central and an executive committee; the other was instead more horizontal, with, for instance, the allocation of some positions by lot (Rendueles and Sola 2015). More generally, while one faction stressed efficacy, through the construction of 'a machinery for electoral war', others wanted to experiment with organizational innovations, giving more power to the grassroots. Tensions remained between those members who had previous experience in movements and parties, and those instead who were mobilizing for the first time. In fact, coexistence of these two groups has not been easy. While Podemos leaders have attempted to maintain the engagement of the less ideological and less experienced members, internal recruitment processes tended to privilege activists with previous experience in movements and parties (della Porta, Fernández et al. 2017, 52).

Additionally, there was a tension between a formal grassroots participatory structure and a personalized style of decision-making (Font et al. 2015). In fact,

> Podemos' (initial) success and electoral prospects have been closely tied to the charismatic leadership of Pablo Iglesias. Thanks to his convincing public speaking skills and his critical stance against economic–political elites and austerity policies, he became a regular television talk show guest before Podemos' launch. Iglesias and his collaborators designed a strategy oriented to use television as a platform to extend a political discourse and, furthermore, a political project. The personalization around the figure of Iglesias is seen as a strategic device, also as part of the populist hypothesis, where the personal leadership plays (or pretends to play) the particular role of representing the whole idea around the concept of people (*el pueblo*). In this sense, the decision of Podemos to print Iglesias' face on the voting ballots of the European elections was highly contested by social activists, who ridiculed this decision. But,

electorally, it worked due to the higher level of his social recognition compared to the name of the new party. Extreme importance has been given by high-ranking members of Podemos to political communication as a strategic mechanism to connect with its constituencies and build up social hegemony in terms of discourse. This is something that has traditionally been absent in the left and alternative social movements in Spain. (della Porta, Fernández et al. 2017, 98)

The organizational structure of Podemos mixes traditional elements of the left-wing party model with some participatory innovations, generating tensions between horizontal networking and a centralization and personalization of the leadership (Galindo et al. 2015; Rendueles and Sola 2015). The organizational model adopted by the Constituent Assembly in November 2014 mentions the use of digital media and various tools for facilitating a decentralized and participatory organization. According to Article 6 of the Organizational Principles of Podemos (OPP), the three main organizational principles are participation, transparency and democratic control. Members (older than 14) join by filling in a form on Podemos' website (Article 12, OPP). They can then participate in various decisions online through a permanent voting code. There are no membership fees, only a voluntary contribution.

The main organisms of the party are the circles, the Citizen Assembly, and the citizens in general. Membership goes from mere online subscription to activism in the local circles (Pérez-Nievas et al. 2018). While membership is a requirement to vote in primaries, members have no obligation to attend meetings. Participation through registration online involves very different degrees of identification with the party and participation in its activities. This brings about unclear borders between notions of registered participants and effective participants. As an activist noted: 'I do not really know if I am actually a member of Podemos. Some days I feel I am, but others I feel myself very far away from the project' (in della Porta, Fernández et al. 2017, 79). Blurred boundaries between the inside and the outside of the party have been described as an importation from the 15M movement, aiming 'to add a greater number of citizens to the analysis, the decision-making and the management of the public' (Article 6, OPP). At the end of 2018, there were about 595,000 people registered in Podemos, according to its website.

More activist forms of membership happen in the circles, which maintain high levels of autonomy, often developing from the local assemblies of the 15M movement. The circles are 'the basic unit of organization in Podemos' and 'the tool that can promote participation, debate and active linkages with society' (Article 6, OPP), including social movements (Article 58, OPP). Shortly after the foundation of the party, there were already about 1,000 sectorial and territorial circles, which were initially self-organized structures with a sort of 'liquid' militancy (Galindo et al. 2015). Following the Constituent Assembly, however, they underwent a ratification process which also saw a decrease in their activism, with, instead, a growing role for the citizen councils, that grew to support local candidates (della Porta, Fernández et al. 2017, 79–80).

In parallel to these attempts to increase participation, a more traditional party structure was put in place. The highest decision-making body is the Citizen Assembly (Article 10, OPP), in which all registered members can participate, with voting rights on- and offline. It must be consulted before major decisions are made on strategic orientation, electoral lists, programme elaboration, election/recall of members of different internal bodies, agreements with other political forces, statute amendments, etc.

The executive body of the party is the Citizen Council (Article 17, OPP), composed of eighty-one members: the General Secretary, seventeen regional general secretaries, a member elected by the registered people outside Spain, and sixty-two members elected directly by the Citizen Assembly. As, during the Constituent Assembly, all of the members elected by the assembly belonged to the team presented by Pablo Iglesias, criticisms emerged about a lack of pluralism. As observed by a member of the party from Madrid: 'We have spoken out much about transversality and inclusiveness but inwardly I think we have had a problem in managing the internal plurality and incorporating it into the spaces of decision' (in della Porta, Fernández et al. 2017, 80).

The Citizen Assembly also elects the General Secretary, who proposes for ratification by the Citizen Assembly the (ten to fifteen) members of the Coordination Council, with the task of supporting him/her in the daily activities of coordination and public representation (Article 25, OPP). A Committee of Guarantee is appointed with the task of safeguarding the rights of registered members and the fundamental principles and rules of the party (Article 26, OPP). Elected by the Citizen Assembly, it is formed by five permanent members plus five substitutes, at least half of them lawyers (Article 27, OPP). This organizational model is replicated in the cities and villages with more than 100 people registered in the party (Article 30, OPP).

Participatory channels were also introduced in the selection of party candidates. Citizen Assemblies have the task of organizing primaries open to all party members to form the list of candidates at general elections. The process is inclusive, even if candidates need to be endorsed by at least one *círculo* or by one of the elected organs of the party. While, in the primaries to select the candidate for prime minister, members can cast only a single vote, in the primaries for Congress, voters can express up to 350 preferences (that is, the number of MPs in Congress). There are then some corrections, to ensure gender equality and to respect obligations with coalition partners, as well as the possibility for the directive organs to reserve positions for independent candidates. In sum, given a voting system that incentivizes block voting, primaries have proven uncompetitive, with results closely resembling the preferences of the leadership (Pérez-Nievas et al. 2018).

The organization of open primaries to select candidates, first introduced for the election of candidates to the European Parliament, aims at avoiding the activists' nuclei isolating the party from society (Iglesias 2015b, 19). The implementation of the primaries, however, created internal conflicts, especially between the group formed around Pablo Iglesias – *Claro que Podemos* ('Sure We Can') – and other critical groups, with some emerging polarization and factionalism (Rose 1964). The management of a deep internal heterogeneity in terms of political positions is in fact a main challenge to the party that eventually triggered the exit of some leaders and activists.

Participatory tools were also looked for in the use of new media. To increase participation, Podemos has experimented with existing commercial online platforms that have seldom been used by social movements (Romanos and Sádaba 2016), in particular through Plaza Podemos and Appgree. The former has been defined as a digital square, 'with collective life which thinks, debates and cooperates, socializing information and generating debates and processes of collective intelligence' (Toret 2015, 132). In it, the community of participants should feel that they are deciding on some of the most relevant topics, by expanding certain threads and closing others (Romanos and Sádaba 2016). In the period of the Constituent Assembly more than 2.4 million page views and 280,000 unique users were counted (Ardanuy and Labuske 2015, 102), with later a decrease in the level of participation. Appgree is used for the organization of mass protests as it allows for a quick poll on the opinions of participants (Romanos and Sádaba 2016). Citizens' inquiries have been used to make binding decisions on relevant issues which are not among the exclusive competences of the Citizen Assembly. They can be called at the national level by the General Secretary, by the absolute majority of the Citizen Council, by 10 per cent of the registered members, or by 20 per cent of the circles. Inquiries have addressed especially the choice of electoral coalitions (at national and regional levels), the support for regional socialist presidents and the form in which to participate in the local elections.

The intensive use of participatory tools does not preclude, however, a plebiscitary relationship between leaders and members. Rather, while digital platforms may favour participation, the definition of the issues on which members are consulted can still be top-down and oriented towards ratifying decisions already made in small circles (della Porta, Fernández et al. 2017, 83; also Galindo et al. 2015).

A mix of tradition and innovation is also to be found in party financing. While Spanish parties have traditionally relied upon state financing and bank credit (van Biezen 2000; Méndez Lago 2007; Vergé 2012; Casal et al. 2014), in open contestation of that system Podemos adopted an innovative model to finance its activities, based upon principles of independence and transparency. As one of its founders explained, 'if people did not support us, if they did not give money, then nothing would be possible. But people supported us also economically' (in della Porta, Fernández et al. 2017, 80). To state funding, in the form of public subsidies to parties distributed according to electoral results, Podemos added crowd-funding for specific initiatives (such as micro-credits, but also the financing of the electoral campaigns), as well as the contribution withdrawn from the salaries of the representatives in public institutions. Moreover, the Ethical Code states that representatives may earn no more than three times the Spanish minimum salary (about 1,880 euro in total), devolving the rest to the party, which assigns part of it to the 'Impulsa' ('Boost') project, which finances social projects through a public competition. As for transparency, the financial situation of Podemos is detailed on its website, updated quarterly, with monitors and external auditors. This system of financing is strongly supported by party members, even the most critical ones. As one of them explained, 'it is clear that although I think that Podemos has been increasingly becoming a traditional party, the funding system makes a difference' (in della Porta, Fernández et al. 2017, 84).

In sum, Podemos attempted to develop an organizational structure that addresses in part the critique of representative democracy that was widespread in the 15M, with particular emphasis on grassroots participation. The party 'generated a great social effervescence: hundreds of circles were created in the first months, an intense public scrutiny of the different programs and projects of the organization took place, and tens of thousands periodically participated in votes through the Internet' (Rendueles and Sola 2018, 37). In October 2014, the founding congress (Vista Alegre I) followed an innovative model, with no delegates, and the possibility to vote online for all attendees (Sola and Rendueles 2018).

The frequent elections in 2015 and 2016 pushed, however, towards a rapid institutionalization oriented towards capturing the opening of electoral opportunities (Rendueles and Sola 2018). In time, the leadership chose to strengthen its control at the expense of a greater plurality, in order to maximize its chances of success in the upcoming elections. As electoral politics pushed the privileging of efficacy over internal pluralism, tensions emerged inside the party.

The relationship with social movements was also discussed intensively. On the one hand, the General Secretary, Iglesias, suggested that 'the current political task is to make visible the damage ("politicize the pain") that austerity has wreaked on the different social sectors represented by the social movements (evictions, pensions, salaries, education, health, etc.) to which Podemos needs to connect in order to serve as a channel for their demands' (in Franzé 2018, 65). On the other, the political secretary, Errejón, stated that the party had to take the political initiative (Franzé 2018). In February 2017, during the second congress (Vista Alegre II), the party was split between a more institutionally oriented faction (34%), an anti-capitalist one (13%) stressing the importance of social movements, and one led by Iglesias (51%) in between them.

While concentrating attention on elections and representation within Parliament and government, Podemos also at times calls for protest events, and endorses protest events promoted by social movement organizations. In particular, on 31 January 2015, The Rally for Change in Puerta del Sol mobilized between 100,000 and 300,000 people from all over the country to address issues of sovereignty, democracy and rights. The march was called to 'maintain the idea that they are a hybrid movement/party that primarily seeks to give expression to popular feelings and needs' (Flesher Fominaya 2015). Additionally, Podemos has participated in protest events organized by various platforms against the Transatlantic Trade Investment Partnership (TTIP), in support of refugees, as well as the transnational Euro-Marches, feminist protests around 8 March, and LGBT Pride Day on 28 June. Podemos' elected representatives have also participated in international protests such as the Blockupy events and the World Social Forum in Tunisia. The chosen name for the party, 'We can', signals the willingness to capitalize on the sense of empowerment emerging from virtual and physical plazas and to take tactics of spatial occupation into the Spanish parliamentary system (Martinez Guillem 2018).

The action of Podemos also links the square and institutions through a subversive use of institutional spaces. So, the performances of Podemos in the institutions challenge the traditional conceptions of institutional politics. The representatives of Podemos call into question the formal character of Parliament by engaging in performances aiming at a re-appropriation of this space. Podemos has in fact presented an alternative image in Parliament, first of all thanks to the age of its representatives – much younger than average (41 years old against an average of 48) – as well as gender parity. Besides a plural background in terms of age, gender, race and class, Podemos' MPs challenged the existing rules by refusing to use official government cars; substituting suits, ties, leather bags and traditional hairstyles with jeans, backpacks, dreadlocks and T-shirts with printed political messages; engaging in public displays of affection such as hugging and kissing; or replacing the traditional acceptance formula 'I swear to abide by the Constitution' with the statement 'I promise to abide by the Constitution in order to change it; never again a country without its people' (Martinez Guillem 2018). Non-conformist behaviour, including kissing on the lips between two congressmen and breastfeeding by a congresswoman, was presented by the party as supporting an image of Podemos as 'a factory of love'. Contesting the aggressive style of some male leaders, feminist members called, with some success, for depatriarchalization (Caravantes 2018). In the representative assemblies, Podemos' elected members also aim, however, at acquiring a public image of accuracy and reliability. As one activist stated, 'for us, institutional work is a big challenge because there we cannot fail, our adversaries are really looking forward to seeing us making evident mistakes at the institutional level. So we have to show much rigor to appear as a solid alternative' (in della Porta, Fernández et al. 2017, 85).

Reflecting the social composition of the anti-austerity protests, Podemos has gained support especially among citizens who are young, urban, well educated, from the North and East of the country, and actively use new technologies (Galindo et al. 2015). In particular, according to data referring to 2015, it is the most preferred party among young people, with 27 per cent of support among the very young (18–24 years). The party also became, however, 'more and more supported by social groups punished by the economic crisis and frustrated by the lack of opportunities' (Fernández-Albertos 2015, 100), and it was even presented as a class-based party (Galindo et al. 2015, 102). As for the class background, 'Podemos' support is similar among the service class, non-manual workers, and skilled and unskilled workers (four approximately equal groups that together represent 80 per cent of the population), but it obtains much lower percentages among owners and supervisors, agricultural workers and, to lesser extent, the self-employed' (Rendueles and Sola 2018, 40). As for employment status, support is drawn over-proportionally from the unemployed, temporary workers and students, and instead falls among housewives and retirees. As for subjective indicators of class belonging, support for Podemos grows as perception of the economic situation worsens (Rendueles and Sola 2018). While more Eurosceptic than those of IU, supporters of Podemos are not, however, the losers in globalization that have emerged in research on right-wing populism (Ramiro and Gomez 2017).

Looking at political attitudes, Podemos has more support among those showing the highest levels of distrust towards politicians, parties, justice, the EU, banks and unions (Cordero and Montero 2015), especially among those who had previously voted for centre-left and Left parties (PSOE and IU) and self-located on the Left (Galindo et al. 2015). In particular, 32% of Podemos voters came from the PSOE; 26% from IU; and 10% had abstained in 2011 (Galindo et al. 2015). Voters locate Podemos on the Left (2.3 on the Left–Right scale, ranging from 1 to 10, with PSOE located at 4.5 and IU 2.5); about 70% of its voters self-identify as being left-wing (18% self-identify as centrist, and 10% did not respond) (Sola and Rendueles 2018). As should be expected, Podemos electors support participatory forms of democracy and are instead hostile to the delegation of power to experts (Lavezzolo and Ramiro 2017). Thus, Podemos has managed to locate itself at the centre of the Left, and obtained support from non-ideological voters as well as from disappointed PSOE voters (Galindo et al. 2015; Rendueles and Sola 2015).

Framing alternatives

Podemos' counter-hegemonic strategy has pointed towards transforming the political status quo through a radical change in discourse. Here as well, transformations were noted with the increasing focus on electoral politics that brought about a growing need to attract voters located on the centre-left, as well as to find party allies on the centre-left.

Especially at the launch of Podemos, some of the party leaders' familiarity with the idea of hegemony in the work of Antonio Gramsci, or discourse analysis in the work of Ernesto Laclau, brought about what was defined as Podemos' 'populist hypothesis', with attempts to trigger the development of a leftist populism (Errejón 2014). The narrative developed by the party pointed towards a crisis, defined by 'a breakdown of the social and political consensus and a dismantling of traditional identities. This breakdown makes possible the existence of a populist Left, which is not located in the symbolic distribution of positions of the regime, but is seeking to create another dichotomy, articulating a new political will with the possibility of becoming the majority' (Errejón 2014). It thus challenged the traditional division between Left and Right as, Pablo Iglesias noted, 'in Spain, the spectre of an organic crisis was generating the conditions for the articulation of a dichotomizing discourse, capable of building the 15M's new ideological constructs into a popular subject and in opposition to the elites' (Iglesias 2015b, 14).

In the attempt to construct a new subject, a new political language should allow 'making transversal interpellations to a disappointed social majority which went beyond the Left–Right axis, upon which the regime shares positions and ensures its stability. We are proposing a dichotomy based on the axis "democracy/oligarchy" or "citizenship/caste" or even "new/old": a distinct border which aims to isolate the elites and create a new identification in front of them' (Errejón 2014). Especially in the beginning, main signifiers in Podemos' discourse have been the people (*gente*) and the caste. The caste is a floating signifier, made up of privileged groups, including politicians, corporations, the media and speculators of various types. Following the 15M discourse, the notion of the people refers to ordinary citizens beyond ideological belonging (Rendueles and Sola 2018). The people are considered then as opposed to the elite – as in the slogan, *el pueblo versus la casta* ('the people against "the caste"', a term imported from the Italian Five Star Movement's vocabulary), resonating with the contrast between those below and those above that had been singled out in the 15M mobilizations (Stobart 2014). A broad coalition is promoted through an anti-corruption discourse. As corruption came to be conceived as the second largest political problem in Spain, Podemos targeted the collusion that emerged, for instance, through the 'revolving door' between government and the advisory and executive boards of corporations (Flesher Fominaya 2014; Stobart 2014). Defining itself as 'neither leftist nor rightist', and differentiating between ordinary lay people and corrupt politicians, Podemos claimed 'we are the people, not politicians', as stated in the Electoral Program for Regional Elections (EPRE 2015, 8).

From the 15M, Podemos also took inspiration for its demand for real democracy, considering that movement to be a political space for the convergence of a variety of identities, which allowed for a new way of doing politics and the emergence of a new political scene. Following Laclau and Mouffe, Podemos' discourse challenges the primacy of class, 'defining hegemony as contingent, unstable and rhetorically constructed; and . . . proposing a transversalist vision that utilizes "empty signifiers" working as synecdoche metaphors, which aggregate different identities into a common construct, the people' (Agustín and Briziarelli 2018, 13). In this perspective, the main site of struggle moves beyond relations of production, addressing the sphere of signification. As the crisis challenges the hegemonic structure, 'fissures appear in the form of empty signifiers, which remain temporarily available for alternative political subjects to be re-signified. Discursive hegemony assumes that social relations are inherently unstable and that meanings are relational and historically contingent' (Agustín and Briziarelli 2018, 14). In Podemos' discourse, the concept of an 'anti-political politics' builds upon the distinction, in Autonomist Marxism, between politics as activity around the state and politics as social struggle, as 'anti-politics implies rejecting the political representation for a direct and active fight for the interests of the sub-altern class' (Agustín and Briziarelli 2018, 16). Finally, the notion of transversality is inspired by the 15M, which was considered to be a prime example of commonality within diversity, going beyond pre-existing ideological identities (Agustín and Briziarelli 2018).

Again, in line with the discontinuity the 15M had aimed at producing in public discourse, Podemos often referred to Gramsci's concept of an organic crisis in which new ideas, perspectives and practices emerge, as a profound drop in the legitimacy of existing institutions challenges 'the cementing function of dominant ideology, the link between state and civil society, and the incorporating capability of the ruling class of subaltern classes' interests and views' (Briziarelli 2018, 100). As transformations require agency, concepts emerged within the 15M such as *sentido comun* ('common sense'), *ciudadania* ('citizenship'), justice or *soberania* ('sovereignty'), used to define an oppositional historical bloc through 'an intellectual and moral reform based on the forging of a "common sense", a "political sense" and a new sense of sociability based on fraternity and solidarity' (Briziarelli 2018, 102).

Also at the level of discourse, however, an adaptation to institutional politics can be identified. In time, the reference to a caste faded away, given the need to adapt to a new situation in which representatives of the party were elected to institutions and the party allied with others at local and national level. The narrative about the transition to democracy also changed then, from that of a pact between the old elites and the old Left, and the defeat of the people, into a more complex process (Franzé 2018).

The call to the people had increasingly focused on popular sovereignty. Concepts such as 'patriot' or 'homeland', traditionally banned by the Spanish Left, were linked to the defence of social welfare and solidarity (Eklund 2018), as well as economic self-determination, in a way resonant with Third World liberation struggles rather than nationalist movements. As Agustín (2018, 154) noted, the fatherland is understood as the people – that is, 'a wide and transversal aggregation which acquires sense against the existing order and its elites'. Connecting social rights to the nation, 'the term "patriot" has been strategically used to criticize political corruption ("those politicians who have the money in Switzerland are betrayers"), the privatization of public services ("to be a patriot is to defend our public services"), and the lack of sovereignty ("to be a patriot is to defend sovereignty, as they are selling the country and our rights")' (della Porta, Fernández et al. 2017, 117). As Pablo Iglesias argued, in an emergency situation the reference to the homeland is meant to rally around the party a broad majority of citizens:

> It is pretty obvious that I am leftist, but I think that the fact of being a leftist at this point is irrelevant. I think that we're in an exceptional social situation in which emergency measures are required. Measures that all Spaniards who love their country should defend. They are merely democratic measures: recovery of decency, dignity and sovereignty and

a perspective of building a different Europe that protects its citizens, the social rights and assumes that popular sovereignty is the basis for building democracy. (Iglesias 2015d)

According to Pablo Iglesias (in Agustín 2018, 164), patriots

work and do not need to be covered by a flag. They wake up early to go to work or to search for a job. The real patriots care about their people ... To us the fatherland is the people. To us defending the fatherland is to defend that there are public hospitals, public schools, having the best services. The fatherland should be more like its people and less like its elites.

The fatherland is, moreover, made by institutions that guarantee equality and defend the interests of the vulnerable against the powerful.

While still aiming at forming a new subject, party discourse also became more clearly oriented towards the Left. Initially, the term 'caste' was used as a floating signifier, diffuse enough to include various groups, political and economic, allowing Podemos to go beyond the ideological discourse traditional for the Left, even if its programme was clearly left-wing. In time, the broad definition of the people was, however, difficult to sustain when specific policies needed to be proposed that advantaged (or convinced) some but not others. The positioning on the Left thus became more and more explicit, with calls for progressive taxation, tax on selling and buying transactions on the stock exchange, the establishment of a public bank, the repeal of the labour market austerity reforms, a 35-hour week and women's rights (Lobera and Parejo 2019), but also migrants' rights, measures against corruption and for political renewal to increase citizens' participation – including voting rights for migrants – citizen petitions, popular legislative instruments and citizen counsellors. In regional assemblies, Podemos focused on public audits, emergency plans, anti-eviction laws, and cuts to the salaries and expenses of institutions and representatives. With increasing electoral success, and entering into several local governments, a move towards more moderate claims has been noted, as calls for a basic universal wage for all citizens were substituted by state aid to those in need, the nationalization of strategic economic sectors of the economy by more public intervention in the economy; the proposed lowering of the retirement age rose from 60 to 65 years, and the cancellation of the Spanish state's debt was tamed into a call for renegotiation.

Already by 2015, a shift in Podemos' relation to the political order from antagonistic to agonistic can be identified, as the party's critique focused more on the behaviour of elites than on the institutions coming from the transition. Recognizing the importance of socialism in Spanish history, the transition was redefined as promoted by an 'impetus created by what is best about our country' (Franzé 2018, 62). The limits of the constitutional process set up at the time were to be overcome by a second transition, with a new constitutional moment. Alliance with IU and intensification of the relations with PSOE also reduced the stress on the above-versus-below discourse. This was accompanied by a shift from targeting *La Casta* to targeting *La Trama*, 'which was understood as a social plot and therefore allowing a more complex reading of the structure of power and its capability to create consent. *La Trama*, in fact, describes a social arrangement rather than an isolated class, . . . i.e. an entire regime defined by power and corruption' (Briziarelli 2018, 103).

In a national context characterized by a general consensus on Europeanization (Barreiro and Sánchez-Cuenca 2001; Vázquez-García et al. 2014; Vázquez-García 2012), with no 'hard Euroscepticism' (Szerbiak and Taggart 2003; Benedetto and Quaglia 2007), Podemos articulated a quest for another Europe. As Iglesias (2015c, 27) stated: 'the strategy we have followed is to articulate a discourse on the recovery of sovereignty, on social rights, even human rights, in a European framework'. At the same time, as stated in the initial party manifesto, there is a 'crisis of legitimacy of the EU', with a 'financial *Coup d'Etat* against Southern European countries'. The lack of democracy is stigmatized in the Programme for the 2014 European elections, but 'more Europe' is called for. As an activist notes:

> There is a paradox on this because most of Podemos' voters are the more Eurosceptic ones in Spain. However, Podemos' discourse on Europe has been very pro-European but critical. For me this has been very interesting and similar to the one displayed by Syriza: we are against the EU as it is constituted but we are in favour of a new type of relations in Europe, we need more Europe to overcome the crisis, we are against a Europe of two speeds, the centre and the periphery, etc. It is true that even the discourse was not Eurosceptic. The perception was that Podemos was the party challenging more the neoliberal order in Europe, maybe because Podemos put much emphasis on the issue of sovereignty. That is, to exit the crisis, overcome austerity and restore democracy we need to recover the national sovereignty that has been taken from us by the EU and globalization. And this, I think it's an interesting balance. We need to recover the ability and the power to decide, but we do not want to be isolated. (in della Porta, Fernández et al. 2017, 120)

Podemos' supporters in the EU elections emerge, in fact, as more interested in the EU than the average citizen (62.4% versus 42.9% of the general sample), but also more often 'quite or very much against' the EU (23.4%

against 13.4%) (CIS June 2014). In the European Parliament, Podemos clearly located itself on the Left, joining the European Left (GUE/NGL). Podemos also often expressed support not only for Syriza but also for Jeremy Corbyn during primary elections in the British Labour Party.

In 2016, as windows of opportunity seemed to close, the party moved towards a conception of a 'war of position', oriented towards forging a 'historic bloc', by broadening the basis of reference and by more participatory politics. Inspired by Gramsci, Podemos aimed at politicizing the masses into a national popular movement through an interaction of political, economic, cultural and social struggles. A hegemonic crisis was therefore seen as an 'impasse of signification, as the meanings at the base of the chain of equivalence of the historic bloc start losing sense' (Briziarelli 2018, 108). Resignification had to happen through the appropriation of public spaces with a re-politicization of the masses (Briziarelli 2018). In a war of position, various groups are called to bridge their social claims in a common front.

These changes notwithstanding, Podemos still presents itself as a movement for a political renewal of the symbols and identities of the traditional Left. Resonant with the 15M discourse, the critique of the Old Left is expressed in the choice of the party name, its colour and its logo. As mentioned, the name Podemos refers to the sense of empowerment that the *acarnpadas*, during the 15M, had been able to transmit to large parts of the Spanish society, with a persistent effect of polarization (Agustín and Briziarelli 2018, 7). It stresses empowerment beyond the already existing classes and ideologies, aiming at the construction of a new subject, as 'recognizing political action as a performative practice means moving away from the mechanistic base–superstructure theory and acknowledging the constructive capacity of the political' (Agustín and Briziarelli 2018, 7). The purple breaks with the red, traditional for the Left, referring instead to feminism. As for the logo, the circle 'prioritizes the world of the citizen over the world of the worker; the latter dominates the symbolic repertoire of the traditional Left, with its images of tools of production and instruments of culture, understood as routes to "enlightenment" and social "improvement"', also referring to the internal organization of the 15M working groups (Vélez 2016). The new politics proposed by the party continues to value participation, increasing public control over political institutions, and ending the privileges of elected representatives. The 15M conception of real democracy is kept alive as an alternative to liberal democracy, which is considered as in crisis. The call to 'We, the democrats' is a call to defend a democracy which is 'robbed and kidnapped by the oligarch', bridging political and social rights against an oligarchy made of political and economic power (in della Porta, Fernández et al. 2017, 118).

Mobilization is supported by a stress on change, excitement and hope. Hope is mobilized against the fear spread by the crisis, as expressed in the slogan *Sí se puede* ('Yes, it is possible') imported from the Plataforma de Afectados por la Hipoteca (PAH, 'Platform of Those Affected by Mortgages'). This is linked to passions and joy – as in the electoral spot that asked, 'When was the last time you voted with excitement?' The need and possibility for change has been reflected in the *Marcha del Cambio*, or the naming of 2015 as 'the year of change', when an electoral victory could have opened the opportunity for building 'a new country' through a constituent process: as stated in the Electoral Programme for Regional Elections, 'change means to achieve by ourselves the higher levels of democracy' (EPRE 2015, 63).

The movement and the party

In the party's self-definition, the anti-austerity protests are consistently considered as a source of inspiration, and Podemos itself as the 'principal political expression of the 15M' (Iglesias 2015b, 10), even if not built on the appropriation of the movement. The programmatic proximity with the movement is often claimed. Even if presenting itself as 'beyond Left and Right', Podemos' political programme developed from a radical leftist one in the 2014 European elections to a typical social democratic project by 2015 (Rendueles and Sola 2015). The five resolutions approved by the Constituent Assembly included 'defending public education – our right and not a business; anti-corruption; winning the right to housing and putting an end to financial impunity; for the right to health – a public health system for all; audit and debt restructuring' (della Porta, Fernández et al. 2017, 122). These resolutions reflect the proximity of Podemos' framing to the main claims expressed by the movements during the anti-austerity wave of protests. While proposals had been elaborated by experts (on the economy, culture and the care system), in many cases these positions were indeed launched by social movement activists who were also Podemos members (della Porta, Fernández et al. 2017). In the general elections of 2015, the programmatic manifesto listed five demands resonating with those put forward by the anti-austerity protests: (1) a new democratic model reinforcing participatory democracy; (2) independence of the judiciary; (3) measures oriented towards fighting corruption; (4) the constitutional guarantee of social rights; (5) a territorial model for the country defending 'unity within diversity' (http://unpaiscontigo.es/#acuerdos). Thus, Podemos has been defined as the result of the political incorporation of a part of the 15M, the one with more political experience. In fact, 'the programmatic inclusion of movements' claims and more generally the framing adopted by Podemos reflect the existing continuities between the party and the 15M, which are also to be found in the use of a consensual approach introduced by the movement with the goal of ideological transversality, as well as the use of ICTs for organizational and participation purposes' (Calvo and Álvarez 2015, 118).

The interactions between the party and progressive social movements continue to be facilitated also by personal experiences and overlapping membership (della Porta, Fernández et al. 2017, 122). Besides the experiences of leaders such as Iglesias or Errejón in the Global Justice Movement and the student movement, thirteen members of the Citizens' State Council had participated in the 15M (seven in Juventud Sin Futuro, six in the student movement), and three in the PAH (Martín 2015, 110). Many elected representatives have also mobilized in grassroots activities, in trade unions, social centres, ecologist or feminist groupings, and many ordinary members have been social movement activists. Thus, as an activist stated, 'all these social movements have been those who have fed Podemos. Podemos does not have a single cadre not coming from those spaces' (in della Porta, Fernández et al. 2017, 125). In fact, as Pablo Iglesias remarked, 'many of those who acquired an experience of leadership came to join Podemos; the party's leading ranks are by and large filled with people from the social movements. It was a natural outcome: the 15M movement politicized civil society, then followed this process of activist formation, and that led to taking the next step, of giving the movement a political and electoral expression' (Iglesias 2015c, 35).

In order to improve relations with existing social movements, Podemos launched the Area of Civil Society, led by an ex-lawyer for the PAH, which in July 2015 organized the Forum for Change, with the participation of more than 2,500 activists. Its opening call stated that the meeting was to:

> include the main demands and citizen proposals that will serve as raw material for the elaboration of the 'People's Programme', the electoral programme for the general elections. Today we face a historic opportunity to transform the institutional, social and economic reality of our country and therefore we consider essential to create a large space for dialogue where we can first listen to the proposals of social movements and civil society. (Public call for the Forum for Change)

Yet tensions between Podemos and the social movements clearly remained, at times intensifying. As Iglesias himself admitted:

> The crisis brought to the fore by this upsurge, which surprised the world, was also a crisis of the existing Spanish left. The 15M held up a

mirror to the left, revealing its deficiencies. It also put on the table the main component of a new common sense: rejection of the dominant political and economic elites, systematically labelled as corrupt. The 15M also crystallized a new culture of contestation that could not be grasped by the categories of left and right – something that the leaders of the existing left refused to acknowledge from the start. The logic of the 15M movement led to its exhaustion; it didn't achieve the effects desired by its committed activists, who hoped that the social could substitute for the institutional. Aiming to reduce politics to the mere expression of countervailing social powers, built through mobilization and patient activism, was one of the major blunders of the movementist intelligentsia in Spain, which failed to realize that the 'in the meantime' was precisely that: a way of working up until the arrival of the moment for audacity, which would require quite different political techniques. (Iglesias 2015b, 12–13)

Podemos remains, therefore, a two-fold party, one part of which is connected to horizontal and grassroots processes, and the other focusing on the party field and the creation of links with the non-mobilized constituency (della Porta, Fernández et al. 2017, 124; also Galindo et al. 2015). This is recognized by party members, one of whom affirmed:

I think that there is an on-going tension with social movements. On the one hand, Podemos needs to disassociate from the movements in order to appear as a serious and governing political force, but not too much because its social base comes directly from the movements and that is still present. On the other hand, it is obvious that Podemos, even with its problems and defects, remains the political expression of the struggle against austerity. (in della Porta, Fernández et al. 2017, 124–5)

In sum, the relation between the party, the 15M, and the other social movements that followed 'exists, but is partial, is not institutionalized and is causing a certain internal tension' (Martín 2015, 109). While the relationship between Podemos and the 15M is indubitable, however, its electoral successes have oriented party activities towards institutions, with declining focus on its original constituency (della Porta, Fernández et al. 2017, 136). In the attempt to go beyond the already mobilized social movements, the 'common sense' discourse has to appeal to shared conceptions about democracy, the crisis and austerity (Subirats 2015b; Errejón 2015), with the aim of gaining support from those majorities that had suffered during the financial crisis and had been deeply disappointed by the mainstream parties, on the centre-right and the centre-left. Certainly, developments such as the economic recovery (even if partial), or, especially, the emergence of the Catalan call for independence as a main contentious issue, challenged the party to adapt its position. If the 15M is said to have opened opportunities for deep transformation by changing Gramscian 'common sense', strategies need, nevertheless, to be adapted to further changes.

*   *   *

Developing a comparison: MAS in Bolivia

The emergence of new parties related to social movements against austerity has also been noted in Latin America, where a wave of left-wing electoral victories started with Hugo Chavez in 1998, continuing with socialist Ricardo Lago in 2000 in Chile, Lula da Silva for the Partido dos Trabalhadores (PT, 'Worker's Party') in 2002 in Brazil, left Peronist Néstor Kirchner in 2003 in Argentina, Tabarè Vasquez of Broad Front in 2004 in Uruguay, Movimiento al Socialismo (MAS, 'Movement towards Socialism') with Evo Morales in 2005 in Bolivia, and Rafael Correa in 2006 in Ecuador (Levitsky and Roberts 2011). Focusing on MAS, I will highlight in particular the similar dynamics regarding the emergence of the party within social movements, and the impact it had on party strategies and framing.

Appropriating opportunities: the neoliberal juncture and party politics

Long-term causes for left-wing revival in Latin America include persisting inequality and severe poverty, notwithstanding growth, with particularly destructurating effects during the economic crisis of the years 1998–2002. While all left-wing parties promised to reduce inequalities, there were differences, however, between the institutionalized left-wing parties in countries such as Brazil, Chile and Uruguay and the so-called populist Left of Chavez in Venezuela, with Argentina, Bolivia and Ecuador in between.

In parallel, the societal resistance to neoliberalism had found different expressions in the different Latin American countries: from social movement protests – using action repertoires such as strikes and demonstrations, but also riots, highway blockages, and occupations of land or public buildings – to electoral action, either through support for the left-wing opposition or through the foundation of new parties on the Left. As Kenneth Roberts (2015a, 61–2) noted, the different forms of resistance were influenced by party alignments as well as the institutional outcomes of neoliberalism:

> The countries with the most explosive patterns of social protest – Venezuela and Ecuador during the critical juncture, and Argentina, Bolivia, and Ecuador in the aftermath period, were all cases of bait-and-switch market reform that programmatically de-aligned party systems and fostered powerful reactive sequences, including partial or complete party system decomposition and the rise of new and more polarizing

electoral protest movements with populist or leftist tendencies. . . . The political expression of societal resistance was quite different where conservatives imposed market reforms over staunch leftist opposition and critical junctures left in place party systems that were both institutionalized and programmatically aligned – the outcome of contested liberalism. Under contested liberalism, societal resistance could be channelled towards established parties of the left, thus weakening anti-systemic forms of social or electoral protest. This outcome moderated the reactive sequences of the aftermath period, which largely consisted of the progressive electoral strengthening of these institutionalized leftist or centre-left parties, including the PT in Brazil, the Socialist/PPD bloc in Chile, the Broad Front in Uruguay, the PRD in Mexico, and the FMLN in El Salvador. In short, reactive sequences produced moderate electoral shifts that reinforced and reproduced the institutional underpinnings of contested liberalism.

While in Brazil, Chile and Uruguay, it was the centre-right that pushed for neoliberalism, with centre-left parties in opposition, in Venezuela, Bolivia and Ecuador there was instead a mass protest against the neoliberal process seen as embraced by all established parties. So:

> where this resistance cleaved party systems – that is, where clearly-differentiated partisan alternatives existed in support and opposition to the neoliberal model – electoral competition was more stable and institutionalized in the post-adjustment era, moderating the eventual turn to the left. Where this resistance was left largely outside party systems, and partisan competition was not clearly structured by programmatic distinctions, post-adjustment reactive sequences destabilized party systems and outflanked them with new and more radical leftist alternatives. (Roberts 2015a, 40)

Massive protests triggered the emergence of new parties when they de-stabilized the existing party system, given 'the representational failures produced by particular types of partisan alignments around the process of market reform. Whereas some partisan alignments channelled societal resistance to market orthodoxy towards institutionalized parties of the Left, other alignments channelled such resistance into extra-systemic forms of social and/or electoral protest, including populism' (Roberts 2015b, 686). As, from the late 1980s and early 1990s, social movements targeting austerity grew in all of Latin America, their development was influenced by domestic political opportunities, in particular the partisan alignment around neoliberal policies. Protests were, in fact, more intense and radical where existing parties seemed unwilling to represent emerging demands for more social justice. In countries such as Chile, Brazil or Uruguay, in which neoliberal reforms were carried out by centre-right parties, the existing left-wing parties could provide an electoral channel for discontent, which led to left-wing presidents. By contrast, in Argentina, Bolivia, Ecuador and Venezuela, the centre-left or the labour-oriented populist parties in power had promoted neoliberal policies that they had initially campaigned against. Thus, lacking party channels, dissent instead took the form of massive protests as well as populist outsiders or left-wing movement parties, with total or partial breakdown of the party system (Roberts 2015b).

Once the Left took power, the two paths led to different outcomes, with a distinction between a 'liberal Left', which adopted moderate market-oriented economic policies, and an 'interventionist Left', which preferred instead more state control and increased public spending. As Madrid (2010, 587–8) noted, the two differed

> in terms of political strategies and their foreign and social policies, with the interventionist left being more critical of the United States, more willing to act aggressively to address social inequalities, and more determined to overhaul or work outside of the existing political institutions. Finally, the liberal and interventionist left also have varied in terms of their organizational structure. Whereas the liberal left has been composed largely of older, relatively well-institutionalized parties, the interventionist left consists mostly of new, fluid, and highly personalistic movements. . . . Older left parties have tended to be more moderate and market-oriented than newer left movements.

These differences can also be explained by the role played by the left-wing parties in the implementation of neoliberal policies:

> Powerful interventionist left movements arose predominantly in those Latin American countries in which traditional leftist or centre-left parties had gained power and implemented market-oriented policies during the 1990s. In these countries, the traditional left's shift to the centre opened up political space on the left, which was occupied by new, more interventionist left movements. As frustration with neoliberal policies grew, disenchanted voters abandoned the traditional left in favour of the new, more radical movements. By contrast, in the countries in which the traditional left remained in the opposition during the 1990s, it won or retained the support of many of those voters who were disenchanted with neoliberal reforms. In these countries, traditional left parties were able to head off the rise of new, more-radical left movements by criticizing neoliberal policies and the parties that implemented them, even while they reached out to more centrist voters by abandoning certain radical features of their platforms and embracing the more popular aspects of the market model, such as free trade. (Madrid 2010, 588)

The interventionist path was led by new left-wing parties, characterized by low institutionalization, strong attachment to the leader, movement-like structures and the use of disruptive tactics. Given that legitimacy declined faced with systematic violations of the rule of law and corruption, as dominant parties tried to prevent access to new groups (Hawkins 2010, 95), movement parties emerged especially in reaction to the perceived betrayal of traditional left-wing parties in defending their social constituency (Handlin and Collier 2011).

While movement parties were rooted in similar social conditions, research pointed towards differences in particular between Bolivia, on the one hand, and Venezuela and Ecuador, on the other (Silva 2009; Roberts 2015a). These three countries, in fact, went through different experiences in terms of the relationship between mass movements and the governments that they had contributed to creating or were in close relations with. It was only in Bolivia that a proper movement party developed from within a long and successful movement against social inequality.

Organizational mobilization

In Bolivia, the Movimiento al Socialismo (MAS) emerged from a long process of setting-up an alternative party on the Left, which had already started in the early 1990s. Participation in local elections in 1999 (in which MAS obtained eighty-one local council seats) provided experience in party politics, and protest activities reached a climax during the 'water war' in 2000. As heavy repression produced solidarization, MAS, campaigning against neoliberalism and for national sovereignty, surprisingly came second in the national elections of 2002, channelling many of the disgruntled voters of the left-wing party Conscience of the Fatherland, which had been the first large national party to refer to indigenous cultural identities but had supported austerity measures. In the next elections in 2005, after US threats in the case of a MAS victory, Morales achieved a resounding majority with 53.74 per cent. After MAS entered government, a new Constitution strengthened the power of the president, and Morales, in 2009, won re-election with 64 per cent of the vote.

In a country characterized by the highest proportion of indigenous people in Latin America (62 per cent), MAS was able to overcome the traditional conflict between the (more politicized) Aymara in the highlands, and the Quechua in the lowlands. In addition, faced with the weakening of the left-wing parties, which had traditionally defended indigenous rights, the party mobilized on the indigenous discourse, which was, however, successfully bridged with a class discourse. In fact, former activists of the traditional Left provided the indigenous movements with experienced leaders, as well as inclusive frames. From the mid-1990s, massive Marches for Sovereignty and Dignity allowed for networking of indigenous organizations around the call for a constitutional process.

In Bolivia, as in Spain, an important condition for the organization of a party was massive mobilization. A social movement for indigenous peoples' rights emerged, renewing left-wing discourse and practices. MAS grew, in particular, from inside a very strong movement by coca growers (*cocaleros*), led by Evo Morales, after the US had pushed for the eradication of coca production. From MAS' inception, movement and party overlapped as the latter was set up as a political instrument for the former (van Cott 2008, 103). Not only did MAS emerge 'organically from social movements themselves' (van Cott 2008, 103), but social movements remained relevant for the party even after its power notably grew. In particular, the party leader Evo Morales 'undoubtedly played an important role in forging a common political project out of the diverse rural and urban movements that ultimately converged in the MAS, his leadership was deeply rooted in an autonomous and bottom-up dynamic of socio-political mobilization – in short, a highly participatory form of popular subjectivity' (Roberts 2015b, 689).

Coca growers were particularly successful in their mobilization as protest spread. Due also to a deep-rooted acceptance of coca use in Bolivia, where its criminalization (under pressure from the US) happened later than in other countries, the movement succeeded in forming a positive collective identity upon the defence of a questionable good. Mobilization was also facilitated by low state repression against coca production in the 1980s, and a tradition of structured relations between the peasants and the state during the left-wing military regime. After the economic crisis, with the collapse of mining and increased dependency on coca, miners relocated as coca growers, bringing new resources of militancy to an already rooted labour union. Activists therefore bridged their identity, as peasants producing coca and as trade unionists, with an ensuing politicization of ethnic identities (Ochoa 2014).

Born from within the *cocaleros* movement, MAS has been defined as 'the direct creation of militant movement activists and grassroots leaders forged in the heat of social mobilization, who decide to enter into the electoral arena and compete for office while sustaining collective action in the streets' (Anria 2018, 8). Movement organizations, particularly of the *cocaleros*, constituted its core constituencies, in a bottom-up genetic process, with blurred boundaries to separate the party and the movement. While not an indigenous party, MAS aimed at bridging class and ethnic references. In a document in 2002, called 'Our Ideological Principle', MAS referred in particular to the failure of internal colonialism and of the Left, and to the potential of indigenous culture instead (Anria 2018).

From its peasant constituency, MAS broadened its appeal to a broad alliance of teachers, street vendors and factory workers, as well as associations of neighbours, with inclusive forms of support for indigenous culture. The party developed, in fact, as:

> a hybrid organization whose electoral success has been contingent on the construction of a strong rural–urban coalition, built on the basis of different linkages between the MAS and organized popular constituencies in rural and urban areas. Whereas the MAS's rural origins gave rise to grassroots control over the leadership, its expansion to urban areas has fostered the emergence of top-down mobilization strategies. (Anria 2013, 19)

Among the preconditions at the birth of the party, Anria has identified the following:

> One was the implementation of neoliberal reforms, which created economic losers who would then resist neoliberal policies, and the crisis of neoliberalism, which opened up space on the left. The second factor was the resistance to coca eradication programs and the state repression associated with such programs, which acted as a unifying force and strengthened peasant and indigenous movements around the defense of their interests. A third factor was a changing institutional context associated with decentralization reforms, which provided opportunities for indigenous social movements and new parties to compete and thrive in local elections. Fourth was a crisis of Bolivia's political party system and state institutions that became acute in the context of anti-neoliberal protests in the early 2000s. (Anria 2018, 69)

As with Podemos, opportunities for the party to break through opened up thanks to unexpected success in specific elections (in this case, at the local level) that paved the way for rapid gains at the national level as well, thanks to an extension of the constituency from the periphery to the centre. Thanks to the opening of opportunities at the local level, the precursor of MAS, the Assembly for the Sovereignty of the Peoples (which to comply with electoral law took over the name of the United Left), was successful first of all in the Chapare region, where the party – in 1999, with the name MAS – achieved some electoral victories. An upward scale-shift at national level happened then in the early 2000s, as the economic crisis of neoliberalism fuelled massive protests, with ensuing decomposition of the party system, especially as the parties that implemented market-oriented reforms were the same ones that had initially campaigned against them.

In particular, the protests against water privatization, especially in Cochabamba (the 'Water War'), played an important role in helping MAS to move into urban areas and to expand its social base through a 'supraclass' or 'plural popular' strategy of coalition building, defined as:

> one in which indigenous issues became the framing plank for successful political articulation among groups as diverse as *cocaleros*, indigenous movements, peasant associations, urban labor unions, and neighborhood associations. Morales played a key role – mostly via charismatic appeals – uniting a remarkably diverse set of subordinate actors into a powerful coalition that converged around the MAS. . . . Clearly, these relationships were less organic than what the MAS had with *cocaleros*, yet in the process the party was able to become their 'instrument' as well. (Anria 2018, 74)

Together with electoral mobilization, social protest, especially within the Water War, allowed for the formation of a heterogeneous coalition against neoliberalism. With twenty-seven MPs in 2002, MAS increased its influence, allowing for further networking between social movements:

> While some of these deputies were representatives from the Chapare and had been selected by the bases through mechanisms of direct participation, others were directly 'invited' by the leadership, had no history of militancy in the MAS, and had few checks from below. Many of the 'invited' leaders quickly became the voice of the MAS, as they related to the media very effectively and knew how to operate within representative institutions (Anria 2013, 27)

In this process, the organizational structure of the party changed, with the opening up of party lists to local leaders of unions, cooperatives and workers in the so-called informal sector. At the organizational level, given its connections to a rural social movement rooted in an assembleary tradition of grassroots participation, MAS kept some horizontal characteristics, including a loose structure that still remained in place, in part at least, as the party achieved national power. This allowed for ties with various rural and urban social movement organizations to be retained. While the *cocaleros* organizations continued to play a pivotal role in setting the party's priorities, the expansion into urban areas through ties with neighbourhood associations as well as trade unions broadened the party's constituency. At the urban level, 'the electoral strategy used to attract these peripheral constituencies combined attempts to co-opt the leadership of popular organizations with the pursuit of political alliances with established center-left parties in hopes of reaching middle class segments' (Anria 2018, 68). As deeply rooted social movements mobilized, their capacity for sustaining autonomous mobilization contributed to maintaining some accountability.

After its important gains in the presidential elections in 2002, in a period of widespread protests (with the so-called Gas War developing in 2004), MAS then succeeded in representing a broad and varied base, providing for a common programmatic ground. Since the 2005 elections,

> Organizations representing groups as diverse as artisans, microenter-prises, pensioners, transportation, street vendors, miners working for cooperatives, and other forms of community organization, such as neighborhood associations, perceived the alliance with the MAS as an opportunity to achieve parliamentary representation, occupy important positions in the government, and gain access to government jobs for their affiliates. For the MAS's part, by forging links to groups with great mobilizational capacity, the party dramatically expanded its support base and thereby its influence. Given that some of these organizations had been key protagonists in the protests that forced the resignation of two consecutive presidents, forging alliances with them was also seen as a way to ensure some degree of governability. (Anria 2018, 86)

As with Podemos, MAS reflected the organizational preferences of social movements, even if bridged with high levels of personalization of the leadership, as Evo Morales used repeated electoral events and social mobilization in order to push for its political agenda. MAS cultivated, in fact, forms of direct participation. As mentioned, its origins are rooted in the Assembly for the Sovereignty of the People (ASP), a social movement organization of peasants and coca growers that, in the second half of the 1990s, had received support from a declining left-wing party, the United Left (IU), to which coca growers gave electoral support. The ASP gave birth to an electoral platform, the Political Instrument for the Sovereignty of the Peoples (IPSP) and then MAS, based on the principle of self-representation. Within a supraclass strategy, MAS aimed at attracting part of the urban middle classes as well as intellectuals (Anria 2018, 27).

Indigenous traditions were kept alive in some innovative forms of internal democracy, bridging participatory and deliberative practices. At its fifth congress in 2003, MAS stated the importance of 'a true participatory democracy of consensus, respect and recognition of the diverse social organizations, where the communities and the people find their liberation from all forms of poverty, misery and discrimination. . . . The Movement towards socialism expresses its profound commitment to the development of a Communitarian democracy, of consensus and participation, of social and economic content' (van Cott 2008, 3). The innovative organizational model based on indigenous traditions also resonates with an anti-capitalist discourse, with calls for redistributive policies against growing poverty, and opposition to the policies of trade liberalization and privatization, which had been supported by all major existing parties.

Social movements were also influential in the selection of candidates for elections. In MAS, the highest decision-making authority is the Regular National Congress (*Congreso Nacional Ordinario*). According to the statute, the party has to keep special linkages with some peasants' unions that had played an important role in its foundation. A requirement for candidacy at the National Directorate is to have experience as leader of a peasant union. The party congress then selects its leaders in free elections, either through absolute majority of the delegates attending the congress, or through consensus (Anria 2018). The National Directorate must also coordinate candidate selection for election at various levels, with significant influence from grassroots social movement organizations. This allows for multiple strategies, allowing for the intervention of various social movement organizations, which has brought about a very plural representation in the congress, with the growing presence of women, as well as indigenous peoples, peasants, and urban poor social groups in the formal and informal labour sectors (Anria 2018).

Changes towards more top-down forms of politics have, however, also been noted. While expanding its contacts with social movements in urban areas, such as La Paz and El Alto, MAS built alliances with various groups. This penetration of civil society, reduced the autonomy of these organizations. As a *masista* noted, 'we can't deny we do that. We aim for our people to become leaders in these organizations. It is an effort to control the social organizations from the top' (in Anria 2013, 34). Another agreed:

> The project we have had as MAS is to be able to take control over the social organizations. In order to do that, you need to start from working at the district level and from there you can start climbing. The MAS became a national-level force only insofar as it played an articulatory role among the experiences, demands, and internal structures of various base organizations in urban settings. (Anria 2018, 34)

Framing alternatives

Relations with social movements affected party policy from when it assumed office in January 2006, as Morales met the anti-neoliberal claims put forward in massive protests, including with the partial nationalization of the hydrocarbon industry (with an increase in royalty payments for multinational companies), an agrarian reform, an anti-corruption law, and a call for a constituent assembly to establish the foundations of a plurinational state (Anria 2018). To a certain extent, MAS also continues to represent movement claims, in Parliament and in government, even if changes have happened over time. Elected on a radical programme, MAS proceeded to implement some of it through a constitutional process. Especially in the beginning, a radical democratic attitude prevailed, with various channels of communication opened for social movements of different types, particularly within the National Coordinator for Change. Once in power, the Morales administration was rhetorically very radical, with more ruptures in foreign than in economic policies, where various constraints pushed for continuity towards heterodox policies, with, however, high fiscal discipline. The partial nationalization of natural gas industries allowed for collecting resources to be invested in welfare services, even if unemployment and poverty are still high and land reform still limited.

While tensions certainly existed between MAS and the social movements, MAS' fluidity, informal features and absence of routinization leave wide room for manoeuvre for the social organizations allied with it. In many cases, these organizations maintain considerable autonomy from MAS, and they mobilize both for and against the government, placing limits on Morales' authority by mobilizing resources even if Morales does not approve (Anria 2018, 38–9). Also, in MAS, 'tensions emerge between the government, the parliamentary representatives, the party leadership, and the leaders and grassroots members of sponsoring organizations that configure the governing coalition' (Anria 2018, 38). In particular, as a ruling party, MAS has increasingly distanced itself from social movement organizations (Anria 2018, 35). Not by chance, the participation of representatives of social movement organizations in the legislature and executive has been reduced, even if it still remains significant (Zegada et al. 2008; Anria 2013).

Even when in power, MAS, however, maintained strong ties with its core constituency of coca growers, who were able to have some influence on agrarian policy, also expanding 'a network of informal alliances with base organizations' (Anria 2013, 36). This informality, with the exception only of the Pacto de Unidad active during the constitutional reform, has been seen as an effect of resistance to institutionalization, as party leaders fear that a formalization of linkages might transform MAS into a conventional party, 'jeopardizing the assembly-like (*asambleísta*) style of decision-making in grassroots organizations' (della Porta, Fernández et al. 2017, 170).

If power is increasingly concentrated in the hands of the leader Evo Morales, there are nevertheless still openings for representatives of the various social movements. Several of MAS' political leaders still reject the label of 'party', as they tend to consider parties to be divisive and fear institutionalization. Based on principles of self-representation of the masses,

> leaders do not want to speak 'for' their constituencies. Instead, they stress that they are spokespeople, or messengers, for their constituencies. That they do not intend to build a conventional party has much to do with this. While functioning as a ruling organization has pushed the MAS to institutionalize the party–movement relationships in some ways, its political core has clearly privileged the sustaining of political mobilization in regard to the institutionalization of the movement as a party. (Anria 2013, 23)

Social movements are especially capable of constructing veto coalitions, creating pressure through their mobilization capacity.

The analysis of candidate selection confirms a complex relation between the party and social movement organizations, with a consistently large number of representatives of social movement organizations in Parliament. In fact, around 70 per cent of MAS representatives in Congress in the legislature during 2009 to 2015 came from various rural and urban social movement organizations. Also, at the local level, 'while the capacity of grass-roots actors to generate decisions from below may initially seem limited, their influence should not be overlooked because decision-making is an interactive, negotiated, and contestatory process' (Anria 2013, 23). This happens through frequent consultation of representatives of grassroots organizations with the Regular National Congress, but also within ad hoc committees and with the president himself.

Conclusion

In sum, movement parties have emerged as neoliberalism challenged previous assets, and social movements expressed discontent with austerity policies. Especially when existing parties on the Left were perceived as moving towards the Right, and therefore unable to represent emerging claims, a de-freezing of the party system was reflected in declining trust and high electoral volatility. New parties then developed on the Left, having overlapping memberships with social movements, through processes of polarization and galvanization.

While the downward trend in party–movement relations had pushed scholars towards expectations of further separation, a new wave of movement parties emerged during the *anti-austerity protests*. This became visible, first, in Latin America in the 1990s, with the foundation of a party such as MAS in Bolivia, followed by a parallel move in Europe more than a decade later. In Southern Europe in particular, the neoliberal critical juncture set in motion a two-fold process that proved most important for a transformation of pre-existing party systems: on the one hand, new energies were mobilized; on the other, competitors (especially on the Left) weakened. New parties such as Podemos in Spain developed as inheritors of energies which grew during the wave of protest, but which were also frustrated by a lack of success in intense and lengthy mobilizing processes.

Also important were *traditions of social movement activity*. While civil society has been considered as weakly organized in Southern Europe (Gunther et al. 1995), it proved, however, very contentious, with high levels of unconventional mobilization. Here, too, resources for the creation of new parties were nurtured within social movements in different ways, and in different moments of the protest cycle against austerity measures in late neoliberalism that developed in each country. In Latin America as in Southern Europe, massive anti-austerity protests acted as critical junctures themselves, faced with the neoliberal crisis (della Porta 2015b).

The cycle of protest started with more conventional forms and within institutions, continued with massive and innovative repertoires of collective action, and then declined in terms of mobilization capacity, but had nonetheless a long-term *empowering effect*. Both in Latin America and in Europe, mobilizations have been indeed empowering – if there was no perceived institutional response, they in fact generated a contentious political culture. The protest cycle offered channels through which to articulate grievances and organize discontent, rather than reverting to apathy. On the contrary, the strong critique of the political class brought about intense politicization.

Electoral alternatives tended to develop, especially, in the *declining phases of the movements*. As protesting for months and years in the streets proved unsuccessful, various alternatives were explored. MAS and Podemos emerged from a double condition: the empowering effects of protest but also its decline faced with a lack of institutional response. The movement parties grew out of the decline of the other parties in the party systems, developing from a mix of institutional closure to movements' demands, but also electoral opportunities provided for by electoral de-alignment, while organizational resources grew within the protests.

The anti-austerity movements reflected, and at the same time strengthened, the *crisis of trust* in centre-left parties. While very critical of representative institutions, movement activists and sympathizers challenged especially the convergence of parties of the (centre) Right and the (centre) Left into a stigmatized bipartisanism with a corruptive impact on democracy. The main left-wing parties in Bolivia, much like the PSOE in Spain, were in fact perceived as having lost touch with their former constituencies and being no longer able to articulate a left-wing alternative to dominant neoliberal policies (della Porta, Andretta et al. 2016). A general *organizational weakness* of parties, even if coupled with traditional clientelist roots, was aggravated by their development as state structures, rather than being civil society-based (Gunther et al. 1995; Roberts 2015a).

An *unholy alliance of the centre-left with the right-wing parties* was all the more stigmatized given the long histories of polarized bipartisanism. During the crisis, evidence of corruption then increased a delegitimation of institutional politics. The declining differences, especially on socioeconomic issues, between the two major parties opened up a space for a new party on the Left. Protests spiralled, with *growing electoral volatility*, as the escalation in contentious politics was produced by and then fuelled a deep drop in trust. In both countries, the critical juncture of the neoliberal crisis produced, in fact, the breakdown of the party systems around which democracy had been constructed. The new parties were successful when they took over the *anti-austerity claims* that had been put forward during protest waves.

Given these conditions, some causal mechanisms worked towards the development of successful movement parties.

First of all, through *organizational appropriation*, movement activists occupied existing parties or created new ones. Through the exploitation of overlapping membership, Podemos grew from within a movement that had strongly mobilized a young generation heavily hit by unemployment and precarity. On the one hand, (young) activists attempted to try and test the electoral approach after other parties had been perceived as failing. On the other, participation in protests had deep transformative effects on party activists, who also acquired personal trust – or at least acceptance – from the social movement activists. In parallel, first the *cocaleros'* movement, and – later on – other movements, had a strong impact on MAS.

Additionally, through a mechanism of *galvanization*, the initial electoral victories acted as turning points. The successful movement parties proved, in fact, capable of exploiting this window of opportunity. Podemos participated in European elections that, given their proportional electoral system, were more favourable for achieving a first electoral success. Electoral successes tended then to be, to a certain extent, self-sustained as they themselves had transformative effects. The 8 per cent which the party obtained activated a virtuous circle, followed by a jump in resonance, not only by increasing recruitment but also by a different type of membership. Initial victories then had cumulative effects in terms of party transformations. The basis of supporters broadened beyond the movement activists, in two directions: to marginalized groups, traditionally not represented in the political system; but also to those who were previously members of centre-left and left-wing parties (such as PSOE and IU in Spain). It thus expanded from informed activists to excluded people, and also from the middle classes to the lower classes. In a similar way, the growth of MAS was accelerated by initial electoral success at the regional level, which then prompted a national development, adding new constituencies to the original *cocaleros* ones.

A sort of *reverse reputational effect* accelerated movement parties' success, as the critiques by those who were perceived as responsible for the suffering of the people gave credit to their enemies. The blame from stigmatized actors increased support and sympathy for the emerging parties. The delegitimation of the elites reduced, therefore, their capacity to resist the new party's rhetoric. Even virulent campaigns by the mass media against the new parties as populist and/or radical tended to increase sympathy for them. Bipartisan attacks against Podemos backfired. Accusations by the elites of the new party being Eurosceptic, anti-modern and culturally underdeveloped had the unwanted effect of legitimizing it. As dissent was stigmatized and protest repressed, the protesters gained increasing popular support. Austerity produced polarization, bringing about chances for solidarization between party activists and movement activists. Similarly, in the case of MAS, the attack upon the party, with open intervention by the United States, favoured the victory of Evo Morales.

Movement parties developed then with different degrees of proximity to, but also tensions with, social movements, as they competed in the electoral arena. At the *organizational* level, movement parties supported a participatory vision, even if they often transformed themselves the nearer they came to power. As for their *strategies*, the disappointment of their former voters with the centre-left parties has often created broad electoral opportunities for the new parties, with some tensions between the strategies of the square and strategies inside the institutions. With reference to the *framing* of the self and others, movement parties tend to reflect the movements' attempts to develop new subjectivities, as traditional definitions on the Left enter into tension with a perceived reshuffling of old cleavages and the emergence of new ones.

The research also points towards challenges for movement parties on the Left as, developing at the intersection between the barricades and the ballot box, these hybrid actors have to address several dilemmas. In their organizational structure, but also repertoires of action and framing, movement parties emerged as often split between their electorate and the movement activists, as well as between what is traditionally considered as the party apparatus and the party in office. On the plus side, social movement linkages provide for a structured constituency, block recruitment, committed activists and high identification. However, loyalty to a core movement can also reduce the appeal to a broader electorate, as well as the capacity to bridge different movements. Disruptive action can not only be difficult to sustain when the streets demobilize, but can also enter into tension with a necessary reputation for reliability and effectiveness within institutions. At the organizational level also, the innovative openings to rank and file as well as external activists can enter into tension with concerns for electoral effectiveness. The more the party approaches the institutions, the more realism prevails over utopian framing of the aims and means to achieve them. In addition, here as well, party victories are resisted by the establishment, both by their party opponent on the Right but also by their party competitors on the centre-left. It is exactly the more radical democratic innovations, in terms of participation and deliberation, that might fall victim to an institutionalization process.

5

Progressive Movements and Democratic Innovations: Some Conclusions

Born abruptly from a Facebook post by a single citizen calling for protests against a new tax raising fuel costs, in France the Gilets Jaunes *(GJ, 'Yellow Vests') have developed into a heterogeneous social movement calling for less social inequality and more direct participation by the people. The protest wave, which started on 17 November 2018 with 2,000 blockades all over France, has used quite radical repertoires of contention, spiralling with escalating police strategies that enraged, rather than scared, protesters. The very loose network that coordinated the protests appealed to the principle of direct democracy, with assembleary decision-making and a rejection of not only parties but also other associations as formal allies. With support from the public that opinion polls have estimated at a very high 70 per cent of citizens, and a parallel drop of trust in the president and his government (down to about 20 per cent), the* Gilets Jaunes *have obtained not only the withdrawal of the specific decision that had sparked the protests, but also the promise, by French President Emmanuel Macron, of some state intervention against social inequality (among which an increase in the minimum wage). Suspected of being infiltrated by the radical Right and the radical Left, alternatively presented as a new* Vendée, *coming from the periphery against the cosmopolitan centre; as a progressive 1968, with a combination of calls for justice and freedom; or even as a multifarious revolt, the movement of the* Gilets Jaunes *still engages in identity work. What is, however, most interesting for a movement that has been defined as prepolitical, is that, at the core of its claims, is*

*a participatory and deliberative conception of democracy, with specific
references to a citizen-initiated referendum and 'sortition chambers', as
public assemblies composed of people chosen by lot that would share
power with elected institutions.*

The *Gilets Jaunes* are merely the most recent example of increasing
calls for a democratic transformation from below that in France have
already been put forward by another massive wave of protest, La Nuit
Debout (Standing Night) (Felicetti and della Porta 2018). As observed in
this volume, democratic innovations have often been promoted by progressive social movements – that is, social movements oriented towards
implementing values of inclusion and social justice – but they have also
moved beyond them. Progressive social movements have been pushing
for a democratic deepening, conceptualizing and experimenting with
democracy. They have called for changes in democratic institutions as
well as prefiguring different forms of democracy and, in this way, they
have historically contributed to democratic innovations, which have
transformed institutions especially in moments of perceived challenges to
existing practices and values. Internally, social movements have engaged
in a continuous process of experimentation and social learning, with
protest cycles producing ever new democratic norms and practices. As
self-reflexive actors, progressive social movements have often singled
out the limitations of the concrete implementation of their normative
conceptions of democracy and tried to overcome them, without ever
finding a fully satisfactory way to address several dilemmas.

The democratic innovations I have analysed have developed in times
of crisis of really existing democracies that were based on established
parties, welfare and nation states. At the turn of the millennium, these
conditions were challenged, as neoliberal globalization, as well as other
general evolutions in contemporary democracies, fuelled a shift of power
from parties (and representative institutions) to the executive, from the
nation state to international governmental organizations, and from
the state to the market. This has accelerated the development of post-
democracies, based upon an elitist conception of electoral participation
for the mass of citizens and free lobbying for stronger interests, along
with low levels of state intervention on social inequality (Crouch 2003,
5). While mass, ideological political parties had in fact acted as channels
for citizens' participation, their decline has broken important linkages
between society and politics (della Porta, Fernández et al. 2017). Further,
capitalist transformations have weakened those channels of functional
representation via unions and interest groups that had supported societal
integration, bringing about in some cases even a criminalization of civil
society organizations (della Porta 2018).

In general, progressive social movements have put forward a participatory and deliberative conception of democracy, struggling to increase channels of access to institutions. The labour movement, as well as the women's movement, struggled for the expansion of voting rights up to universal suffrage (della Porta 2015b). Additionally, civil rights movements have pushed for expanding citizens' rights, urban movements for decentralization, student movements for participation in decisions about the educational system, and so on. Participation has therefore been established as an important democratic quality to counterbalance representation, but also to make democratic decisions more just and effective. Furthermore, discursive qualities have been counterpoised to majoritarian decision-making as important conditions for a democratic process (Polletta 2002). What is more, progressive social movements have also experimented internally with forms of direct participation, as well as high-quality deliberation, with ever more sophisticated techniques oriented towards inclusion.

While recognizing that a perfect balance between different democratic qualities can never be found, progressive social movements, as with other collective actors, have tried to balance efficacy with compliance to normative standards. Contextual conditions, filtered through traditions and learning processes, have influenced claims for institutional change as well as internal democratic practices (della Porta 2009). Specific interactions in different fields have also contributed to different conceptions within progressive social movements themselves – for instance, between trade unions and squatted youth centres, transnational networks and local groups, cooperatives and self-help groups (della Porta and Mattoni 2015).

What this volume has shown, however, is that the boundaries between institutional and non-institutional activities are quite porous, since social movements experiment with different conceptions of democracy also acting within institutions. In fact, social movements are not just 'strangers at the gate' (Tarrow 2012). To use Easton's (1953) metaphor, they have not waited for a gatekeeper to be activated, but have often penetrated the black box where institutional decisions are made. This happened through grassroots involvement in Constitution-making, referendums and electoral participation – the latter through the construction of political parties. As the empirical cases presented have revealed, progressive social movements do intervene in institutional politics, bringing with them substantive attention to policy changes, but also procedural attention towards the development of participatory and deliberative ways of achieving decisions. Under some conditions, their attempts might be successful in putting new topics on the agenda and even influencing democratic transformations, but also in practising new democratic repertoires in the internal life of social movements themselves.

In this concluding chapter, I will first summarize the democratic innovations from below that I have analysed in the three previous chapters. Then, returning to the theoretical questions presented in particular in the introductory chapter, I will review some main research results and arguments presented in the volume in the light of their contributions to two main fields of knowledge in the social sciences: social movement studies, with particular attention to social movement outcomes, and so-called empirical theories of democracy, with particular attention to democratic changes. I will end with some reflections on the way forward.

Innovating from below

Crises have been considered as important triggers for change, especially when there are historical experiences with direct democracy. As Altman (2019, 22) noted, 'elected representatives do not, by their own volition, give up their exclusive domain over the legislative agenda without a strong reason to do so. The adoption of citizen-initiated mechanisms of direct democracy tends to occur in times of political instability: times when, for one reason or another, lawmakers believed that a new page in a nation's history is being turned.

The research presented in this volume has pointed to the potential, in times of crisis, for progressive social movements to intervene at different stages of a process of democratic innovation. As observed by della Porta and Felicetti (2019), 'Social movements, together with other civil society actors, are at times co-producers of citizen-led democratic innovations. Unlike top-down democratic experiments, in which institutions and the interests they pursue are of primary importance, bottom-up ones, which give citizens the central stage, spring from protest and respond to the need for radical democratic reform.' In fact, democratic innovations from below have substantial potential to relieve the democratic stress we are currently experiencing. Developing in these intense moments, citizen-initiated mechanisms of direct democracy can strengthen the normative foundation of democracy – that is, freedom and equity among citizens – by empowering citizens, channelling social demands and defusing violence. Even when the results do not match the original goals of their promoters, they have positive spillover effects on democratic life affecting both 'the political game itself (by generating incentives for political consensus, moderating circumstantial majorities, and expanding the political playing field), and the relationship between representative institutions and the citizenry (by augmenting policy congruence, women's empowerment, civic participation, satisfaction with democracy, and broadening the topics subject to popular consideration)' (Altman 2019, 23).

The analysis of crowd-sourced constitutional processes has indicated that, in particular in times of crisis, social movements have some capacity to exert constitutive powers. The sociology of constitutions has pointed towards the general importance of constitutional processes, as well as towards changes in the conception and practice of Constitution-making. In moments of democratic malaise, the direct involvement of citizens in the writing and re-writing of constitutions is a way to restore collective identity. Reflecting the shift in constitutional thinking from a legalistic vision of constitutionalism as a technical process, to a participatory one oriented towards creating a founding moment, progressive social movements have in fact triggered constitutional processes in which citizens' participation in deliberative arenas has been considered to be necessary in order to construct normative agreements.

In Iceland and in Ireland, citizens' initiatives prompted some initial experiments in Constitution-making through the appointment of citizens assemblies, which have endowed themselves with instruments for interactions with the outside. Plural sources of information, civilized interactions, mutual respect, publicity and inclusive participation characterized the constitutional arenas in which citizens took part. Critical junctures as moments of crisis contributed to innovations in repertoires of progressive movements by pushing them to engage in the writing of the basic norms and rules for society. Social movements then acquired constituent power by calling for the constitutional protection of public goods against privatization, and also for the recognition of the value of the participation of citizens in public life (Bailey and Mattei 2013). In doing so, those progressive movements have also created public spheres that, as Habermas (1989 [1962]) has influentially stated, are public in the triple sense of being open to the public, venues for acting in public, and devoted to the discussion of public issues against an increasing retrenchment of the public itself through the privatization trend dominant within the liberal constitutional order. Constitutional processes work, then, as a potential moment of regeneration of the political against the apolitical message of neoliberalism (Mouffe 2018).

Referendums and other mechanisms of direct democracy have also been more and more used in times of democratic malaise, as a response to the increasing mistrust of representative institutions. While the uses of referendums have varied greatly – as too has their democratic quality – progressive social movements have at times perceived the potential advantages (in terms of legitimacy, but also of efficiency) of handing the right to decide directly to citizens. On issues as contested as the conception of public services or national independence, instruments of direct democracy can contribute not only to legitimating public decision through participation, but also to enriching public life. As in the cases I analysed, the participation of social movement organizations in campaigns along the referendum process contributed substantially to increasing not only the number of participants but also the plurality of the arguments, by multiplying the public arenas in which the referendums' issues have been discussed.

In participating in referendum processes, progressive social movements increase the capacity for referendums effectively to extend the constitutional safeguards against the excessive power of elected representatives (Qvortrup 2014c), balancing delegation with participation (Marxer and Pállinger 2007). Protest activities organized by broad networks of social movement activists help in the formation of citizens' wills, contributing to improving the quality of public life also by increasing citizens' abilities to make considered judgements (della Porta, O'Connor et al. 2017a). In Italy, as in Catalonia and Scotland, processes of direct democracy have been prompted by the opening up of political opportunities, but also by their closing down in the representative institutions. Regardless of their final results, social movements' engagement in referendums seems to have empowered progressive ideas by making topics more relevant to the public and improving citizens' awareness. Referendums from below – involving a larger degree of extra-institutional mobilization, either through citizen-initiated referendums or by the wide-scale appropriation of state-endorsed ones – are, in fact, particularly conducive to broadening participation and deliberation.

Finally, in moments of crisis, movement parties have emerged and achieved broad support in a very short time-span. As late neoliberalism triggered a crisis of political legitimacy through the evident lack of capacity (or willingness) of public institutions to ensure citizenship rights, the ensuing electoral earthquake opened up spaces for new parties on the Left as well as on the Right. On the Left, progressive social movements have triggered the development of political parties that not only represented their claims, but also were influenced by their conceptions and practices of democracy. Besides de-freezing once-frozen political cleavages, the growing discontent was expressed in the electoral arenas not only (or mainly) by abstention, but rather by the emergence of hybrid movement parties. As centre-left parties moved towards the centre, accepting the main tenets of neoliberal trust in the free market and abandoning social protection, and as calls for social justice and against inequality spread among the citizens through massive campaigns of protest, new parties emerged on the Left. While sometimes entering into tension with their initial base of supporters, they expanded their capacity to attract disappointed voters from the centre-left parties in disarray. While therefore increasing scepticism towards representative democracy that produced the expectation of anti-political developments, movement parties (for instance, in Spain or in Bolivia) testify to attempts to bring into representative institutions participatory and deliberative ideals nurtured by progressive social movements. Anti-austerity protests therefore had empowering effects too in terms of democratic innovations, experimented with in the internal life of the movement parties, but also innovating within the public institutions they gained access to. As protest campaigns spread a contentious political culture, and the strong critique of the political class brought about intense politicization, party alternatives developed, especially in the declining phases of the movements.

The progressive movement parties I have studied grew out of the decline of the centre-left parties, fuelled by a mix of institutional closure to movements' demands, but also the opening of electoral opportunities given electoral de-alignment and increasing volatility. In the cases of Podemos in Spain and MAS in Bolivia, given a sharp drop in trust in the centre-left parties, left-wing movement activists and sympathizers, even if critical of representative forms of democracy, took the opportunity of occupying a political and electoral space that had been left empty, as they successfully built support by putting forward anti-austerity claims developed during the protest cycle. Mechanisms of organizational appropriation allowed for the occupation of these institutional channels, while initial electoral victories galvanized movement activists who were in search of new repertoires of action, given the insufficiency of street protests in obtaining the demanded changes. In fact, their electoral successes were facilitated by a reverse reputational effect, as the attacks by political and mass media actors, who were considered to be part of the neoliberal elite, contributed to focus attention and sympathies on the new movement parties. In all cases, while adapting to representative political institutions, progressive movement parties supported participatory and deliberative visions at the organizational level, maintained disruptive and unconventional repertoires of action and reflected movements' frames and claims.

Conditions and limits for democratic innovations

The crowd-sourced constitutionalism, referendums from below and movement parties that I have analysed sprang up under conditions of deep crisis, from progressive social movements, with claims for social justice and democratic deepening. These movements appropriated political opportunities which they themselves contributed to generating, occupying what they perceived as empty spaces in institutional politics. They are certainly worth studying, because – as Boaventura de Sousa Santos (2014, 241) suggested – we need to develop a 'sociology of emergences' able to 'identify and enlarge signs of possible future experiences, under the guide of tendencies and latencies, that are actively ignored by hegemonic rationality and knowledge'. The construction of alternative futures or possible utopias requires, in fact, an art of organizing hope towards the building of realist utopias (Dinerstein 2014, 1; Gastil and Wright 2018). Studying democratic innovations is therefore important in order to understand how changes from below might happen through the development of alternative practices (Reiter 2017).

My research indicates that democratic innovations are far from easy to pursue, and the solutions they suggest in relation to participatory and deliberative democracy often imperfect. While empowering citizens, they are, however, subject to backlashes from many and powerful enemies, in the forms of both taming and repressing. First and foremost, they need the development of progressive coalitions between institutional actors and social movement actors. While opportunities are appropriated and resources mobilized in action, the relations between movements and institutions proved most important for the development of innovations. These relations are, however, often precarious, and often put at risk by, among other things, the difficulties in sustaining pressure from the street, as well as the resilience of the establishment.

The US could provide, to a certain extent, a contrast case to the ones I studied. While the Occupy movement has clearly pointed towards the need for participatory and deliberative conceptions of democracy, no broad-scale transformations have been promoted in the institutional political system. Notwithstanding the lack of crowd-sourced constitutional attempts, referendums from below or movement parties, some experiments with different conceptions of democracy have been launched. Among them, the Town Hall meetings have tried to bridge representative with direct democracy, and the Oregon Citizens' Initiative Review Commission has in some ways inspired the Irish deliberative constitutional process; and groups like Move On or Indivisible have attempted to transform party politics. These processes have, however, developed with no connection to anti-austerity protests, which had in fact, in the US, a more marked scepticism about institutional politics (della Porta 2015b). A brief look at them shows that, while certainly interesting in their experimentation with participatory and deliberative conceptions, they have more limited innovative aspiration than the ones I have analysed in contexts where social movements have been involved in their promotion.

A traditional form of bringing citizens into institutional decisions, often cited when talking about democratic innovation in the US, are Town Hall meetings, still taking place in about 1,000 towns in New England. Here, assemblies open to all voters are called yearly to decide on priorities in public spending. Before the meeting, which can last for an entire day, a board publishes an agenda of issues to discuss and vote upon (Reiter 2017). While research comparing participation in Town Hall meetings indicated that this is lower with higher educational level and income level (Bryan 2004), and higher in small-size polities, their scope is quite limited and so is the quality of participation and deliberation.

The aim of combining democracy by lot with electoral procedures found institutional recognition in the Oregon Citizens' Initiative Review Commission (CIRC), established in 2011 by the Oregon Legislature, which was in fact a point of inspiration for the Irish constitutional process. Here, as well, from the procedural point of view, the process relies upon the creation of groups of lay citizens, based on random selected representatives and then corrected in order to match the demographics of the Oregon electorate in terms of age, gender, ethnicity, education, partisan affiliation and place of residence. The five-day gathering is then devoted to debates among the panellists about a statewide initiative (Gastil et al. 2014). Here, too, in the process, neutral experts, along with proponents and opponents, provide testimony to the panellists; this information is then used to write a statement identifying key facts and arguments relevant to the initiative. As Gastil et al. (2014) summarized:

> at the end of their deliberations, each panel of citizens wrote a page of analysis about their assigned initiative for the official Oregon State Voters' Pamphlet, which the Secretary of State delivered along with mail-in ballots to every registered voter in the state. Such widespread use allows the Citizens' Statements produced by the CIR to play a prominent role in voter education and subsequently influence the outcome of binding governmental decisions. Initially promoted by a civic organization, Healthy Democracy Oregon, the process developed with a CIR Commission now empowered as an official state agency. The Oregon CIR is, in fact, the first deliberative innovation established by law that grants a random sample of the public substantial political power.

While aiming at offering citizens a dispassionate account of a public topic, CIRCs have, however, limited effects in terms of enlarging public debate. Differently from the crowd-sourced constitutional processes, the CIRC aims only at presenting '"neutral information developed by peers" to citizens, using pedagogical language and providing a fair treatment of both sides of a contentious issue' (Altman 2019, 185). As Gastil et al. (2014) noted:

the CIR was intended to provide informed, non-partisan information that voters could use when deciding how to vote. This was viewed as a supplement to the more narrowly focused explanatory statement and financial impact statements that already appeared in the state's Voters' Pamphlet, while also serving as an alternative to the more inflamed rhetoric that came to voters through paid campaign messages in that same Pamphlet.

Neither can anything similar to a movement party be singled out in the US, where we found instead attempts to develop processes of collective lobbying of decision-makers, including visible mass activities, for progressive aims. The best-known and most influential example is MoveOn, which emerged with an online petition launched by two tech entrepreneurs during the tense debate on President's Clinton impeachment in 1998, and is now a nonprofit organization focusing on education and advocacy, providing tools for civic engagement for progressive communication campaigns. The aim of making the ordinary citizens' voice more audible is pursued through the running of virtual phone banks, crowd-sourced TV ad production, and the online coordination of massive telephone and door-to-door canvassing for primaries and elections. A federal political action committee, financed through very small donations, supports progressive policies and candidates at elections, through developing tools for telephone calls, phone parties and in-district meetings, as well as ads and counter-information. MoveOn-related ActionForum.com also promotes public debates online. While endorsing some candidates – prominently Barack Obama and Bernie Sanders – MoveOn is not developing any party structure, and the same can be said for the Democratic Socialists of America (DSA), which presents itself as not a party, but a political and activist organization, which also endorses some candidates.

Emerging as a reaction to the election of Donald Trump to the presidency, Indivisible also works rather as a lobby, targeting Members of Congress. Formed by professionals with experience within Congress, the group has described its strategy as inspired by the Tea Party, especially in its choice of targeting individual Members of Congress (MoCs) at local level, and of developing a defensive strategy aimed at stalling the president's agenda, especially on the most important symbolic issues. The group advocated the use of existing political channels, focusing pressure on institutional targets, especially MoCs, through collective action. Defensive and locally focused, the strategy advocated 'working with fellow challengers, choosing specific and narrow goals and engaging in persistent and visible action' (Brooker 2018). The use of lobbying, even if in visible and collective forms, is a decision that matches the social basis of the group's promoters. The founders of what has been dubbed 'the

Tea Party of the Left' are in fact 'well-connected political insiders seeking to manipulate conventional politics to advance a progressive agenda. . . . [they] felt that, given their know-how as a group of political insiders, they could both inspire action and channel it based on what they'd seen work in Washington' (Brooker 2018).

In sum, while participation and deliberation are important qualities in these initiatives as well, the lack of interaction between social movements and institutional actors is reflected in limited aspirations towards emancipatory aims.

Democracy and the populist Right

Not only do democratic innovations therefore seem sensitive to certain contextual conditions, but also calls for participation and deliberation, such as those I have analysed, are developed by collective actors that have inclusive and emancipatory conceptions of citizenship. In this sense, the progressive innovations that I have analysed are not to be confused with the challenges that right-wing populists bring to democracy. While movement parties have emerged also on the Right, and right-wing actors have promoted constitutional reforms appealing to the people, as well as calling for referendums, the vision of democracy they refer to is very different from the participatory and deliberative one I have addressed in this volume.

Certainly, social movements and movement parties, like any other type of party, can also emerge on the regressive side of the political spectrum. In general, 'Far-right collective actors are part of a large mobilization process by which they managed to politicize issues previously neglected by mainstream parties (e.g. immigration, minority issues, "law and order", welfare chauvinism; . . .). In this respect, the far right has been read through the lens of those economic and cultural grievances brought about by the process of globalization' (Castelli Gattinara and Pirro 2018, 7). These actors have, however, expressed very different types of critique of liberal democracy from the progressive actors I have focused upon.

In reaction to the financial crisis, movement parties have emerged, or been strengthened, on the radical Right (Caiani and Cisar 2019). For sure, the ensuing political turmoil, affecting also the centre-right parties, has given an advantage to their competitors on the extreme Right, especially those bridging traditional right-wing positions with populist rhetoric. While, in some cases, these parties and movement organizations also complain about the limits of representative democracy, both their internal practices and their proposals for change differ from those of the progressive movement parties we have analysed. First and foremost, the radical Right movement parties have linked the socioeconomic crisis to the opening of borders and the alleged threat that migrants pose to national identity (Wodak 2015). While criticizing the establishment and the 'old parties', right-wing movement parties support conservative and authoritarian values, singling out groups of citizens (first of all, migrants and other minorities) who should be excluded from the definition of the people.

In general, the very conception of relations with movements is different from the one we found on the Left, as they tend to be either seen as subordinated to the party hierarchy, or kept at some distance, while the linkages between parties and movements are often less explicit and more contested on the Right than on the Left. For instance, Alternative für Deutschland (AFD, 'Alternative for Germany') not only had a group of ultra-liberal economists, rather than a social movement, at its origins, but also initially criticized the xenophobic PEGIDA (Patriotische Europäer gegen die Islamisierung des Abendlandes, 'Patriotic Europeans Against the Islamization of the Occident') movement, also maintaining ambivalent relations later on (Schwoerer 2019; Weisskircher and Berntzen 2019). Similarly complex were the relations with social movements of the UK Independence Party (UKIP), which emerged in 1993 as a fringe party within elite circles focusing on specific concerns relating to UK membership of the EU. UKIP 'has been a vehicle for a range of different and, at times, competing movements with different and occasionally conflicting interests and ideas' (Hanna and Busher 2019, 47). Even the Front National in France, despite being accompanied during its inception in the 1980s by a larger reactionary network of grassroots organizations, has nonetheless had ambivalent relations with the right-wing movement that developed outside it, with only weak organizational links to it (Frigoli and Ivaldi 2019, 70). In sum, the very definition of movement organizations is deceptive for groups which are considered as at the root of the movement parties on the Right. All in all, even if with some exceptions, the substitutive relationship between the electoral and the protest arenas that has been noted on the Right but not on the Left (Hutter 2014, 138–9) has, if not hampered, certainly shaped the interactions between movements and parties.

Movements and parties on the Right also differ from those on the Left in terms both of the content of their criticism of liberal democracy, and in their internal organizational structures, which build upon strong and personalized leadership rather than on citizens' participation (della Porta 2017b). As recent research has demonstrated, the anti-gender movement, which claims to defend freedom of speech, thought and conscience, has politicized religious actors and discourse, targeted women's and LGBTQ rights, and attacked, in particular, sexual and reproductive rights, same-sex marriage, adoption by same-sex parents, sexual education, the protection of women and gender minorities from violence, and new reproductive technologies, as well as what they consider to be sexual permissiveness (Paternotte and Kuhar 2018). Developed within the Catholic Church and promoted by right-wing movement organizations and parties, these ideas have been bridged to the defence of traditional values and identities. In this discursive strategy, the rhetorical toolkit also includes the spreading of fear against minority groups, who are portrayed as perpetrators of attacks upon the nation (Fassin 2014; Stambolis-Ruhstorfer and Tricou 2018). While there is an appeal to 'return the word to the people' – including at times the call for popular referendums – anti-gender activists promote an exclusive understanding of the people through the binary opposition of good and evil (Paternotte and Kuhar 2018). The claim of resisting attempts to curtail the freedom of speech of a 'silent majority', self-represented as victims of discrimination, is accompanied by attacks on equal access to rights by LGBTQ individuals and women, with a rejection even of laws against violence towards women and sexual minorities (Bracke et al. 2018; Mayer and Sauer 2018). While the anti-gender movement has been said to instrumentally adopt protest strategies developed by their adversaries (even copying the carnivalesque atmosphere of Gay Pride, with music and disco music), it continues to rely more on lobbying by powerful (often Catholic conservative) associations, as is the case of 'La Manif pour tous' in France or the *sentinelle* in Italy (Garbagnoli 2018; Stambolis-Ruhstorfer and Tricou 2018). Research on racist and xenophobic movement organizations has pointed towards similar appeals to the people – coupled, however, with hierarchical structures and exclusivist framing (Caiani and della Porta 2019).

Additionally, right-wing movements and right-wing parties in power have promoted constitutional changes in what has been defined as populist constitutionalism (Kaidatzis 2018). In general, right-wing populists have been said to be impatient with procedures (Müller 2017, 590), aiming rather at reducing checks and balances. Distrust for laws and regulations has found expression in a compression of civil rights, disempowering rather than empowering citizens. Populist constitutionalism also differs from popular constitutionalism in that the 'will of the people' finds expression in the former in confirmatory plebiscites rather than in the grassroots participation proposed by the latter.

In general, first of all, while the participatory democracy proposed by social movements points towards horizontal relations with an empowerment of the people, the populist conception put forward by right-wing actors 'does not require that mass constituencies engage in collective action at all, beyond the individual act of casting a ballot in national elections or popular referendums. Although both forms of popular subjectivity contest established elites, social movements mobilize such contestation from the bottom-up, whereas populism typically mobilizes mass constituencies from the top-down behind the leadership of a counter-elite' (Roberts 2015). While, certainly, there is also dissatisfaction on the Right with what is seen as an elitist trend, the people are there perceived in an exclusive and nativist form as the *ethnos*, rather than as the empowered citizens that we have seen as at the basis of progressive movements' visions.

Deliberative democracy is also far from technocratic solutions, which aim at reducing the range of decisions in the hands of elected politicians and handing them to an elite of self-appointed experts. Rather, deliberative democracy as proposed by progressive movements relies upon the knowledge, commitment and goodwill of citizens, who are trusted to be able to make good decisions. As the competence of experts is challenged by processes of politicization of science (della Porta, Keating et al. 2018), critiques of democratic accountability and praise for technical knowledge are not a solution to the democratic stress. Rather, technocratic visions risk reducing not only the legitimacy of decision-makers, but also the efficacy of decisions, as they do not help individuals learn to be good citizens, but rather push them to the margins and make them more responsive to populist leaders.

In what follows, I will refer to the contributions of this analysis for social movement studies as well as empirical democratic theories.

Democratic innovations as social movement outcomes

The democratic innovations addressed in this volume can be analysed within the social science literature on social movement outcomes. While initially a marginal subject in research on social movements, various types of outcomes (from policy to biographical ones) have attracted more and more interest (Bosi et al. 2016, for a review). Research has considered procedural impacts – as social movements achieve acceptance and come to be recognized as a legitimate counterpart by their opponents – and substantive impacts – such as advantages and concessions to their claims (Kitschelt 1986). Movements might produce structural impacts, changing political institutions, and sensitizing impacts, influencing political debate (Kriesi 2004) as well as culture, contributing to political socialization (Giugni 2004). While assessing the outcomes of movements is certainly not an easy task, given the complex interactions during long-lasting processes, as well as the plurality of tactics used by movements themselves (della Porta and Diani 2006, ch. 9), discussions concerning what determines their outcomes have been central to the debate on social movements.

A number of social movement characteristics have frequently been cited as particularly influential. While some research has singled out a minimalist strategy ('thinking small'), the adoption of direct action, and a centralized and bureaucratic organization as favouring success, others have pointed instead towards broad claims, radical action strategies and horizontal organization as more propitious for challenging actors (Gamson 1990 [1975]; Piven 2006). Prefigurative strategies, sometimes counterposed to instrumental action, can, however, be effective in experimenting with new ideas (della Porta 2018). If some scholars have opposed prefigurative politics to political strategy (e.g. Smucker 2014), others have instead considered it as a specific form of strategic action that links means and aims. In this sense, prefiguration might rather be considered as 'the most strategic means for bringing about the social change' as it removes 'the temporal distinction between the struggle in the present and the goal in the future; instead the struggle and the goal, the real and the ideal, become one in the present' (Maeckelbergh 2011, 2, 4). Beyond the conception of ethical practices (in which the means are not in tension with the aims), prefiguration is linked to the experimentation with concrete utopias (Gordon 2017), 'reaching ahead and acting as if a goal has already been achieved' (Swain 2017, 6). As community is built within a sort of laboratory of experience (Yates 2015), sites of protests such as camps might be able to assert a 'counter-temporality' (Petrick 2017, 1), thus experimenting with potential futures.

Not only, then, do social movements combine different strategies, but their effects vary, depending upon institutional constraints and opportunities as well as the availability of allies and their own power (Cress and Snow 2000). In fact, social movement organizations often operate in conjunction with political parties and even public institutions, so that 'the outcome of bargaining is not the result of the characteristics of either party, but rather is the function of their resources relative to each other, their relationships with third parties, and other factors in the environment' (Burstein et al. 1995, 280).

The analysis of democratic innovations points towards the importance of social movements as incubators of emerging ideas about democracy. In their use of a broad range of action repertoires, entering political institutions is an option that becomes particularly interesting when other forms – such as protest in the streets (or the squares) – are exhausted, but there is still the perception of broad support from public opinion. Additionally, the chances of success increase when social movements are able to build broad coalitions, with ensuing politicization and a scale-shift in framing, from specific policy claims to the meta-issue of democracy. As for the political context, democratic innovations seem to be favoured by some openings of opportunities, but also fuelled as opportunities close down.

The paths through which challenges might obtain (small or large) concessions are complex. In fact, 'changes do not happen in a direct modality or in a linear fashion: as their ideas are vulgarized and domesticated, the early risers in a protest cycle often disappear from the scene. But a portion of their message is distilled into common frameworks of public or private culture while the rest is ignored' (Tarrow 1994, 185). In this process, there are forward steps and backward steps, moments in which public policies approach the demands made by social movements, and others in which the situation deteriorates. Social movements frequently obtain successes in the early phases of mobilization, but this triggers opposing interests and often a polarization in public opinion, or even the creation of counter-movements.

In fact, social movements address various steps in the decision-making process: the emergence of new issues; the elaboration and implementation of new legislation; and the effects of public policies in alleviating the conditions of those mobilized by collective action (Kolb 2007). Their results have, therefore, been assessed at various levels of responsiveness within the political system: '*access responsiveness*', referring to authorities' availability to listen to claim-makers; '*agenda responsiveness*', when demands are then put on the public agenda; '*policy responsiveness*', when policies are adopted which are congruent with the movement's claims; '*output responsiveness*', when those policies are implemented; and '*impact responsiveness*', when they are effective in addressing movements' claims (Schumaker 1975, 494–5, emphasis added).

All these levels have their relevance when assessing the responsiveness to demands for democratic innovations. Past research has pointed towards the specific tensions emerging in social movement participation in various mechanisms, such as participatory budgeting or citizens' juries or, even more recently, sortition chambers (citizens' assemblies formed by lot), which have been experimented with in order to increase participatory and deliberative institutional qualities. As Julien Talpin noted:

> First, their adversarial cognitive frames, seeing protest and bargaining as the means of promoting their cause, might not fit the more collaborative attitude required in democratic innovations. Also, activists might not acquire the skills required by participatory engagement: protest implies capacities other than the facilitation and organization of democratic processes. Finally, the most powerful SMOs [Social Movement Organizations] might not be ready for engagement in institutions taking place mostly at the local level. (Talpin 2015, 783)

These tensions notwithstanding, the involvement of social movements within participatory experiments is an important condition for their success (Talpin 2015). As in the cases I analysed, social movement organizations do in fact participate as institutional designers, promoters and practitioners of various democratic experiments (Dryzek 2010, 8–9). In doing this, they tend to improve participation, which is a fundamental condition for high-quality deliberation (Hauptmann 2001, 408; see also della Porta and Felicetti 2017 and della Porta 2019). As empirical research points towards the difficulties of institutional experiments in involving citizens (Ryfe 2002, 365) and to the risk of reproducing (or even increasing) social inequalities (something already observed in other forms of political participation), social movements might help to broaden the social distribution of participants (Smith 2009, 41ff.), with greater involvement by the popular classes (as in the participatory budget, see Gret and Sintomer 2005, 77; Baiocchi and Ganuza 2016). Additionally, inputs from below tend to improve the deliberative working of democratic innovations by playing a 'countervailing power' in reducing the potential dominance of some groups, given asymmetries in resources, knowledge and oratory skills (Fung and Wrights 2003). Progressive social movements might also increase public awareness and ensure public authorities are held accountable in the implementation of the results of democratic innovations, so empowering new democratic arenas (Talpin 2015, 784). Research has highlighted a generally low level of power attribution to these participatory experiments. As Graham Smith (2009, 17) noted, empirical evidence suggests that 'the deep scepticism expressed by citizens about their capacity to affect the decision-making process is often justified. . . . The prevailing division of powers between public authorities and citizens is far from challenged.' It is, in particular, still unclear how participatory experiments relate to those formal institutions that organize representation along territorial lines, and 'how deliberative procedures themselves might operate within both secondary associations and more formal political institutions' (Johnson 1998, 175–6). In this context, social movements put pressure on the authorities so that decisions made 'from below' are implemented by the administration (Santos 2005).

The research presented in this volume also points towards the importance of political innovations in some specific moments of widespread crisis. At the origin of social movement studies, the Chicago School addressed changes as happening through the sudden breaking of established paths, the reproduction of ruptures, and their stabilization. Collective behaviour was the concept used to define forms of social behaviour in which 'usual conventions cease to guide social action and people collectively transcend, bypass or subvert established institutional patterns and structures' (Turner and Killian 1987 [1974, 1957], 3). Even if the collapsing of social movements and crowds into a common category has been very much criticized, some insights of that approach could be usefully discussed in order to explain social movements in extraordinary times. Not by chance, this approach has been revisited during the Great Recession. While, since the 1970s, social movement studies have in fact looked at stable democracies, within analytic approaches that aimed at embedding movements in normal political circumstances, there are, however, times and places in which protests and social movements are emerging phenomena (Johnston 2018). In fact, as symbolic interactionist approaches had put it, social movements trigger social change by the spreading of emergent norms (Turner 1996) that, by defining 'what's going on here', 'guide new and different ways that participants express their attitudes, beliefs, and values' (Johnston 2018, 8).

While research on protests has focused on long waves (Markoff 2016) as well as short(er) cycles (Tarrow 1989) as analytic concepts, an emerging concern in social movement studies with 'great transformations' triggering big mobilizations (della Porta 2015b) can be noticed. The reflection on the relevance of some specific moments as catalysts for change speaks to the capacity of social movements to contribute to emerging norms by breaking routine and introducing new ethical concerns (Wagner Pacifici 2017). Although still largely a silence in social movement studies, protests as momentous events have been reflected upon, in particular by research looking at contentious politics as triggering an intensification of the perception of time (della Porta 2017a). As Mark Beissinger noted, analysing *extraordinary times*, protest events are in fact 'contentious and potentially subversive practices that challenge normalized practices, modes of causation, or systems of authority' (Beissinger 2002, 14). In sum, the research confirms that, in the cases I have analysed, the perception of a crisis as a condition for, and at the same time effect of, a broad wave of protests has been pivotal in the development of alternative practices and conceptions of democracy, and the attempt to put them into practice within political institutions. The crisis has, in fact, produced voids that social movements tried to fill.

Institutional change in empirical theories of democracy

In political science, empirical democratic theory is a definition used to distinguish empirically based, middle-range theories of democracy from normative theories. Empirical theories of democracy have traditionally focused on really existing democratic institutions. In doing so, they have tended to normatively legitimate a specific liberal conception founded on representation and majoritarian decision-making, even if tempered by various forms of checks and balances. As David Held (2006, 166) noted:

Their 'realism' entailed conceiving of democracy in terms of the actual features of Western polities. In thinking of democracy in this way, they recast its meaning and, in so doing, surrendered the rich history of the idea of democracy to the existent. Questions about the nature and appropriate extent of citizen participation, the proper scope of political rule and the most suitable spheres of democratic regulation – questions that have been part of democratic theory from Athens to nineteenth-century England – are put aside, or, rather, answered merely by reference to current practice. The ideals and methods of democracy become, by default, the ideals and methods of the existing democratic systems. Since the critical criterion for adjudicating between theories of democracy is their degree of 'realism', models which depart from, or are in tension with, current democratic practice can be dismissed as empirically inaccurate, 'unreal' and undesirable.

The definition of democracy is, however, ever debated in the scientific field, as well as in the public sphere. Even classical normative definitions underline the legitimating role of citizens as well as the importance of dialogue and consensus. Really existing democracies (Dahl 2000) combine, in fact, in their institutional assets, different conceptions, as 'the history of real democracies has always involved tension and conflict' (Rosanvallon 2006, 11). The emphasis placed on elections often risks obfuscating the fact that even electoral accountability, to be effective, requires critical citizens who make governors accountable – in fact, 'When the electoral institution is chosen as the institution characterising democratic regimes the much more important presence of a sphere that is both public and distinct from the regimes is obscured. Deprived of this, deprived that is of open public discourse, and despite being governed by persons regularly elected, such a regime could only misleadingly be called democratic' (Pizzorno 2010, xiii). To be accountable, democratic institutions need, in fact, a set of controls – what Rosanvallon calls counter-democracy, that is: 'a particular form of political intervention that involves neither decision making nor exercise of the will, but is still a fundamental aspect of the democratic process' (Rosanvallon 2006, 40). A circuit of surveillance (or vigilance) over the action of the representatives is anchored outside state institutions within plural public spheres and multiple associations (Rosanvallon 2006). Through self-reflexive practices, democracy is in a permanent process of definition and redefinition (Eder 2010). Democratic innovations, such as the ones I have discussed, have highlighted some democratic qualities that balance representation through participation, and majoritarian decision-making through discursive deliberative practices.

In political theory, the dominant liberal (or bourgeois) model of democracy is in fact challenged by other conceptions, variously labelled as: participatory democracy, stressing the importance of participation (Pateman 1970; Polletta 2002); strong democracy, with an enhanced role for citizens (Barber 1984); or associative democracy, with a special role given to public interest groups (among others, Perczynski 2000). In addition to participation, the importance of deliberation is stressed in conceptions of discursive democracy or communicative democracy (Young 1996; Dryzek 2000), and the need for social rights in welfare democracy (Fitzpatrick 2002). Historically, various institutions and actors have contributed to balancing different democratic qualities, maintaining democratic legitimacy.

In periods of stability, empirical theories of democracy have addressed the context for democratic governance, often pointing towards socioeconomic preconditions, but also certain institutional forms, as facilitating democratic consolidation. Constitutions have anchored functional and geographical divisions of power and citizenship rights within nation states; institutions of direct democracy have been considered as ways to complement delegation with some participation in specific (often limited) forms and on allowed topics; political parties have been considered as the most important bi-frontal institutions in bridging the state and civic society. Oriented by the assumption of an independence of the political from other spheres of social action, the empirical theories of democracy have given little consideration to extra-institutional actors. In fact, even in the social science literature I surveyed on constitutionalism, referendums and political parties, the main approaches focused on the role of experts, elites and elected politicians. Constitutions were considered to be technical legal matters, referendums as dominated by elites, political parties as more and more focused on institutions and less and less rooted in society.

Recent evolutions have, nevertheless, been addressed – first of all, through the observation of an acceleration of constitutional processes, the multiplication of referendums and the emergence of new parties. Second, research has explained these trends as an effect of democratic malaise and an expression of attempts to rebuild trust in institutions. Thus, research on constitutionalism included outsiders as relevant actors, research on referendums suggested the potential role of public opinion, and research on political parties looked at external and internal linkages.

These trends opened up spaces for interaction between social movement studies and empirical theories of democracy. In fact, as already mentioned, the concepts and theories used to explain the relations between established and non-established actors, conventional and unconventional forms of political participation, and contentious and non-contentious politics are limited in social movement studies as, here too, a sort of autonomy from institutions has been (explicitly or implicitly) assumed. The research presented in this volume shows instead their unexpected hybridization, with the penetration of social movements within institutions. While this is not a new phenomenon – suffice it to think about the institutional penetration of the labour movements – this trend has certainly been accelerated in the Great Recession.

Empirical theories of democracy tend also to stress continuities, looking at ways in which institutions structure behaviour, cleavages are frozen, and political socialization reproduces (or not) democratic values. Not only constitutions, but also public policies, have been considered as establishing path-dependent reproduction – or, at the best, gradual, incremental adaptation. Time has been considered especially in what William Sewell (1996) has defined as teleological temporality, with assumptions about big historical trends, such as democratic consolidation or even democratic deepening.

The research I have presented in this volume addresses, instead, times of multiple crises and sudden changes. As times of transition to democracy (O'Donnell and Schmitter 1986), these are under-structured times, in the sense that structures are no longer able to constrain events. Recent times have, in fact, been defined as momentous: 'Great Transformation', 'Great Recession', as well as 'Great Regression' have been frequently used short-cut terms to characterize the period following the financial breakdown of 2008. Moments of rupture such as the ones we are living in are most important in defining new paths, as 'What is important are the significant *breaks* – where old lines of thought are disrupted, older constellations displaced, and elements, old and new, are regrouped around a different set of premises and themes' (Hall 1980, 33). Not by chance, references to special moments as well as momentous events have been more and more frequent as calls for what was expected to be routine protests triggered portentous waves of contentious politics. In the language of political activism, a momentum is now evoked as an act that dares to challenge existing structures, through massive support and at great velocity (della Porta 2018).

Reference to moments of rapid transformations can indeed be found in different sociological analyses addressing institutional change. In particular, in neo-institutional approaches, *critical juncture* is the concept most often used to describe times of deep transformation. It is defined as '(1) a major episode of institutional innovation, (2) occurring in distinct ways, (3) and generating an enduring legacy' (Collier and Munck 2017, 2). In their influential analysis of political incorporation of the lower classes in Latin America, David Collier and Ruth Collier reflected on 'a type of discontinuous political change in which critical junctures "dislodge" older institutional patterns' (1991, 36). While the term 'critical juncture' has been quite stretched to cover a heterogeneous range of phenomena, it convincingly points towards the need to distinguish, also in the analysis of contentious politics, between times of continuity and times of change, normal times and intense times. Among those who have studied the sudden transformations in contentious politics, Kenneth Roberts (2015a, 65) has characterized critical junctures as periods of 'crisis or strain that existing policies and institutions are ill-suited to resolve' – and therefore different from normal politics, when 'institutional continuity or incremental change can be taken for granted'.

In these perspectives, citizen-driven democratic innovations, such as the ones I have presented, have interacted with critical junctures: massive protests have been triggered by sudden shocks, such as the financial crisis, and they have, in their turn, not only highlighted the need for change, but also contributed knowledge for 'another democracy' – that, to a certain extent, they even prefigured. As legitimacy crises, which social movements have contributed to fuelling, have created gaps, the movements' ideas and practices were able to penetrate institutions, via constitutional processes, direct democratic procedures and the emergence of movement parties.

Innovations in intense times: the way forward

In short, both types of literatures I referred to in this volume in general, and in this concluding chapter in particular, converge in analysing social movement-driven democratic innovations, such as the ones I have presented in this volume, as embedded in intense times. These times have been labelled as times of backlash, characterized by the convergence of an intensified networking, increased capacity for collective action, and aggressive framing by reactionary actors (including movements) (della Porta 2018).

The backlash is, however, only part of the story. In intense moments such as the ones we are living through, changes can happen quickly in different directions, as agency and conjunctures play a more important role than in quiet times. Antonio Gramsci (1971) defined similar historical times as an interregnum. As he noted, 'The crisis consists precisely in the fact that the old is dying and the new cannot be born; in this interregnum a great variety of morbid symptoms appear.' In these dangerous times, challenges to really existing democracy also come, in fact, from regressive movements, in forms and with content that should not be confused with the ones put forward by progressive movements. However, it is important to re-instate that these are not only times of threats, but could also be (or become) times of opportunities for democratic deepening.

For sure, these are highly politicized times. As Chantal Mouffe (2018, 1) has noted, in Europe a 'populist moment' signals the crisis of neoliberal hegemony. As the

> democratic discourse plays a crucial role in the political imaginary of our societies through the construction of a collective will, mobilizing common affects in defence of equality and social justice, it will be possible to combat the xenophobic policies promoted by right-wing populism. In redrawing political frontiers, this 'populist moment' points to a 'return of the political' after years of postpolitics.

In these times, as backlashes are visible, there is, however, also space for agency on the side of the progressive actors. In fact, these are times of risks but also of chances.

Against this backdrop, this volume seeks to contribute to the knowledge of democratic innovations from below, as participation and deliberation can help to address the challenges of the Great Regression through their capacity to imagine a future opposed to the 'retrotopic' nostalgia on the Right (Bauman 2017b). In sum, moments of crisis can in fact be expected to fuel both pressures for progressive change and regressive backlash, utopias and retrotopias. In order to overcome the challenges and keep democracy alive, calls for a cultural sovereignty of the ethnic majority (Appadurai 2017; Bauman 2017a, 2017b) must be countered by the development of participatory and deliberative spaces where solidarity can be rebuilt and society revitalized (Mason 2017). It is in these spaces that recognition might happen because, as Alessandro Pizzorno noted, 'The original resource a human being can offer to another is the capacity to recognize the worth of the other to exist – a resource that cannot be produced if it is not shared . . . The good of selfpreservation is achieved when mutual recognition between human beings is achieved' (Pizzorno 1991, 218–19). So, 'the presence of other people is necessary for acting. Before becoming a possible means for individual ends, the interaction with others appears as an end in itself' (Pizzorno 1991, 221).

Even with all their limits, the cases I analysed have been pivotal in spreading some new ideas and practices on how citizens can participate in politics. In sum, while movements remain transient, alternating phases of visibility and phases of latency (and while we can expect the lifespan of movements in 'liquid modernity' to be increasingly short), some movement-produced knowledge seems to survive, becoming embedded in new institutions, which often spread beyond the original examples.

Bibliography

Ackerman, B. (1991). *We the People*. Cambridge, Mass., Belknap Press of Harvard University Press.

Ackerman, B. (1995). 'Higher Lawmaking'. In S. Levinson (ed.), *Responding to Imperfection: The Theory and Practice of Constitutional Amendment*. Princeton University Press, pp. 63–87.

Ackerman, B. (2015). 'Three Paths to Constitutionalism – and the Crisis of the European Union'. *British Journal of Political Science*, 45(4): 705–14.

Agustín, O. G. (2018), 'We the People or We the Republic? The Institutional Dilemma'. In O. G. Agustín and M. Briziarelli (eds.), *Podemos and the New Political Cycle: Left-Wing Populism and Anti-Establishment Politics*. London, Palgrave, pp. 147–69.

Agustín, O. G., and M. Briziarelli (2018). 'Wind of Change: Podemos, its Dreams and Politics'. In O. G. Agustín and M. Briziarelli (eds.), *Podemos and the New Political Cycle: Left-Wing Populism and Anti-Establishment Politics*, London, Palgrave, pp. 1–25.

Allegretti, G. (2003). *L'insegnamento di Porto Alegre. Autoprogettualità come paradigma urbano*. Florence, Alinea.

Allen, A. (2016). *The End of Progress: Decolonizing the Normative Foundations of Critical Theory*. New York, Columbia University Press.

Allern, E. H. (2010). *Political Parties and Interest Groups in Norway*. Essex, ECPR Press.

Allern, E. H., and T. Bale (2012). 'Political Parties and Interest Groups: Disentangling Complex Relationships'. *Party Politics*, 18(1): 7–25.

Altman, D. (2011). *Direct Democracy Worldwide*. Cambridge University Press.

Altman, D. (2019). *Citizenship and Contemporary Direct Democracy*. Cambridge University Press.

Alvarez, R. M., and J. Brehm (2002). *Hard Choices, Easy Answers: Values, Information, and American Public Opinion*. Princeton University Press.

Anria, S. (2013). 'Social Movements, Party Organization, and Populism: Insights from the Bolivian MAS'. *Latin American Politics and Society*, 55(3): 19–46.

Anria, S. (2018) *Movements, Party, and Grassroots Participation: The Exceptional Case of the Bolivian MAS*. Cambridge University Press.

Appadurai, A. (2017). 'Democracy Fatigue'. In H. Geiselberger (ed.), *The Great Regression*. Cambridge, Polity, pp. 1–12.

Ardanuy, M., and E. Labuske (2015). 'El músculo deliberativo del algoritmo democrático: Podemos y la participación ciudadana'. *Revista Teknokultura*, 12(1): 93–109.

Arnstein, S. R. (1969). 'A Ladder of Citizen Participation'. *Journal of the American Institute of Planners*, 35(4): 216–24.

Arribas Lozano, A. (2015). 'Recordar el 15M para reimaginar el presente. Los movimientos sociales en España más allá del ciclo electoral de 2015'. *Interface: A Journal for and about Social Movements*, 7(1): 150–64.

Ársælsson, K. M. (2012). 'Real Democracy in Iceland?' *Open Democracy*, 12 November, www.opendemocracy.net/kristinn-m%C3%A1r-%C3%A1rs%C3%A6lsson/real-democracy-in-iceland.

Baccaro, L., and K. Papadakis (2008). *The Promise and Perils of Participatory Policy Making*. Geneva, International Institute for Labour Studies.

Bacqué, M.-H., H. Rey and Y. Sintomer (eds.) (2005). *Gestion de proximité et démocratie participative*. Paris, La Découverte.

Bailey, S., and U. Mattei (2013). 'Social Movements as Constituent Power: The Italian Struggle for the Commons'. *Indiana Journal of Global Legal Studies*, 20(2): 965–1013.

Baiocchi, G. (2002). 'Synergizing Civil Society: State – Civil Society Regimes in Porto Alegre, Brazil'. *Political Power and Social Theory*, 15: 3–52.

Baiocchi, G., and E. Ganuza (2016) *Popular Democracy*. Stanford University Press.

Balcells, L., S. Dorsey and J. F. Tellez (2018) 'Repression and Dissent in Catalonia', working paper.

Barber, B. R. (1984). *Strong Democracy: Participatory Politics for a New Age*. Berkeley, University of California Press.

Barceló, J. (2018). 'Batons and Ballots: The Effectiveness of State Violence in Fighting against Catalan Separatism', *Research and Politics*, https://journals.sagepub.com/doi/pdf/10.1177/2053168018781747.

Barker, C., and L. Cox (2002). 'What Have the Romans Ever Done for Us? Academic and Activist Forms of Movement Theorizing'. In C. Barker and M. Tyldesley (eds.), *Alternative Futures and Popular Protest VIII: Conference Proceedings*. Manchester Metropolitan University, pp. 1–27.

Barreiro, B., and I. Sánchez-Cuenca (2001). 'La europeización de la opinión pública española'. In C. C. Montero (ed.), *La europeización del sistema político español*. Madrid, Istmo, pp. 29–51.

Barrio, A., O. Barberà and J. Rodríguez-Teruel (2018) '"Spain Steals from Us!" The "Populist Drift" of Catalan Regionalism'. *Comparative European Politics*, https://doi.org/10.1057/s41295-018-0140-3.

Bartels, L. (2014). 'Ideology and Retrospection in Electoral Responses to the Great Recession'. In L. Bartels and N. Bermeo (eds.), *Mass Politics in Tough Times: Opinions, Votes and Protest in the Great Recession*. Oxford University Press, pp. 185–223.

Bartolini, S. (2000). *The Political Mobilization of the European Left 1860–1980: the Class Cleavage*. Cambridge University Press.

Basta, K. 2017. 'The Social Construction of Transformative Political Events'. *Comparative Political Studies*, https://doi.org/10.1177/0010414017740601.

Bauman, Z. (2017a). 'Symptoms in Search of an Object and a Name'. In H. Geiselberger (ed.), *The Great Regression*. Cambridge, Polity, pp. 13–26.

Bauman, Z. (2017b). *Retrotopia*. Cambridge: Polity.

Beissinger, M. R. (2002). *Nationalist Mobilization and the Collapse of the Soviet State*. Cambridge University Press.

Bellamy, R. (2007). *Political Constitutionalism: A Republican Defence of the Constitutionality of Democracy*. Cambridge University Press.

Bellucci, E. (2014). 'The Political Consequences of Blame Attribution for the Economic Crisis in the 2013 Italian National Election'. *Journal of Elections, Public Opinion and Parties*, 24(2): 243–63.

Benedetto, G., and L. Quaglia (2007). 'The Comparative Politics of Communist Euroscepticism in France, Italy and Spain'. *Party Politics*, 13(4): 478–99.

Benford, R. D., and D. A. Snow (2000). 'Framing Processes and Social Movements: An Overview and Assessment'. *Annual Review of Sociology*, 26: 611–39.

Bergmann, E. (2014). *Iceland and the International Financial Crisis: Boom, Bust and Recovery*. Basingstoke, Palgrave Macmillan.

Bernburg, J. G. (2016). *Economic Crisis and Mass Protest: The Pots and Pans Revolution in Iceland*. Oxford, Routledge.

Bernhard, L. (2012). *Campaign Strategy in Direct Democracy*. London, Palgrave.

Bieler, A. (2015). '"Sic Vos Non Vobis" (For You, But Not Yours). The Struggle for Public Water in Italy'. *Monthly Review: An Independent Socialist Magazine*, 67(5); http://monthlyreview.org/2015/10/01/sic-vos-non-vobis-for-you-but-not-yours.

Bieler, A. (2017). "Fighting for Public Water: The First Successful European Citizens' Initiative'. *Interface: A Journal For and About Social Movements*, 9(1): 300–26.

Binzer Hobolt, S. (2007). 'Campaign Information and Voting Behaviour in EU Referendums'. In C. H. de Vreese (ed.), *The Dynamics of Referendum Campaigns: An International Perspective*. Basingstoke and New York, Palgrave Macmillan, pp. 84–114.

Bjørklund, T. (2009). 'The Surge of Referendums and the New Politics Approach'. In M. Setälä and T. Schiller (eds.), *Referendums and Representative Democracy: Responsiveness, Accountability and Deliberation*. London, Routledge, pp. 117–36.

Black, I., and S. Marsden (2016). *The Yes Volunteers: Capturing the 'Biggest*

Grassroots Campaign in Scotland's History'. Edinburgh North & Leith, Common Weal.

Blokker, P. (2010). 'Democratic Ethics, Constitutional Dimensions, and Constitutionalisms'. In A. Febbrajo and W. Sadurski (eds.), *Central and Eastern Europe after Transition: Towards a New Socio-legal Semantics*. Burlington, Vt., Ashgate, pp. 73–98.

Blokker, P. (2013). *New Democracies in Crisis? A Comparative Constitutional Study of the Czech Republic, Hungary, Poland, Romania and Slovakia*. Milton Park, Abingdon, Oxon, Routledge.

Blokker, P. (2017). 'Constitutional Reform in Europe and Recourse to the People'. In X. Contiades and A. Fotiadou (eds.), *Participatory Constitutional Change: The People as Amenders of the Constitution*. Milton Park, Abingdon, Oxon, and New York, Routledge, pp. 31–51.

Blount, J. (2011). 'Participation in Constitutional Design'. In T. Ginsburg and R. Dixon (eds.), *Comparative Constitutional Law*. Cheltenham, UK, and Northampton, Mass., Edward Elgar, pp. 38–56.

Blumer, H. (1951). 'Social Movements'. In A. McClung Lee (ed.), *Principles of Sociology*. New York, Barnes & Noble, pp. 199–220.

Bobbio, L., and A. Zeppetella (1999). *Perchè proprio qui? Grandi opere e opposizioni locali*. Milan, Franco Angeli.

Bordignon, F., and L. Ceccarini (2013). 'Five Stars and a Cricket: Beppe Grillo Shakes Italian Politics'. *South European Society and Politics*, 18(4): 427–49.

Borriello, A., and S. Mazzolini (2018). "European Populism(s) as a Counter-Hegemonic Discourse? The Rise of Podemos and M5S in the wake of the Crisis'. In O. G. Agustín and M. Briziarelli (eds.), *Podemos and the New Political Cycle: Left-Wing Populism and Anti-Establishment Politics*. London, Palgrave, pp. 227–54.

Bosi, L., M. Giugni and K. Uba (2016) *The Consequences of Social Movements: Taking Stock and Looking Forward*. In L. Bosi, M. Giugni and K. Uba, *The Consequences of Social Movements*. Cambridge University Press, pp. 3–38.

Bracke, S., W. Dupont and D. Paternotte (2018). ""No Prophet is Accepted in His Own Country": Catholic Anti-Gender Activism in Belgium'. In R. Kuhar and D. Paternotte (eds.), *Anti-Gender Campaigns in Europe: Mobilizing against Equality*. London, Rowman and Littlefield International, pp. 41–58.

Brennan, J. (2016). *Against Democracy*. Princeton University Press.

Briziarelli, M. (2018). 'Podemos' Twofold Assault on Hegemony: The Possibilities of The Post-Modern Prince and the Perils of Passive Revolution'. In O. G. Agustín and M. Briziarelli (eds.), *Podemos and the New Political Cycle: Left-Wing Populism and Anti-Establishment Politics*. London, Palgrave, pp. 97–122.

Brooker, Megan E. (2018). 'Indivisible: Invigorating and Redirecting the Grassroots'. In D. Meyer and S. Tarrow (eds.), *The Resistance*. Oxford University Press, pp. 162–85.

Bryan, F. (2004). *Real Democracy: The New England Town Meeting and How it Works*. University of Chicago Press.

Buchanan, R. (2006). 'Legitimating Global Trade Governance: Constitutional and Legal Pluralist Approaches'. *Northern Ireland Legal Quarterly*, 57: 1–19.

Burstein, P., R. L. Einwohner and J. A. Hollander (1995). *The Success of Political Movements: A Bargaining Perspective*. In C. Jenkins and B. Klandermans (eds.), *The Politics of Social Protest: Comparative Perspectives on States and Social Movements*. Minneapolis: University of Minnesota Press, pp. 275–95.

Caciagli, M., and P. Uleri (1994). 'Una prospettiva comparata per valutare le consultazioni referendarie'. In M. Caciagli and P. Uleri (eds.), *Democrazie e referendums*. Roma-Bari, Laterza, pp. 3–27.

Caiani, M., and O. Cisar (2019). 'Movement, Parties and Movement Parties of the Radical Right: Towards a Unified Approach?' In M. Caiani and O. Cisar (eds.), *Radical Right Movement Parties in Europe*. London, Routledge, pp. 11–25.

Caiani, M., and D. della Porta (2019). 'The Radical Right as Social Movement Organizations'. In J. Rydgren (ed.), *The Oxford Handbook of the Radical Right*. Oxford University Press, pp. 327–47.

Calvo, K., and I. Álvarez (2015). 'Limitaciones y exclusiones en la institucionalización de la indignación: del 15-M a Podemos'. *Revista Española de Sociología*, 24: 115–22.

Caravantes, P. (2018). 'New versus Old Politics in Podemos: Feminization and Masculinized Party Discourse'. *Men and Masculinities*, 1–26, https://doi.org/10.1177/1097184X18769350.

Carrozza, C. (2013). 'Riforme, attori e conflitti nelle politiche dei servizi idrici italiani'. In C. Carrozza and E. Fantini (eds.), *Si scrive acqua . . . Attori, pratiche e discorsi nel movimento italiano per l'acqua bene comune*. Turin, Accademia University Press, pp. 3–19.

Carrozza, C., and E. Fantini (2013). 'Acqua paradigma dei beni comuni: tra epica e pratica'. In C. Carrozza and E. Fantini (eds.), *Si scrive acqua . . . Attori, pratiche e discorsi nel movimento italiano per l'acqua bene comune*. Turin, Accademia University Press, pp. 75–100.

Carsetti, P. (2014). 'Referendum sull'acqua e sui servizi pubblici locali: un voto per il ritorno al futuro'. *Economia e Società Regionale*, 32(3): 62–75.

Casal, F., J. Teruel-Rodríguez, O. Barberá and A. Barrio (2014). 'The Carrot and the Stick: Party Regulation and Politics in Democratic Spain'. *South European Society and Politics*, 19(1): 89–112.

Casas-Cortés, M. I., M. Osterweil and D. E. Powell (2008). 'Blurring Boundaries: Recognizing Knowledge-practices in the Study of Social Movements'. *Anthropological Quarterly*, 81(1): 17–58.

Castelli Gattinara, P., and A. L. P. Pirro (2018). 'The Far Right as Social Movement'. *European Societies*, https://doi.org/10.1080/14616696.2018.1494301.

Cernison, M. (2014). 'Online Communication Spheres in Social Movement Campaigns: The Italian Referendum on Water'. Ph.D. dissertation, European University Institute.

Cernison, M. (2016). 'The Italian Referendum on Water'. Florence, Cosmos Working Paper.

Cetrà, D., E. Casanas-Adam and M. Tàrrega (2018). 'The 2017 Catalan Independence Referendum: A Symposium'. *Scottish Affairs* 27(1): 126–43.

Chiaramonte, A., and R. D'Alimonte (2012). 'The Twilight of the Berlusconi Era: Local Elections and National Referendums in Italy, May and June 2011'. *South European Society and Politics*, 17(2): 261–79.

Ciervo, M. (2009). *Geopolitica dell'acqua*. Rome, Carocci.

CIS (2014). Report of the Centro de Investigaciones Sociológicas, June 2014; http://datos.cis.es/pdf/Es3029mar_A.pdf.

Citizens' Movement (2009). *The Citizens' Movement*, https://grapevine.is/mag/2009/04/03/citizen-movement-borgarahreyfingin-iceland-elections-2009.

Cohen, J. (1989) 'Deliberation and Democratic Legitimacy'. In A. Hamlin and P. Pettit (eds.), *The Good Polity: Normative Analysis of the State*. Oxford, Basil Blackwell, pp. 17–34.

Collier, R., and D. Collier (1991). *Shaping the Political Arena*. Princeton University Press.

Collier, D., and G. L. Munck (2017) 'Building Blocks and Methodological Challenges: A Framework for Studying Critical Junctures'. *Qualitative and Multi-Method Research*, 15(1): 2–8.

Colon-Rios, J. (2009). 'The Second Dimension of Democracy: The People and their Constitution'. *Baltic Journal of Law & Politics*, 2(2): 1–30.

Colon-Rios, J. (2011). 'The Three Waves of the Constitutionalism–Democracy Debate in The United States (And an Invitation to Return to the First)'. Victoria University of Wellington Legal Research Papers, 1 VUWLRP 23/2011: 1–34.

Colon-Rios, J. (2013). *Weak Constitutionalism: Democratic Legitimacy and the Question of Constituent Power*. London, Routledge.

Conde-Ruiz, J. I., and C. Marín (2013). 'The Fiscal Crisis in Spain'. *Intereconomics*, 48(1): 4–32.

Cordero, G., and J. R. Montero (2015). 'Against Bipartyism, Towards Dealignment? The 2014 European Election in Spain'. *South European Society and Politics*, 20(3): 357–79.

Cox, L. (2014). 'Movements Making Knowledge: A New Wave of Inspiration for Sociology?' *Sociology*, 48(5): 954–71.

Crameri, K. (2015). 'Political Power and Civil Counterpower: The Complex Dynamics of the Catalan Independence Movement'. *Nationalism and Ethnic Politics*, 21(1): 104–20.

Cress D., and D. Snow (2000) 'The Outcomes of Homeless Mobilization: The Influence of Organization, Disruption, Political Mediation, and Framing'. *American Journal of Sociology*, 105: 1063–1110.

Crouch, C. (2003). *Post-Democracy*. Cambridge, Polity.

Crowther, J., V. Galloway and I. Martin (eds.) (2005). *Popular Education: Engaging the Academy. International Perspectives*. Leicester, NIACE.

Crozier, M., S. Huntington and J. Watakuni (1975). *The Crisis of Democracy*. New York University Press.

Curtice, J. (2014). 'Has the Referendum Campaign Made a Difference?' Edinburgh, ScotCen Social Research.

Curtis, K. A., J. Jupille and D. Leblang (2014). 'Iceland on the Rocks: The

Mass Political Economy of Sovereign Debt Resettlement'. *International Organization*, 68(3): 721–40.

Dahl, R. A. (2000). *On Democracy*. New Haven, Conn., Yale University Press.

Dalle Mulle, E. (2016). 'New Trends in Justifications for National Self-Determination: Evidence from Scotland and Flanders'. *Ethnopolitics*, 15(2): 211–29.

Dalton, R. (2004). *Democratic Challenges, Democratic Choices: The Erosion of Political Support in Advanced Industrial Democracies*. Oxford University Press.

Dawson, M., and F. de Witte (2013). 'Constitutional Balance in the EU after the Euro-Crisis'. *The Modern Law Review*, 76: 817–44.

de Vreese, C. H. (2007). 'Context, Elites, Media and Public Opinion in Referendums: When Campaigns Really Matter'. In C. De Vreese (ed.), *The Dynamics of Referendum Campaigns: An International Perspective*. London, Palgrave, pp. 1–20.

de Vreese, C. H., and H. G. Boomgaarden (2007). 'Immigration, Identity, Economy and the Government: Understanding Variation in Explanations for Outcomes of EU-Related Referendums'. In C. De Vreese (ed.), *The Dynamics of Referendum Campaigns: An International Perspective*. London, Palgrave, pp. 185–205.

della Porta, D. (1995). *Social Movements, Political Violence, and the State: A Comparative Analysis of Italy and Germany*. Cambridge University Press.

della Porta, D. (2007). *The Global Justice Movement: Cross-national and Transnational Perspectives*. Boulder, Paradigm.

della Porta, D. (2008). 'Eventful Protest, Global Conflicts'. *Distinktion: Scandinavian Journal of Social Theory*, 9(2): 27–56.

della Porta, D. (ed.) (2009). *Democracy in Social Movements*, Houndsmill: Palgrave.

della Porta, D. (2013). *Can Democracy Be Saved? Participation, Deliberation and Social Movements*. Cambridge, Polity.

della Porta, D. (2015a). *I partiti politici*. Bologna, Il Mulino.

della Porta, D. (2015b). *Social Movements in Times of Austerity: Bringing Capitalism back into Protest Analysis*. Cambridge, Polity.

della Porta, D. (2017a). *Where Did the Revolution Go?* Cambridge University Press.

della Porta, D. (2017b). 'Progressive and Regressive Politics in Late Neoliberalism'. In H. Geiselberger (ed.), *The Great Regression*. Cambridge: Polity, pp. 26–39.

della Porta, D. (2018). 'Protests as Critical Junctures: Some Reflections Towards a Momentous Approach to Social Movements'. *Social Movement Studies*, forthcoming.

della Porta, Donatella (2019). 'For Participatory Democracy: Some Notes'. *European Political Science*.

della Porta, D., and M. Andretta (2013). 'Protesting for Justice and Democracy: Italian Indignados?' *Contemporary Italian Politics*, 5(1): 23–37.

della Porta, D., M. Andretta, T. Fernandes, F. O'Connor, E. Romanos and M. Vogiatzoglou (2016). *Late Neoliberalism and its Discontents in the*

Economic Crisis: Comparing Social Movements in the European Periphery. Basingstoke, Palgrave Macmillan.

della Porta, D., and M. Diani (2006). *Social Movements: An Introduction.* Oxford, Blackwell.

della Porta, D., and A. Felicetti (2017). 'Democratic Innovations and Social Movements'. In *The Governance Report.* Oxford University Press, pp. 127–42.

della Porta, D., and A. Felicetti (2019). 'Innovating Democracy against Democratic Stress in Europe: Social Movements and Democratic Experiments', *Representation,* https://doi.org/10.1080/00344893.2019.1624600.

della Porta, D., J. Fernández, H. Kouki and L. Mosca (2017). *Movement Parties in Times of Austerity.* Cambridge, Polity.

della Porta, D., and M. Keating (eds.) (2008). *Approaches and Methodologies in the Social Sciences.* Cambridge University Press.

della Porta, D., Keating, M., Baiocchi, G., et al. (2018). 'The Paradoxes of Democracy and the Rule of Law'. In IPSP (ed.), *Rethinking Society for the 21st Century: Report of the International Panel on Social Progress,* Vol. II: *Political Regulation, Governance, and Societal Transformations.* Cambridge University Press, pp. 373–411.

della Porta, D., and A. Mattoni (eds.) 2015. *Spreading Protest: Social Movements in Times of Crisis.* Colchester: ECPR Press.

della Porta, D., L. Mosca and L. Parks (2015). 'Subterranean Politics and Visible Protest in Italy'. In M. Kaldor and S. Selchow (eds.), *Subterranean Politics in Europe.* London, Palgrave, pp. 60–93.

della Porta, D., F. O'Connor and M. Portos (forthcoming). 'The Framing of Secessionism in the Neo-Liberal Crisis: the Scottish and Catalan Cases'. In G. Martinico, C. Margiotta and C. Closa (eds.), *Secessionism.* London, Routledge.

della Porta, D., F. O'Connor, M. Portos and A. Subirats (2017a). *Referendums from Below.* Bristol, Policy Press, and University of Chicago Press.

della Porta, D., F. O'Connor, M. Portos and A. Subirats (2017b). '"The Streets Will Always Be Ours" – Catalonia, a Referendum from Below'. *Open Democracy,* 5 October, www.opendemocracy.net/can-europe-make-it/donatella-della-por ta-francis-oconnor-martin-portos-anna-subirats-ribas/streets-w.

della Porta, D., and M. Portos (forthcoming). 'A Bourgeois Story? The Class Basis of Catalan Independentism'. Paper presented at seminar 'The Political Consequences of Inequality: II. Inequalities, Territorial Politics, Nationalism', 22–23 November 2018, Florence, Scuola Normale Superiore.

della Porta, D., and H. Reiter (eds.) (1998). *The Policing of Protest.* Minneapolis, University of Minnesota Press.

della Porta, D., and H. Reiter (2012). 'Desperately Seeking Politics'. *Mobilization: An International Quarterly,* 17(3): 349–61.

della Porta, D., and D. Rucht (1996). 'Social Movement Sectors in Context: A Comparison of Italy and West Germany, 1965–1990'. In J. Craig Jenkins and Bert Klandermans (eds.), *The Politics of Social Protest.* Minneapolis, Minnesota University Press, pp. 299–272.

Dessi, Giulia (2012) 'The Icelandic Constitutional Experiment'. *Open Democracy,*

23 October, www.opendemocracy.net/giulia-dessi/icelandic-constitutional-ex periment.

Diamanti, I. (2007). 'La democrazia degli interstizi. Società e partiti in Europa dopo la caduta del Muro'. *Rassegna italiana di sociologia*, 3: 387–412.

Diamond, L., and R. Gunther (eds.) (2001). *Parties and Democracy*. London, Johns Hopkins University Press.

Dinerstein, A. C. (2014). *The Politics of Autonomy in Latin America: The Art of Organizing Hope*. Basingstoock, Palgrave MacMillan.

Douzinas, C. (2014). 'The "Right to the Event": The Legality and Morality of Revolution and Resistance'. *International Studies in Phenomenology and Philosophy*, 2.

Dryzek, J. S. (2000). *Deliberative Democracy and Beyond: Liberals, Critics, Contestations*. Oxford, UK, and New York, Oxford University Press.

Dryzek, J. S. (2010). *Foundations and Frontiers of Deliberative Governance*. Oxford University Press.

Dyck, J. J. (2009). 'Initiated Distrust: Direct Democracy and Trust in Government'. *American Politics Research*, 37(4): 539–68.

Earle, G., C. Moran and Z. Ward-Perkins (2017) *The Econocracy*. London: Penguin.

Easton, D. (1953). *The Political System: An Inquiry into the State of Political Science*. New York, Alfred A. Knopf.

Eder, K. (2010) 'The Transformations of the Public Sphere and their Impact on Democratization'. In A. Pizzorno (ed.), *La democrazia di fronte allo stato democratico*. Milan, Feltrinelli, pp. 247–83.

Eklund, E. (2018), 'Populism, Hegemony and the Phantasmatic Sovereign: The Ties between Nationalism and Left-wing Populism'. In O. G. Agustín and M. Briziarelli (eds.), *Podemos and the New Political Cycle: Left-Wing Populism and Anti-Establishment Politics*. London, Palgrave, pp. 123–46.

Elkins, Z., T. Ginsburg and J. Melton (2012). 'A Review of Iceland's Draft Constitution from the Comparative Constitutions Project', I-CONnect blog, www.iconnectblog.com/2012/10/a-review-of-icelands-draft-constitution-from-the-comparative-constitutions-project.

Elster, J. (1998). 'Deliberation and Constitution Making'. In J. Elster (ed.), *Deliberative Democracy*. Cambridge University Press, pp. 97–122.

England, P. (2015) 'Changing the Way Politics Works: An Interview with Katrin Oddsdottir'. *Open Democracy*, 25 July. www.opendemocracy.net/ourkingdom/phil-england/changing-way-politics-works-interview-with-katrin-oddsdottir.

EPRE (2015). 'Podemos' Electoral Program for Regional Elections', https://podemos.info/wp-content/uploads/2015/05/prog_marco_12.pdf.

Errejón, Í. (2014). 'Qué es Podemos?' *Le Monde Diplomatique en español* (July), https://mondiplo.com/que-es-podemos.

Errejón, Í. (2015). 'We the People. El 15-M: ¿Un Populismo Indignado?' *ACME: An International E-Journal for Critical Geographies*, 14(1): 124–56.

Eyerman, R., and A. Jamison (1991). *Social Movements: A Cognitive Approach*. University Park, Pennsylvania State University Press.

Fantini, E. (2012). 'Water as Human Right and Commons: Themes and Practices in the Italian Water Movement'. *Pace diritti umani*, 2: 15–40.

Fantini, E. (2013). 'Gli attori e il percorso storico del movimento italiano per l'acqua bene comune'. In C. Carrozza and E. Fantini (eds.), *Si scrive acqua . . . Attori, pratiche e discorsi nel movimento italiano per l'acqua bene comune.* Turin, Accademia University Press, pp. 20–41.

Fantini, E. (2014) 'Catholics in the Making of the Italian Water Movement: A Moral Economy'. *PArtecipazione e COnflitto. The Open Journal of Sociopolitical Studies* 7(1): 35–57, http://siba-ese.unisalento.it/index.php/paco, https://doi.org/10.1285/i20356609v7i1p35.

Farrell, D. M., E. O'Malley and J.Suiter (2013). 'Deliberative Democracy in Action Irish-style: The 2011 We The Citizens Pilot Citizens' Assembly'. *Irish Political Studies*, 28(1): 99–113.

Fassin, E. (2014) 'Same-Sex Marriage, Nation and Race: French Political Logics and Rhetoric'. *Contemporary French Civilization*, 3: 281–301.

Fatke, M. (2015). 'Participation and Political Equality in Direct Democracy: Educative Effect or Social Bias?' *Swiss Political Science Review*, 21(1): 99–118.

Fattori, T. (2013). 'From the Water Commons Movement to the Commonification of the Public Realm'. *South Atlantic Quarterly*, 112(2): 377–87.

Feenstra, R. A., and J. Keane (2014). 'Politics in Spain: A Case of Monitory Democracy'. *International Journal of Voluntary and Nonprofit Organizations*, 25(5): 1262–80.

Felicetti, A., and D. della Porta (2018). 'Between Deliberation and Contestation: The Convergence of Struggles against Austerity and Its World in the Nuit Debout Movement'. *Social Movement Studies*, 17: 658–75.

Fernández, J., and M. Portos (2015). 'Moving from the Squares to the Ballot Box. Podemos, Appropriation of Opportunities and the Institutionalization of Anti-Austerity Protests: A Cycle-Based Approach'. Working paper presented at the Conference 'Movements and Parties', 6 October. Florence, Scuola Normale Superiore.

Fernández-Albertos, J. (2015). *Los votantes de Podemos. Del partido de los indignados al partido de los excluidos.* Madrid, Catarata.

Fernández-Albertos, J., and D. Manzano (2012). 'The Lack of Partisan Conflict over the Welfare State in Spain'. *South European Society and Politics*, 17(3): 427–47.

Fillmore-Patrick, H. (2013). 'The Iceland Experiment (2009–2013): A Participatory Approach to Constitutional Reform'. Democratization Policy Council Policy Note, New Series #02: 1–17.

Finchett-Maddock, L. (2016). *Protest, Property and the Commons: Performance of Law and Resistance.* London, Routledge.

Fishkin, J. S. (1997). *The Voice of the People: Public Opinion and Democracy.* New Haven and London, Yale University Press.

Fishman, R. M. (2011). 'Democratic Practice After the Revolution: The Case of Portugal and Beyond'. *Politics and Society*, 39(2): 233–67.

Fitzpatrick, T. (2002) 'The Two Paradoxes of Welfare Democracy'. *International Journal of Social Welfare*, 11: 159–69.

Flesher Fominaya, C. (2014). '"Spain is Different": Podemos and 15-M'. *Open Democracy*, 29 May, www.opendemocracy.net/can-europe-make-it/ cristina-flesher-fominaya/%E2%80%9Cspain-is-different%E2%80%9D-po demos-and-15m.

Flesher Fominaya, C. (2015). 'Podemos' March for Change'. *Open Democracy*, 31 January, www.opendemocracy.net/can-europe-make-it/cristina-flesher-fo minaya/podemos%E2%80%99-march-for-change.

Foley, G. (1999). *Learning in Social Action. A Contribution to Understanding Informal Education*. London and New York, Zed Books.

Foley, G. (ed.) (2004). *Dimensions of Adult Learning:. Adult Education and Training in a Global Era*. Maidenhead, Open University Press.

Font, J., D. della Porta and Y. Sintomer (eds.) (2014) *Participatory Democracy in Southern Europe*. London, Rowman and Littlefield.

Font, J., and E. Rodríguez (2009). 'Intense But Useless? Public Debate and Voting Factors in Two Referendums in Spain'. In M. Setälä and T. Schiller (eds.), *Referendums and Representative Democracy: Responsiveness, Accountability and Deliberation*. London, Routledge, pp. 162–85.

Font, N., P. Graziano and M. Tsakatika (2015). 'Economic Crisis and Inclusionary Populism: Evidence from Southern Europe'. Paper presented at the Annual APSA Conference, 3–6 September. San Francisco.

Forst, R. (2019) 'The Justification of Progress and the Progress of Justification'. In A. Allen and E. Mendieta (eds.), *Justification and Emancipation: The Critical Theory of Rainer Forst*. University Park, Penn State University Press, forthcoming.

Frankland, E. G., P. Lucardie and B. Rihoux (eds.) (2008). *Green Parties in Transition: The End of Grass-roots Democracy?* Farnham, Ashgate.

Franklin, M. N. (2002). 'Learning from the Danish case: A Comment on Palle Svensson's Critique of the Franklin Thesis'. *European Journal of Political Research*, 41(6): 751–7.

Franzé, Javier (2018), 'Podemos: From Antagonism to Agonism? Populism, Political Frontier and Democracy', in O. G. Agustín and M. Briziarelli (eds.), *Podemos and the New Political Cycle: Left-Wing Populism and Anti-Establishment Politics*. London, Palgrave, pp. 49–74.

Fraser, N. (1990). 'Rethinking the Public Sphere'. *Social Text*, 25/26: 56–80.

Freire, P. (1996). *Pedagogy of the Oppressed*. New York, Continuum.

Frigoli, G., and G. Ivaldi (2019). 'Still a Radical Right Movement Party? Political Opportunities, Party Strategy and the Cultural Context of the Front national in France'. In M. Caiani and O. Cisar (eds.), *Radical Right Movement Parties in Europe*. London, Routledge, pp. 63–80.

Fung, A., and E. O. Wrights (2003). *Deepening Democracy*. London, Verso.

Galindo, J., K. Llaneras, O. Medina, J. San Miguel, R. Senserrich and P. Simón (2015). *Podemos: La cuadratura del círculo*. Madrid, Debate.

Gamson, W. (1990) [1975], *The Strategy of Social Protest*. Homewood, The Dorsey Press.

Garbagnoli, S. (2018). 'Italy as a Lighthouse: Anti-gender Protests between "Anthropological Question" and National Identity'. In R. Kuhar and

D. Paternotte (eds.), *Anti-Gender Campaigns in Europe: Mobilizing against Equality*. London, Rowman and Littlefield International, pp. 115–75.

Garner, R., and M. N. Zald (1985). 'The Political Economy of Social Movement Sectors'. In D. G. Suttles and M. N. Zald (eds.), *The Challenge of Social Control: Citizenship and Institutions in Modern Society*. Norwood, NJ, Ablex Publishing Corporation, pp. 119–45.

Gastil, J., R. Richards and K. Knobloch (2014). 'Vicarious Deliberation: How the Oregon Citizens' Initiative Review Influenced Deliberation in Mass Elections'. *International Journal of Communication*, 8: 62–89.

Gastil, J., and R. Richards. 2013. 'Making Direct Democracy Deliberative through Random Assemblies'. *Politics & Society*, 41(2): 253–81.

Gastil, J., and E. O. Wright (eds.) (2018). *Democracy by the Lot*. London, Verso.

Geiselberger, H. (ed.) (2017). *The Great Regression*. Cambridge, Polity.

Gerbaudo, P. (2012). *Tweet and the Street*. London, Pluto Press.

Gillespie, R. (2017) 'Spain: The Forward March of Podemos Halted? *Mediterranean Politics*, 22(4): 537–44.

Giugni, M. (2004). *Social Protest and Policy Change*. London, Rowman and Littlefield.

Giugni, M., and F. Passy (1998). 'Social Movements and Policy Change: Direct, Mediated, or Joint Effect?' *American Sociological Association Section on Collective Behavior and Social Movements, Working Paper Series*, 1(4).

Goldstone, J. A. (2003). 'Introduction: Bringing Institutionalized and Noninstitutionalized Politics'. In J. A. Goldstone (ed.), *States, Parties, and Social Movements*. Cambridge University Press, pp. 1–24.

Gordon, U. (2007). *Anarchy Alive!* London, Pluto.

Gordon, U. (2017) 'Prefigurative Politics between Ethical Practice and Absent Promise'. *Political Studies*, 66: 521–37.

Goretti, C., and L. Landi (2013). 'Walking on the Edge: How Italy Rescued Italy in 2012'. *Intereconomics*, 48(1): 14–21.

Graeber, D. (2012). *The Democracy Project: A History, a Crisis, a Movement*. London, Allen Lane.

Gramsci, A. 1971. *Selections from the Prison Notebooks*. London, International Publishers.

Gret, M., and Y. Sintomer (2005) *The Porto Alegre Experiment: Learning Lessons for Better Democracy*. London, Zed Books.

Gunther, R., N. Diamandouros and J. H. Puhle (eds.) (1995). *Democratic Consolidation in Southern Europe*. Baltimore, Md., Johns Hopkins University Press.

Gunther, R., and L. Diamond (2003). 'Species of Political Parties: A New Typology'. *Party Politics*, 9(2): 167–99.

Gunther, R., J. R. Montero and J. Botella (2004). *Democracy in Modern Spain*. New Haven, Conn., Yale University Press.

Gunther, R., G. Sani and G. Shabad (1988). *Spain After Franco: The Making of a Competitive Party System*. Berkeley, Los Angeles and London, University of California Press.

Gusfield, J. R. (1963). *Symbolic Crusade*. Urbana-Champaign, University of Illinois Press.

Gylfason, T. (2012). 'From Collapse to Constitution: The Case of Iceland', CESifo Working Paper #3770, pp. 1–44.

Gylfason, T. (2013) 'Democracy on Ice: A Post-Mortem of the Icelandic Constitution'. *Open Democracy*, 19 June, www.opendemocracy.net/can-europe-make-it/thorvaldur-gylfason/democracy-on-ice-post-mortem-of-icelandic-constitution.

Habermas, J. (1985). *The Theory of Communicative Action: Lifeworld and System: A Critique of Functionalist Reason*. Boston, Beacon Press.

Habermas, J. (1989) [1962] *The Structural Transformation of the Public Sphere: An Inquiry into a Category of Bourgeois Society*. Cambridge, Polity.

Habermas, J. (1996). *Between Facts and Norms: Contribution to a Discursive Theory of Law and Democracy*. Cambridge, Mass., MIT Press.

Hall, Stuart (1980) 'Cultural Studies: Two Paradigms'. In R. Collins et al. (eds.), *Media, Culture, and Society: A Critical Reader*. Beverly Hills, Sage.

Hallgrímsdóttir, H. K., and E. Brunet-Jailly (2015). 'Contentious Politics, Grassroots Mobilization and the Icesave Dispute: Why Iceland Did Not "Play Nicely"'. *Acta Sociologica*, 58(1): 79–93.

Halvorsen, S. (2012). 'Beyond the Network? Occupy London and the Global Movement'. *Social Movement Studies*, 11(3–4): 427–33.

Handlin, S., and R. B. Collier (2011). 'The Diversity of Left Party Linkages and Competitive Advantages'. In S. Levitsky and K. M. Roberts (eds.), *The Resurgence of the Latin American Left*. Baltimore, Md., Johns Hopkins University Press, pp. 139–61.

Hanna, J., and J. Busher (2019). 'UKIP and the UK's Radical Right: A Tale of a Movement Party Success?' In M. Caiani and O. Cisar (eds.), *Radical Right Movement Parties in Europe*. London, Routledge, pp. 46–62.

Hardiman, N., and A. Regan (2013). 'The Politics of Austerity in Ireland'. *Intereconomics*, 48: 9–14.

Harmel, R., and J. D. Robertson (1985). 'Formation and Success of New Parties: A Cross-national Analysis'. *International Political Science Review*, 6(4): 501–23.

Hart, V. (2003). 'Democratic Constitution Making', Special Report, United States Institute for Peace, pp. 1–12.

Hauptmann, E. (2001) 'Can Less Be More? Leftist Deliberative Democrats' Critique of Participatory Democracy'. *Polity* 33(3): 397–421.

Hawkins, K. (2010). *Venezuela's Chavismo and Populism in Comparative Perspective*. New York, Cambridge University Press.

Heaney, M. (2010). 'Linking Political Parties and Interest Groups'. In L. S. Maisel, J. M. Berry and G. C. Edwards III (eds.), *The Oxford Handbook of American Political Parties and Interest Groups*. Oxford University Press, pp. 568–87.

Held, D. (2006) *Models of Democracy*, 3rd edn. Cambridge, Polity.

Hirschl, R. (2004). 'The New Constitutionalism and the Judicialization of Pure Politics Worldwide'. *Fordham Law Review*, 75: 722–54.

Hobolt, S. B. (2009). *Europe in Question: Referendums on European I,ntegration*. Oxford University Press.

Hutter, S. (2014). *Protesting Culture and Economics in Western Europe*. Minneapolis: Minnesota University Press.

Iglesias, P. (2015a). 'El espacio de la socialdemocracia quedó vacío y lo hemos ocupado nosotros'. Interview, *La Opinión de Málaga*, 17 May, www. laopiniondemalaga.es/nacional/2015/05/17/espacio-socialdemocracia-quedo -vacio-hemos/766680.html.

Iglesias, P. (2015b). 'Understanding Podemos'. *New Left Review*, 93: 7–22.

Iglesias P. (2015c). 'Spain on Edge Interview', *New Left Review*, 93: 23–42.

Iglesias P. (2015d). 'Recuperar la democracia', speech at the Forum Nueva Economía, 27 June, www.huffingtonpost.es/pablo-iglesias/recuperar-la-dem ocracia_b_5533727.html.

Indridason, I. H. (2014). 'The Collapse: Economic Considerations in Vote Choice in Iceland'. *Journal of Elections, Public Opinion and Parties*, 24(2): 134–59.

Indridason, I. H., et al. (2016). 'Re-electing the Culprits of the Crisis? Elections in the Aftermath of a Recession'. *Scandinavian Political Studies*, 40(1): 28–60.

Johnson, J. (1998) 'Arguing for Deliberation: Some Skeptical Considerations'. In J. Elster (ed.), *Deliberative Democracy*. Cambridge University Press, pp. 161–84.

Johnston, H. (2018). 'The Revenge of Turner and Killian: Paradigm, State, and Repertoire in Social Movement Research'. Paper presented at the conference '1968: 50 Years After'. Florence, Cosmos, Scuola Normale Superiore, 23–25 May.

Jonsson, S. I. (2016) 'Economic Crisis and Real Critical Junctures: On the Decay of the Political Party System of Iceland'. *The Polar Journal*, 6(1): 131–51.

Juris, J. (2012). 'Reflections on #Occupy Everywhere: Social Media, Public Spaces, and Emerging Logics of Aggregation'. *American Ethnologist*, 39(2): 259–79.

Kaidatzis, A. 2018. 'Populist Constitutionalism: Reassessing the Relationship between Public Law and Politics'. Paper submitted to the International Conference on 'The Power of Public Law in the 21st Century', Central and Eastern European Regional Chapter of the International Society of Public Law (ICON-S), 20 April. Budapest.

Katz, R. S., and P. Mair (1995). 'Changing Models of Party Organization and Party Democracy'. *Party Politics*, 1(5): 5–28.

Kitschelt, H. (1986). 'Political Opportunity Structures and Political Protest: Anti-Nuclear Movements in Four Democracies'. *British Journal of Political Science*, 16(1): 57–85.

Kitschelt, H. (1988). 'Left-libertarian Parties: Explaining Innovation in Competitive Systems'. *World Politics*, 40(2): 194–234.

Kitschelt, H. (1989). *The Logics of Party Formation: Ecological Parties in Belgium and West Germany*. Ithaca, NY, Cornell University Press.

Kitschelt, H. (1994). *The Transformation of European Social Democracy*. Cambridge University Press.

Kitschelt, H. (2006). 'Movement Parties'. In R. Katz and W. Crotty (eds.), *Handbook of Party Politics*. London, Sage, pp. 278–91.

Kolb, F. (2007) *Protest and Opportunities: The Political Outcomes of Social Movements.* University of Chicago Press.

Kriesi, H. (2004) 'Political Context and Opportunity'. In D. Snow, S. Soule and H. Kriesi, *The Blackwell Companion to Social Movements.* Malden, Mass.: Blackwell.

Kriesi, H. (2005). *Direct Democratic Choices. The Swiss Experience.* Lanham, Lexington Book.

Kriesi, H. (2007). 'The Participation in Swiss Direct-democratic Votes'. In C. De Vreese (ed.), *The Dynamics of Referendum Campaigns: An International Perspective.* London, Palgrave, pp. 117–42.

Kriesi, H. (ed.) (2012a). *Political Communication in Direct Democratic Campaigns: Enlightening or Manipulating?* London, Palgrave.

Kriesi, H. (2012b). 'The Role of Predispositions'. In H. Kriesi (ed.), *Political Communication in Direct Democratic Campaigns: Enlightening or Manipulating?* London, Palgrave, pp. 143–67.

Kriesi, H. (2012c). 'Conclusion.' In H. Kriesi (ed.), *Political Communication in Direct Democratic Campaigns: Enlightening or Manipulating?* London, Palgrave, pp. 223–40.

Kriesi, H., and L. Bernhard (2014). 'Die Referendumsdemokratie'. In H. Scholten and K. Kamps (eds.), *Abstimmungskampagnen Politikvermittlungin der Referendumsdemokratie.* Wiesbaden, Springer, pp. 3–18.

Kriesi, H., L. Bernhard and R. Hänggli (2007). 'National Political Strategies in Direct-Democratic Campaigns'. *Challenges to Democracy in the 21st Century,* Working Paper No. 8: 1–47. Centre of Competence in Research (NCCR), www.nccr-democracy.uzh.ch/publications/workingpaper/pdf/WP8.pdf.

Kriesi, H., Grande, E., Dolezal, M., et al. (2012). *Political Conflict in Western Europe.* Cambridge University Press.

Kriesi, H., E. Grande, R. Lachat, M. Dolezal, S. Bornschier and T. Frey (2008). *West European Politics in the Age of Globalization.* Cambridge University Press.

Kriesi, H., R. Koopmans, J. W. Duyvendak and M. G. Giugni (1995). *New Social Movements in Western Europe: A Comparative Perspective.* London, UCL Press.

Landomore, H. (2017) 'Inclusive Constitution Making and Religious Rights: Lessons from the Icelandic Experiment'. *The Journal of Politics,* 79(3): 762–79.

Lavezzolo, S., and L. Ramiro (2017) 'Stealth Democracy and the Support for New and Challenger Parties'. *European Political Science Review,* 10(2): 267–89.

Lawson, K. (1980). 'Political Parties and Linkage'. In K. Lawson (ed.), *Political Parties and Linkage: A Comparative Perspective.* New Haven, Conn., Yale University Press, pp. 3–24.

LeDuc, L. (2002). 'Opinion Change and Voting Behaviour in Referendums'. *European Journal of Political Research,* 41(6): 711–32.

LeDuc, L. (2007). 'Opinion Formation and Change in Referendum Campaigns'. In C. de Vreese (ed.), *The Dynamics of Referendum Campaigns: An International Perspective.* London, Palgrave, pp. 21–45.

Letamendia, A. L. (2017). 'Movilización, represión y voto: rastreando las claves del referéndum de autodeterminación del 1 de octubre de 2017 en Catalunya'. *Anuari del Conflicte Social*: 1–32, https://doi.org/10.1344/ACS2018.7.1.

Levitsky, S., and K. M. Roberts (2011). 'Latin America's 'Left Turn': A Framework for Analysis'. In S. Levitsky and K. M. Roberts (eds.), *The Resurgence of the Latin American Left*. Baltimore, Md., Johns Hopkins University Press, pp. 1–28.

Lobera, J. (2015). 'De movimientos a partidos. La cristalización electoral de la protesta'. *Revista Española de Sociología*, 24: 97–105.

Lobera, J., and D. Parejo (2019) 'Streets and Institutions? The Electoral Extension of Social Movements and its Tensions'. In R. Kinna and U. Gordon (eds.), *Routledge Handbook of Radical Politics*. Abingdon, Oxon, Routledge, pp. 123–46.

Loftsdóttir, K. (2016). 'Building on Iceland's "Good Reputation": Icesave, Crisis and Affective National Identities'. *Ethnos: Journal of Anthropology*, 81(2): 338–63.

López, I. (2012). 'Consensonomics: la ideología dominante en la CT'. In G. Martínez (ed.), *CT o la Cultura de la Transición. Crítica a 35 años de la cultura española*. Madrid, Ed. Debolsillo, pp. 77–88.

Madrid, R. L. (2010). 'The Origins of the Two Lefts in Latin America'. *Political Science Quarterly*, 125(4): 587–609.

Maduz, L. (2010). 'Direct Democracy'. *Living Reviews in Democracy* (Center for International and Comparative Studies, University of Zurich), 2: 1–14, www.css.ethz.ch/content/dam/ethz/special-interest/gess/cis/center-for-securities-studies/pdfs/Maduz-2010-DirectDemocracy.pdf.

Maeckelbergh, M. (2011) 'Doing is Believing: Prefiguration as Strategic Practice in the Alterglobalization Movement'. *Social Movement Studies*, 10(1): 1–20.

Mair, P. (1983). 'Adaptation and Control: Towards an Understanding of Party and Party System Change'. In H. Daalder and P. Mair (eds.), *Western European Party Systems: Continuity & Change*. London, Sage, pp. 405–29.

Mair, P. (2009). 'Representative versus Responsible Government'. Working Paper, 09/8, Max Planck Institute for the Study of Societies, Cologne.

Mair, P. (2014). 'Explaining the Absence of Class Politics in Ireland'. In I. van Biezen (ed.), *On Parties, Party Systems and Democracy: Selected Writings of Peter Mair*. Colchester: ECPR Press, pp. 115–42.

Mair, P., and I. van Biezen (2001), 'Party Membership In Twenty European Democracies, 1980–2000'. *Party Politics*, 7(1): 5–21.

Malo de Molina, M. (2004). 'Common Notions, Part 1: Workers-Inquiry, Co-Research, Consciousness Raising', http://eipcp.net/transversal/0406/malo/en.

Mansbridge, J. (1996). 'Using Power / Fighting Power: The Polity'. In S. Benhabib (ed.), *Democracy and Difference: Contesting the Boundaries of the Political*. Princeton University Press, pp. 46–66.

Markoff, J. (2016). 'Historical Analysis and Social Movement Research'. In D. della Porta and M. Diani (eds.), *The Oxford Handbook of Social Movements*. Oxford University Press, pp. 68–85.

Marks, G. (1989). *Union in Politics: Britain, Germany and the United States in the Nineteenth and Early Twentieth Century*. Princeton University Press.

Marsh, M. (2007). 'Referendum Campaigns: Changing What People Think or Changing What They Think About?' In C. de Vreese (ed.), *The Dynamics of Referendum Campaigns. An International Perspective*. London, Palgrave, pp. 63–83.

Marsh, M., and S. Mikhaylov. (2012). 'Economic Voting in a Crisis: The Irish Election of 2011'. *Electoral Studies*, 30: 1–7.

Martín, I. (2015). 'Podemos y otros modelos de partido–movimiento'. *Revista Española de Sociología*, 24: 107–14.

Martinez Guillem, S. (2018) 'Podemos' Performative Power: Transforming Political Culture through Space Struggles'. In O. G. Agustín and M. Briziarelli (eds.), *Podemos and the New Political Cycle: Left-Wing Populism and Anti-Establishment Politics*. London, Palgrave, pp. 75–94.

Marxer, W., and Z. T. Pállinger (2007). 'Stabilizing or Destabilizing? Direct-democratic Instruments in Different Political Systems'. In M. Setälä and T. Schiller (eds.), *Referendums and Representative Democracy: Responsiveness, Accountability and Deliberation*. London, Routledge, pp. 34–55.

Mason, P. (2017). 'Overcoming the Fear of Freedom'. In H. Geiselberger (ed.), *The Great Regression*. Cambridge, Polity, pp. 88–103.

Mattei, U. (2013). 'Protecting the Commons: Water, Culture, and Nature. The Commons Movement in the Italian Struggle against Neoliberal Governance'. *South Atlantic Quarterly*, 112(2): 366–76, http://works.bepress.com/ugo_mattei/48.

Mayer, S., and B. Sauer (2018). '"Gender Ideology" in Austria: Coalitions Around an Empty Signifier'. In R. Kuhar and D. Paternotte (eds.), *Anti-Gender Campaigns in Europe: Mobilizing against Equality*. London, Rowman and Littlefield International, pp. 23–40.

Mayo, P. (1999). *Gramsci, Freire and Adult Education: Possibilities for Transformative Action*. London: Zed.

Mayo, P., and L. English (2012). 'Adult Education and Social Movements: Perspectives from Freire and Beyond'. *Educazione Democratica*, 2(3): 170–208.

Mazzoni, D., and E. Cicognani (2013). 'Water as a Commons: An Exploratory Study on the Motives for Collective Action among Italian Water Movement Activists'. *Journal of Community & Applied Social Psychology*, 23(4): 314–30.

Mazzoni, D., M. van Zomeren and E. Cicognami (2015). 'The Motivating Role of Perceived Right Violation and Efficacy Beliefs in Identification with the Italian Water Movement'. *Political Psychology*, 36(3): 315–30.

McAdam, D., and K. Kloos (2016). *Deeply Divided*. Oxford University Press.

McAdam, D., and S. G. Tarrow (2010). 'Ballots and Barricades: On the Reciprocal Relationship Between Elections and Social Movements'. *Perspectives on Politics*, 8(2): 529–42.

McAdam, D., S. Tarrow and C. Tilly (2001). *Dynamics of Contention*. Cambridge University Press.

McDonough, T., and T. Dundon (2010). *Thatcherism Delayed? The Irish Crisis and the Paradox of Social Partnership*. Rochester, NY, Social Science Research Network.

Meguid, B. M. (2005). 'Competition Between Unequals: The Role of Mainstream Party Strategy in Niche Party Success'. *American Political Science Review*, 99(3): 347–59.

Melucci, A. (1982). *L'Invenzione del Presente. Movimenti, Identità, Bisogni Individuali*. Bologna, il Mulino.

Melucci, A. (1989). *Nomads of the Present*. London, Hutchinson Radius.

Melucci, A. (1996). *Challenging Codes*. Cambridge and New York, Cambridge University Press.

Mendelsohn, M., and F. Cutler (2000). 'The Effect of Referendums on Democratic Citizens: Information, Politicization, Efficacy and Tolerance'. *British Journal of Political Science*, 30(4): 685–98.

Méndez Lago, M. (2007). 'Turning the Page: Crisis and Transformation of the Spanish Socialist Party'. *South European Society and Politics*, 11(3–4): 419–37.

Meyer, D., and S. Tarrow (eds.) (2018). *The Resistance*. Oxford University Press.

Morris, A. (2000). 'Charting Futures for Sociology. Social Organization Reflections on Social Movement Theory. Criticisms and Proposals'. *Contemporary Sociology*, 29(3): 445–54.

Motta, S. C., and A. M. Esteves (2014). 'Reinventing Emancipation in the 21st Century: The Pedagogical Practices of Social Movements'. *Interface* 6(1): 1–24.

Mottier, V. (1993). 'La structuration sociale de la participation aux votations fédérales'. In H. Kriesi (ed.), *Citoyenneté et démocratie directe: Compétence, participation et décision des citoyens et citoyennes suisses*. Zurich, Seismo, pp. 123–44.

Mouffe, C. (2018). *For a Left Populism*. London, Verso.

Muehlebach, A. (2018) 'Commonwealth: On Democracy and Dispossession in Italy'. *History and Anthropology*, 29(3): 342–58, https://doi.org/10.1080/027 57206.2018.1458719.

Müller, J. W. (2017), 'Populism and Constitutionalism'. In C. Rovira Kaltwasser, P. A. Taggart, P. Ochoa and P. Osteguy (eds.), *The Oxford Handbook of Populism*. Oxford University Press

Müller-Rommel, F. (1993). *Gruene Partein in Westeuropa*. Opladen, Westdeutscher Verlag.

Muñoz, J., and M. Guinjoan (2013). 'Accounting for Internal Variation in Nationalist Mobilization: Unofficial Referendums for Independence in Catalonia (2009–11)'. *Nations and Nationalism*, 19(1): 44–67.

Neijens, P., P. van Praag, W. Bosveld and J. Slot (2007). 'Turnout in Referendums: The Dutch Experience. An Analysis of Voter and Referendum Characteristics That Influence Turnout in Referendums'. In C. de Vreese (ed.), *The Dynamics of Referendum Campaigns: An International Perspective*. London, Palgrave, pp. 142–58.

O'Donnell, G. A., and P. C. Schmitter (1986). *Transitions from Authoritarian Rule: Tentative Conclusions about Uncertain Democracies*. Baltimore, Md., Johns Hopkins University Press.

O'Neill, M. (1997). *Green Parties and Political Change in Contemporary Europe*. Aldershot, Ashgate.

Oberhuber, F. (2006). 'The Convention Method: An Institutional Device for Consensus-building'. In S. Puntscher Riekmann and W. Wessels (eds.), *The Making of a European Constitution, Dynamics and Limits of the Convention Experience*. Wiesbaden, VS Verlag für Sozialwissenschaften, pp. 90–120.

Ochoa, U. D. (2014). *The Political Empowerment of the Cocaleros of Bolivia and Peru*. London, Palgrave.

Offe, C. (2011) 'Rethinking Progress and Ensuring a Secure Future for All: What we Can learn from the Crisis.' *Trends in Social Cohesion*, 22: 79–92.

Orriols, L., and T. Rodon (2016). 'The 2015 Catalan Election: The Independence Bid at the Polls'. *South European Society and Politics*, 21(3): 359–81.

Ostaszewski, P. (2013). 'Iceland: Political Implications of the Financial Crisis of 2008 and the Road to Changes in the Economic Policy and in the Model of Democracy'. *Forum Scientiae Oeconomia*, 1(1): 55–74.

Palà, R., and S. Picazo (eds.) (2014). 'Procés'. *Dossier Crític*, special issue.

Palermo, F. (2007). 'La "manutenzione costituzionale": alla ricerca di una funzione'. In F. Palermo (ed.), *La manutenzione costituzionale*. Padua, CEDAM, pp. 1–18.

Papadopoulos, Y. (2001) 'How Does Direct Democracy Matter? The Impact of Referendum Votes on Politics and Policy-Making'. *West European Politics*, 24(2): 35–58.

Parks, L. (2014) 'Framing in the Right2Water European Citizens' Initiative'. Paper prepared for presentation at the ECPR general conference, 3–6 September. Glasgow.

Pateman, C. (1970). *Participation and Democratic Theory*. Cambridge University Press.

Paternotte, D., and R. Kuhar (2018). '"Gender Ideology" in Movement: Introduction'. In R. Kuhar and D. Paternotte (eds.), *Anti-Gender Campaigns in Europe: Mobilizing against Equality*. London, Rowman and Littlefield International, pp. 1–22.

Perczynski, P. (2000). 'Active Citizenship and Associative Democracy'. In M. Saward (ed.), *Democratic Innovation: Deliberation, Representation and Association*. London and New York, Routledge, pp. 161–71.

Pérez-Nievas, S., J. Rama-Caamaño and C. Fernández-Esquer (2018). 'New Wine in Old Bottles? The Selection of Electoral Candidates in General Elections in Podemos'. In G. Cordero and X. Coller (eds.), *Democratizing Candidate Selection*. London, Palgrave Macmillan, pp. 123–46.

Petrella, R. (2001). *The Water Manifesto: Arguments for a World Water Contract*. London and New York, Zed Books.

Petrick, K. (2017). 'Occupy and the Temporal Politics of Prefigurative Democracy'. *Triple C: Communication, Capitalism & Critique*, 15(2): 492–506.

Picot, G., and A. Tassinari (2014). 'Liberalization, Dualization, or Recalibration? Labor Market Reforms under Austerity, Italy and Spain 2010–2012'. Nuffield College, Working Paper Series in Politics.

Piven, F. (2006) *Challenging Authority. How Ordinary People Change America.* New York, Rowman & Littlefield Publishers.

Pizzorno, A. (1991). 'On the Individualistic Theory of Social Order'. In P. Bourdieu and J. Coleman (eds.), *Social Theory for a Changing Society.* Boulder, Colo., Westview Press, pp. 209–44.

Pizzorno, A. (1993). *Le radici della politica assoluta.* Milan, Feltrinelli.

Pizzorno, A. (2010) Introduzione. In A. Pizzorno (ed.), *La democrazia di fronte allo stato democratico.* Milan, Feltrinelli, pp. xi–xxvii.

Poguntke, T. (1993). *Alternative Politics: The German Green Party.* Edinburgh University Press.

Poguntke, T. (2002). 'Party Organizational Linkage: Parties Without Firm Social Roots?' In K. R. Luther and F. Müller-Rommel (eds.), *Political Parties in the New Europe: Political and Analytical Challenges.* Oxford University Press, pp. 43–62.

Poguntke, T. (2006). 'Political Parties and Other Organizations'. In R. S. Katz and W. Crotty (eds.), *Handbook of Party Politics.* London: Sage, pp. 396–405.

Polletta, F. (2002). *Freedom is an Endless Meeting.* University of Chicago Press.

Přibáň, J. (2007). *Legal Symbolism: On Law, Time and European Identity.* Aldershot, and Burlington, Vt., Ashgate.

Quarta, A., and T. Ferrando (2015). 'Italian Property Outlaws: From the Theory of the Commons to the Praxis of Occupation'. *Global Jurist*, 15(3): 261–90.

Qvortrup, M. (2012). 'The History of Ethno-national Referendums 1791–2011'. *Nationalism and Ethnic Politics*, 18(1): 129–50.

Qvortrup, M. (2014a). 'Referendums in Western Europe'. In M. Qvortrup (ed.), *Referendums Around the World: The Continued Growth of Direct Democracy.* London, Palgrave, pp. 43–64.

Qvortrup, M. (2014b). 'Conclusion'. In M. Qvortrup (ed.), *Referendums Around the World: The Continued Growth of Direct Democracy.* London, Palgrave, pp. 246–51.

Qvortrup, M. (2014c). 'Referendums on Independence, 1860–2011'. *The Political Quarterly*, 85(1): 57–64.

Rahat, G. (2009). 'Elite Motives for Initiating Referendums: Avoidance, Addition and Contradiction'. In M. Setälä and T. Schiller (eds.), *Referendums and Representative Democracy: Responsiveness, Accountability and Deliberation.* London, Routledge, pp. 98–116.

Ramiro, L., and R. Gomez (2017). 'Radical-Left Populism during the Great Recession: Podemos and Its Competition with the Established Radical Left'. *Political Studies*, 65: 108–25.

Ranney, A. (1994). 'Nuove pratiche e vecchia teoria'. In M. Caciagli and P. Uleri (eds.), *Democrazie e referendums.* Rome-Bari, Laterza, pp. 29–48.

Rashkova, E. R., and I. van Biezen (2014). 'The Legal Regulation of Political Parties: Contesting or Promoting Legitimacy?' *International Political Science Review*, 35(3): 265–74.

Reiter, B. (2017). *The Crisis of Liberal Democracy and the Path Ahead: Alternatives to Political Representation and Capitalism.* London, Rowman and Littlefield International.

Rendueles, C., and J. Sola (2015). 'Podemos and the Paradigm Shift'. *Jacobin Magazine: A Magazine of Culture and Polemic*, 13 April, www.jacobinmag. com/2015/04/podemos-spain-pablo-iglesias-european-left.

Rendueles, C., and J. Sola (2018). 'Podemos and the Overturn of Spanish Politics'. In O. G. Agustín and M. Briziarelli (eds.), *Podemos and the New Political Cycle: Left-Wing Populism and Anti-Establishment Politics*. London, Palgrave, pp. 25–47.

Rico, G., and R. Liñeira (2014). 'Bringing Secessionism into the Mainstream: The 2012 Regional Election in Catalonia'. *South European Society and Politics*, 19(2): 257–80.

Ritter, D. (2014). 'Comparative Historical Analysis'. In D. della Porta (ed.), *Methodological Practices in Social Movement Research*. Oxford University Press.

Roberts, K. M. (2015a). *Changing Course in Latin America: Party Systems in the Neoliberal Era*. New York, Cambridge University Press.

Roberts, K. M. (2015b). 'Parties, Populism, and Social Protest in Latin America's Post-Adjustment Era'. In D. della Porta and M. Diani (eds.), *The Oxford Handbook of Social Movements*. Oxford University Press, pp. 686–95.

Rohrschneider, R. (1993). 'Impact of Social Movements on the European Party System'. *The Annals of the American Academy of Political and Social Sciences*, 528(1): 157–70.

Rokkan, S. (1970). *Citizens, Elections, and Parties*. Oslo University Press.

Romanos, E. (2014). 'Evictions, Petitions and Escraches: Contentious Housing in Austerity Spain'. *Social Movement Studies*, 13(2): 296–302.

Romanos, E., and Sádaba, I. (2016). 'From the Street to Institutions through the App: Digitally Enabled Political Outcomes of the Spanish Indignados Movement'. *Revista Internacional de Sociología*, 74(4): e048.

Rootes, C. (1995). 'A New Class? The Higher Educated and the New Politics'. In L. Maheu (ed.), *Social Movements and Social Classes*. London and Thousand Oaks, Sage, pp. 220–35.

Rosanvallon, P. (2006). *La contre-démocratie: la politique à l'âge de la défiance*. Paris, Seuil.

Rose, R. (1964). 'Parties, Factions and Tendencies in Britain'. *Political Studies*, 12(1): 33–46.

Rüdig, W. (1990). *Explaining Green Party Development: Reflections on a Theoretical Framework*. Strathclyde Papers on Government and Politics 71. Glasgow, Department of Government, University of Strathclyde.

Ruzza, C. (2004). *Europe and Civil Society: Movement Coalitions and European Governance*. Manchester University Press.

Ryfe, D.-M. (2002) 'The Practice of Deliberative Democracy: A Study of 16 Deliberative Organizations'. *Political Communication*, 19(3): 359–317.

Sacchi, S. (2015). 'Conditionality by Other Means: EU Involvement in Italy's Structural Reforms in the Sovereign Debt Crisis'. *Comparative European Politics*, 13(1): 77–92.

Sager, F., and M. Bühlmann (2009). 'Checks and Balances in Swiss Direct

Democracy'. In M. Setälä and T. Schiller (eds.), *Referendums and Representative Democracy: Responsiveness, Accountability and Deliberation*. London, Routledge, pp. 186–206.

Sampedro, V., and J. Lobera (2014). 'The Spanish 15-M Movement: A Consensual Dissent?' *Journal of Spanish Cultural Studies*, 15(1–2): 61–80.

Santos, B. de Sousa (2014). *Epistemologies of the South*. Boulder, Colo.: Paradigm.

Santos, B. de Sousa (ed.) (2005) *Democratizing Democracy: Beyond the Liberal Democratic Canon*. London, Verso.

Sartori, G. (1976). *Parties and Party Systems*. Cambridge University Press.

Schavelzon, S., and J. Webber (2018), 'Lessons from Latin America: The Path to Progressive Party'. In O. G. Agustín and M. Briziarelli (eds.), *Podemos and the New Political Cycle: Left-Wing Populism and Anti-Establishment Politics*. London, Palgrave, pp. 173–99.

Schiller, T. (2007). 'Direct Democracy and Theories of Participatory Democracy: Some Observations'. In Z. T. Pállinger, B. Kaufmann, W. Marxer and T. Schiller (eds.), *Direct Democracy in Europe*. Wiesbaden, VS Verlag für Sozialwissenschaften, pp. 52–63.

Schiller, T. (2009) 'Conclusions'. In M. Setälä and T. Schiller (eds.), *Referendums and Representative Democracy: Responsiveness, Accountability and Deliberation*. London, Routledge, pp. 207–19.

Scholl, B. (2006). *Europas symbolische Verfassung: nationale Verfassungstraditionen und die Konstitutionalisierung der EU*. Wiesbaden, VS Verlag für Sozialwissenschaften.

Schumaker, P. (1975) 'Policy Responsiveness to Protest-Group Demands'. *Journal of Politics*, 37: 488–521.

Schumpeter, J. A. (1943). *Capitalism, Socialism and Democracy*. London, Allen & Unwin.

Schwoerer, J. (2019). 'Alternative fuer Deutschland: From the Streets to the Parliament?' In M. Caiani and O. Cisar (eds.), *Radical Right Movement Parties in Europe*. London, Routledge, pp. 29–45.

Sciarini, P., N. Bornstein and B. Lanz. (2007). 'The Determinants of Voting Choices on Environmental Issues: A Two-level Analysis'. In C. de Vreese (ed.), *The Dynamics of Referendum Campaigns: An International Perspective*. London, Palgrave, pp. 234–66.

Scott, J. (1985). *Weapons of the Weak: Everyday Forms of Peasant Resistance*. New Haven, Conn., Yale University Press.

Scott, J. (1990). *Domination and the Art of Resistance: Hidden Transcript*. New Haven, Conn., Yale University Press.

Setälä, M. (2009). 'Introduction'. In M. Setälä and T. Schiller (eds.), *Referendums and Representative Democracy: Responsiveness, Accountability and Deliberation*. London, Routledge, pp. 1–14.

Setälä, M., and T. Schiller (eds.) (2012). *Citizens' Initiatives in Europe: Procedures and Consequences of Agenda-Setting by Citizens*. Basingstoke, Palgrave Macmillan.

Sewell, W. H. (1996). 'Three Temporalities: Toward an Eventful Sociology'. In

T. J. McDonald (ed.), *The Historic Turn in the Human Sciences*. Ann Arbor, University of Michigan Press, pp. 245–80.

Silva, E. (2009). *Challenging Neoliberalism in Latin America*. New York, Cambridge University Press.

Sitter, N. (2009). 'To Structure Political Conflict: The Institutionalization of Referendums on European Integration in the Nordic Countries'. In M. Setälä and T. Schiller (eds.), *Referendums and Representative Democracy: Responsiveness, Accountability and Deliberation*. London, Routledge, pp. 77–97.

Smith, D. A., and C. J. Tolbert (2004). *Educated by Initiative: The Effects of Direct Democracy on Citizens and Political Organizations in the American States*. Ann Arbor, University of Michigan Press.

Smith, G. (2009) *Democratic Innovations: Designing Institutions for Citizen Participation*. Cambridge University Press.

Smucker, Jonathan M. (2014). 'Can Prefigurative Politics Replace Political Strategy?' *Berkeley Journal of Sociology*, 58: 74–82.

Sola, J., and C. Rendueles (2018) 'Podemos, the Upheaval of Spanish Politics and the Challenge of Populism'. *Journal of Contemporary European Studies*, 26(1): 99–116.

Stambolis-Ruhstorfer, M., and J. Tricou (2018) 'Resisting "Gender Theory" in France: A Fulcrum for Religious Action in a Secular Society'. In D. Paternotte and R. Kuhar (eds.), *Anti-Gender Campaigns in Europe: Mobilizing against Equality*. London, Rowman and Littlefield International, pp. 79–88.

Stobart, L. (2014). 'Understanding Podemos 1/3: 15M and Counter-politics'. *Left Flank*, 5 November, http://left-flank. org/2014/11/05/explaining-podemos-1-15-m-counter-politics.

Streeck, W. (2014). 'Taking Crisis Seriously: Capitalism on its Way Out'. *Stato e Mercato*, 1(100): 45–68.

Streeck, W. (2017). 'The Return of the Repressed as the Beginning of the End of Neoliberal Capitalism'. In H. Geiselberger (ed.), *The Great Regression*. Cambridge, Polity, pp. 157–72.

Subirats, J. (2015a). '¿Desbordar el "dentro"–"fuera"?' *Revista Teknokultura*, 12(1): 161–8.

Subirats, J. (2015b). 'Todo se mueve. Acción colectiva, acción conectiva, Movimientos, partidos e instituciones'. *Revista Española de Sociología*, 24: 123–31.

Suiter, J., D. M. Farrell and C. Harris (2016). 'The Irish Constitutional Convention: A Case of "High Legitimacy?"' In M. Reuchamps and J. Suiter (eds.), *Constitutional Deliberative Democracy in Europe*. Colchester, ECPR Press, pp. 33–51.

Suteu, S. (2015). 'Constitutional Conventions in the Digital Era: Lessons from Iceland and Ireland'. *Boston College International & Comparative Law Review*, 38: 251–329.

Swain, Dan (2017). 'Not Not but Not Yet: Present and Future in Prefigurative Politics'. *Political Studies*, 67: 47–62.

Sweet, A. S. (2008). 'Constitutionalism, Rights, and Judicial Power'. Faculty Scholarship Series, 77.

Szerbiak, A., and P. Taggart (2003). 'Theorising Party-Based Euroscepticism: Problems of Definition, Measurement and Causality'. SEI Working Paper 69; European Parties, Elections and Referendums Network Working Paper 12. Sussex European Institute.

Talpin, J. (2015) 'Democratic Innovation'. In D. della Porta and M. Diani (eds.), *The Oxford Handbook of Social Movements*. Oxford University Press, pp. 781–92.

Tarrow, S. G. (1989). *Democracy and Disorder: Protest and Politics in Italy, 1965–1975*. Oxford University Press.

Tarrow, S. G. (1994). *Power in Movement*. Cambridge University Press.

Tarrow, S. G. (2011). *Power in Movement: Social Movements and Contentious Politics*. Cambridge University Press.

Tarrow, S. G. (2012). *Strangers at the Gate*. Cambridge University Press.

Tarrow, S. G. (2015). 'Contentious Politics'. In D. della Porta and M. Diani (ed.), *The Oxford Handbook of Social Movements*. Oxford University Press, pp. 86–107.

Teubner, G. (1992). 'The Two Faces of Janus: Rethinking Legal Pluralism'. *Cardozo Law Review*, 13: 1443–62.

Thorarensen, B. (2014) 'Why the Making of a Crowd-sourced Constitution in Iceland Failed'. *Constitution Making and Constitutional Change*, https://constitutional-change.com/why-the-making-of-a-crowd-sourced-constitution-in-iceland-failed.

Thoreau, H. D. (1948). *Walden or On Life in the Woods: On the Duty of Civil Disobedience*. Norman Holes, Pearson.

Thornhill, C. (2011). *A Sociology of Constitutions: Constitutions and State Legitimacy in Historical-Sociological Perspective*. Cambridge University Press.

Thornhill, C. (2012). 'The Formation of a European Constitution: An Approach from Historical-Political Sociology'. *International Journal of Law in Context*, 8(3): 354–93.

Tierney, S. (2012). *Constitutional Referendums: The Theory and Practice of Republican Deliberation*. Oxford University Press.

Tilly, C. 1986. *The Contentious French*. Cambridge, Mass., Harvard University Press.

Tilly, C. (2004). *Contention and Democracy in Europe, 1650–2000*. Cambridge University Press.

Tilly, C. (2008). *Contentious Performances*. Cambridge University Press.

Torcal, M. (2006). 'Political Disaffection and Democratisation History in New Democracies'. In M. Torcal and J. R. Montero (eds.), *Political Disaffection in Contemporary Democracie:. Social Capital, Institutions, and Politics*. London, Routledge, pp. 157–89.

Torcal, M. (2014). 'The Incumbent Electoral Defeat in the 2011 Spanish National Elections: The Effect of the Economic Crisis in an Ideological Polarized Party System'. *Journal of Elections, Public Opinion and Parties*, 24(2): 203–21.

Toret, J. (2015). 'Una mirada tecnopolítica al primer año de Podemos. Seis hipótesis'. *Revista Teknokultura*, 12(1): 121–35.

Touraine, A. (1985). 'An Introduction to the Study of Social Movements'. *Social Research*, 52: 749–88.

Tully, J. (2007). 'A New Kind of Europe? Democratic Integration in the European Union'. *Critical Review of International Social and Political Philosophy*, 10: 71–86.

Tully, J. (2008). 'The Imperialism of Modern Constitutional Democracy'. In M. Loughlin and N. Walker (eds.), *The Paradox of Constitutionalism: Constituent Power and Constitutional Form.*, Oxford University Press, pp. 315–38.

Turner, Ralph. 1996. 'The Moral Issue in Collective Action'. *Mobilization: An International Quarterly*, 1: 1–15.

Turner, R., and L. Killian (1987) [1974, 1957]. *Collective Behavior.* Englewood Cliffs, NJ: Prentice Hall.

Uleri, P. (1994). 'Dall'istaurazione alla crisi democratica. Un'analisi in chiave comparata del fenomeno referendario in Italia'. In M. Caciagli and P. Uleri (eds.), *Democrazie e referendums.* Rome-Bari, Laterza, pp. 390–429.

van Biezen, I. (2000). 'Party Membership in Twenty European Democracies, 1980–2000'. *Party Politics*, 6(3): 329–42.

van Biezen, I., P. Mair and T. Poguntke (2012). 'Going, Going, . . . Gone? Party Membership in the 21st Century'. *European Journal of Political Research*, 51(1): 24–56.

van Cott, D. L. (2005). *From Movements to Parties in Latin America: The Evolution of Ethnic Politics.* New York, Cambridge University Press.

van Cott, D. L. (2008). *Radical Democracy in the Andes.* New York, Cambridge University Press.

Vázquez-García, R. (2012). 'The Spanish Party System and European Integration: A Consensual Europeanization'. In E. Kulahci (ed.), *The Domestic Party Politics of Europeanisation.* London, ECPR Series, pp. 109–24.

Vázquez-García, R., S. D. Fernández and A. Sojka (2014). 'Spain'. In N. Conti (ed.), *Party Attitudes Towards the EU in the Member States: Parties for Europe, Parties Against Europe.* Oxford, Routledge, pp. 99–114.

Vergé, T. (2012). 'Party Strategies Towards Civil Society in New Democracies: The Spanish Case'. *Party Politics*, 18(1): 45–60.

Wade, R. H., and S. Sigurgeirsdóttir (2011). 'Iceland's Meltdown: The Rise and Fall of International Banking in the North Atlantic'. *Brazilian Journal of Political Economy*, 31(5): 684–97.

Wagner Pacifici, R. 2017. *What is an Event?* University of Chicago Press.

Weber, M. (1922). *Wirtschaft und Gesellschaft.* Tübingen, Mohr.

Weisskircher, M., and L. E. Berntzen (2019). 'Remaining on the Streets: Anti-Islamic PEGIDA Mobilization and its Relationship to Far Right Party Politics'. In M. Caiani and O. Cisar (eds.), *Radical Right Movement Parties in Europe.* London, Routledge, pp. 114–30.

Welton, M. (1993). 'Social Revolutionary Learning: The New Social Movements as Learning Sites'. *Adult Education Quarterly*, 43(3): 152–64.

Wirth, W., C. Schemer, R. Kühne and J. Matthes (2012). 'The Impact of Positive and Negative Effects in Direct-democratic Campaigns'. In H. Kriesi (ed.),

Political Communication in Direct Democratic Campaigns: Enlightening or Manipulating? London, Palgrave, pp. 205–24.

Wodak, R. (2015) *The Politics of Fear: What Right-Wing Populist Discourse Means.* London, Sage.

Yashar, D. J. (2005). *Contesting Citizenship in Latin America: The Rise of Indigenous Movements and the Postliberal Challenge.* New York, Cambridge University Press.

Yates, L. (2015). 'Rethinking Prefiguration: Alternatives, Micropolitics and Goals in Social Movements'. *Social Movement Studies*, 14(1): 1–21.

Young, I. M. (1996) 'Communication and The Other: Beyond Deliberative Democracy'. In S. Benhabib (ed.), *Democracy and Difference: Contesting the Boundaries of the Political.* Princeton University Press, pp. 120–35.

Young, I. M. (2003). 'Activist Challenges to Deliberative Democracy'. In J. S. Fishkin and P. Laslett (eds.), *Debating Deliberative Democracy.* Oxford, Blackwell, pp. 102–20.

Ypi, L. (2012) *Social Justice and Avant-garde Political Agency.* Oxford University Press.

Zaller, J. R. (1992). *The Nature and Origins of Mass Opinion.* New York, Cambridge University Press.

Zegada, M. T., Y. F. Torrez and G. Cámara (2008). *Movimientos sociales en tiempos de poder: articulaciones y campos de conflicto en el gobierno del MAS, 2006–2007.* La Paz, Centro Cuarto Intermedio / Plural Editores.

Index